Mediatized Religion in As

This edited volume discusses mediatized religion in Asia, examining the intensity and variety of constructions and processes related to digital media and religion in Asia today. Individual chapters present case studies from various regions and religious traditions in Asia, critically discussing the data collected in light of current mediatization theories. By directing the study to the geographical, cultural and religious contexts specific to Asia, it also provides new material for the theoretical discussion of the pros and cons of the concept mediatization, among other things interrogating whether this concept is useful in non-"Western" contexts.

Kerstin Radde-Antweiler is Professor of Religious Studies at the University of Bremen, Germany. Her research focuses on mediatized religion, mediatization theory, video gaming, Pagan and Christian traditions and ritual studies. She edited special issues on the interrelation of culture and digital media and published several articles. She is co-editor-in-chief of *gamevironments*, the first academic journal with a specific focus on video gaming and religion.

Xenia Zeiler is tenure track Professor of South Asian Studies at the University of Helsinki, Finland. Her research is situated at the intersection of digital media, religion and culture in India and the worldwide Indian community. Other foci are Digital Humanities and Tantric traditions. She is the author of numerous articles and book chapters on digital and mediatized Hinduism, and co-editor-in-chief of *gamevironments*, the first academic journal with a specific focus on video gaming and religion.

Routledge Research in Digital Media and Culture in Asia
Edited by Dal Yong Jin, Simon Fraser University

Mediatized Religion in Asia
Studies on Digital Media and Religion

Edited by
Kerstin Radde-Antweiler and
Xenia Zeiler

Routledge
Taylor & Francis Group
New York London

First published 2019 by Routledge
52 Vanderbilt Avenue, New York, NY 10017

2 Park Square, Milton Park, Abingdon, Oxon OX14 4RN

First issued in paperback 2020

Routledge is an imprint of the Taylor & Francis Group, an informa business

Library of Congress Cataloging-in-Publication Data
CIP data has been applied for.

ISBN 13: 978-0-367-66393-3 (pbk)
ISBN 13: 978-1-138-04824-9 (hbk)

Typeset in Sabon
by codeMantra

Contents

List of Figures

List of Tables

List of Contributors

Heidi A. Campbell is Professor of Communication and affiliate faculty in Religious Studies at Texas A&M University. She is the director of the Network for New Media, Religion and Digital Culture Studies and the author of over 90 articles and books including *When Religion Meets New Media* (Routledge 2010) and *Networked Theology* (Baker Academic 2016).

Pauline Hope Cheong, PhD, is Professor at the Hugh Downs School of Human Communication, Arizona State University. Her award-winning pedagogy and research includes more than 80 publications in the complex interactions between communication technologies and different cultural communities around the world, including changing religious authority practices and how voluntary groups use digital media to interact and form local and global communities.

Gregory Price Grieve is Professor and Head of the Department of Religious Studies at the University of North Carolina at Greensboro. The author of numerous books and articles, Grieve teaches at the intersection of Asian religions and popular culture. He specializes in digital religion, particularly the emerging field of video games and value systems, and is currently researching video games and the problem of evil.

Sam Han is Senior Lecturer of Anthropology and Sociology at the University of Western Australia. He is the author most recently of *Technologies of Religion: Spheres of the Sacred in a Post-Secular Modernity* (Routledge, 2016) and *Digital Culture and Religion in Asia* (Routledge, 2015) (with Kamaludeen Mohamed Nasir).

Christopher Helland is Associate Professor of Sociology of Religion at Dalhousie University in Canada. Helland's research examines the role of new media in relation to issues of religious authority and power, religious information-seeking behavior, ritual practices, and even changing belief systems. His most recent research project is investigating the effects of computer-mediated communications on diaspora religious groups.

Hew Wai Weng is research fellow at Institute of Malaysian and International Studies, National University of Malaysia (IKMAS, UKM). He has been writing on Chinese Muslim identities, Hui migration, and cultural politics of urban Muslim middle classes in Malaysia and Indonesia. He is the author of *Chinese Ways of Being Muslim: Negotiating Ethnicity and Religiosity in Indonesia* (NIAS Press 2018).

Dhanya Fee Kirchhof is a doctoral candidate at the Department of Gender and Media Studies for the South Asian Region at Humboldt-Universität zu Berlin. Her research explores the interrelatedness of changing communicative configurations, affiliations and socioreligious change in anti-caste contexts. She has published on those issues in the *South Asia Chronicle*.

Kerstin Radde-Antweiler is Professor of Religious Studies at the University of Bremen, Germany. Her research focuses on mediatized religion, mediatization theory, video gaming, Pagan and Christian traditions and ritual studies. She edited special issues on the interrelation of culture and digital media and published several articles. She is co-editor-in-chief of *gamevironments*, the first academic journal with a specific focus on video gaming and religion.

Birgit Staemmler is researcher at the Japanese Department of Tübingen University, Germany, currently funded by the Horst- und Käthe-Eliseit-Foundation for research on Shamanism on the Japanese Internet. Her PhD is entitled *Chinkon kishin: Mediated Spirit Possession in Japanese New Religions* (published 2009). She is co-editor of *Japanese Religions on the Internet: Innovation, Representation and Authority* (2011, with Erica Baffelli and Ian Reader).

Tan Meng Yoe is lecturer of Communications in the School of Arts and Social Sciences at Monash University Malaysia. His current research interest focuses on how religious and political communication among Malaysians are expressed on online spaces. He is the co-founder of the Southeast Asia Internet Research Network.

Ruth Tsuria is Assistant Professor in the Department of Communication, Journalism, and Public Relations at Seton Hall University. Her research investigates the intersection of digital media, religion and feminism. She has published articles on Digital Religion in various academic outlets, and is currently working on her first book.

Rohit Singh has a PhD in Religious Studies from the University of California, Santa Barbara. He is Assistant Professor in the Department of Philosophy and Religious Studies at Middle Tennessee State University. He is the author of "Reimagining Tibet through the Lens of Tibetan Muslim History and Identity" in *The Oxford Handbooks Online* (2015), and his current research focuses on historical and contemporary Buddhist-Muslim interactions in South Asia and the Tibetan Cultural Sphere.

Narges Valibeigi is a PhD candidate in Communication and Media studies at Carleton University. Her primary research interest is the representation of religious identity and rituals on the Internet and how social media become a new platform of practicing religion. Since 2008, her focus has been on new communication technologies and their impacts on Shia Iranian community.

Wai-yip Ho is Associate Professor of Education at the University of Hong Kong and Marie Curie fellow. He is the author of *Islam and China's Hong Kong: Ethnic Identity, Muslim Networks and the New Silk Road* (Routledge, 2015). His research includes Christian-Muslim relations, new media, madrasah and Muslim youths in China.

Xenia Zeiler is tenure track Professor of South Asian Studies at the University of Helsinki, Finland. Her research is situated at the intersection of digital media, religion and culture in India and the worldwide Indian community. Other foci are Digital Humanities and Tantric traditions. She is author of numerous articles and book chapters on digital and mediatized Hinduism.

Introduction

1 Mediatized Religion in Asia

Interrelations of Media, Culture and Society beyond the "West"

Xenia Zeiler

Media are part of our everyday life. This statement is true on a global scale, that is, for most parts of Asia as much as for North America or Europe. The mediatization of basically all aspects of daily life constantly intensifies – among them, not surprisingly, religion. Today, each and every world region and each and every religious tradition is mediatized, if not necessarily to the same extent or level of saturation. Media, among other things, offer a much-used platform for (re)negotiations, (re)interpretations and (re)constructing of religious beliefs, symbols and practices. As the number and diversity of studies on media and religion in Asia rapidly increase, it seems to be time to reflect on the various approaches as well as theoretical and methodical frameworks which are applied in this field and to advance promising new perspectives.

Mediatization – which is a metaconcept as well as an approach with practical methodical consequences – certainly is among these, offering specific perspectives to study the increasingly important interrelation of media, religion and society at large in Asia. But what is mediatization precisely, what constitutes mediatized religion, and how is it relevant for and applicable to the study of media and religion in Asia? This volume is intended to contribute to our understanding of what constitutes mediatized religion in Asia, empirically as well as theoretically, by applying mediatization approaches to critically discussed novel case studies from various Asian regions.

Specifically, this volume includes chapters focusing on regions within Asia with heterogeneous cultural, linguistic, ethnic and religious backgrounds – that is, it defines Asia geographically. In order to present the varied spectrum of what we understand to constitute the field of mediatized religion in Asia overall, the volume goes beyond the often, if so far not primarily, studied regions of South, Southeast and East Asia. Namely, it includes chapters focusing on mediatized religion in West Asia, such as in Israel and Iran.

Overall, this volume critically discusses the application of the existing mediatization approaches as well as newly developed approaches closely based on them, particularly for studying religious traditions in contemporary Asia. In doing so, it also contributes to the debate on the broader implications of digital media and religion in Asia, a debate that must be supported by empirical and verifiable evidence. As such, this book seeks not only to discuss and develop further the application of theoretical concepts, but also to situate this research within the wider discourse of how digital media intersect with the religious world of the 21st century.

The Study of Media and Religion in Asia

The interrelation of media and religion in Asian contexts so far has been studied with a number of foci, approaches and methods. When applying a broad definition of media, the term includes a diverse variety of genres and formats, ranging from modern mass media, such as print media, to digital media, such as social media, in detail. The term additionally includes journalistic media. It is thus not surprising that the existing studies are based in various disciplinary backgrounds, ranging from Asian studies over religious studies to media and communication studies, to name but a few. Also and not surprisingly, many of the existing publications – largely book chapters in edited volumes and journal articles – are interdisciplinary. As specified below, we find studies focusing on particular media genres as well as (much more seldom) applying cross-media perspectives and studies analyzing empirical material within regional as well as (much more seldom) transregional scopes. In many cases, such articles or book chapters are located in journal issues or edited volumes focusing on one specific region within Asia and/or focusing on just one of the two fields in Asia, either media or religion. In short, studies on intersections of media, especially but not exclusively digital media, and religion in Asia so far have been published in a vast array of widespread venues and scopes, with more structured and systematized overview publications still largely lacking.

When looking at the existing chapters and articles on media and religion in Asia, it also becomes clear that many concentrate on specific geographical regions. China, India and partly Korea and Japan belong to the more extensively researched regions, while the Siberian regions of North Asia, Central Asia and the Arab-speaking Asian regions, including the Middle East and the Arabian Peninsula, are among the less researched regions in Asia. Insular Asia, including the Philippines, Malaysia and Indonesia, lies somewhat in between these two poles when it comes to research coverage on intersections of media and religion.

More comprehensive works – be they monographs, edited volumes or special journal issues – on media and religion in Asia are overall rare. To the more closely related publications belong those which focus on the field of religion and technology scholarship in Asia. Among the first to take up this theme for Asian contexts is *Mediating Piety: Technology and Religion in Contemporary Asia* (Lim 2009) which, among other things, also touches on questions of media and religion. *Asian Religions, Technology and Science* (Keul 2015) then covers several regions within Asia and includes a number of chapters specifically on media and religion. To the same field belongs *Religion and Technology in India: Spaces, Practices and Authorities* (Jacobsen and Myrvold 2018) which presents discussions of various religious traditions and technology in India, including chapters on religion and media. In contrast to these publications, this edited volume entirely concentrates on the interrelation of media – especially digital media – and religion in various Asian regions, by specifically applying mediatization approaches.

The undoubtedly largest number of studies appeared in volumes which have a regional focus within Asia. The pioneering edited volume *Media and the Transformation of Religion in South Asia* (Babb and Wadley 1995) was the first comprehensive work of this kind and today belongs to the classics in the field. Many other region-specific monographs and volumes have been published since then. *Media and New Religions in Japan* (Baffelli 2016), *Celebrity Gods: New Religions, Media, and Authority in Occupied Japan* (Dorman 2012), *Drawing on Tradition: Manga, Anime, and Religion in Contemporary Japan* (Thomas 2012) and *Japanese Religions on the Internet: Innovation, Representation, and Authority* (Baffelli, Reader and Staemmler 2011) concentrate on Japan. *Digital Judaism: Jewish Negotiations with Digital Media and Culture* (Campbell 2015) contains chapters on Israel.

Many of the existing studies on media and religion in Asia have been published in works which focus on a combination of two out of three parameters: media, religion, Asia. For example, we find a number of edited volumes with a focus on media in Asia – that is, they are not restricted to one region in Asia but comprise studies on several Asian regions – and contain some chapters on religion. Among them are *Contemporary Culture and Media in Asia* (Black, Khoo and Iwabuchi 2016), which stands out as it takes a pronounced trans-Asia approach; the *Routledge Handbook of New Media in Asia* (Hjorth and Khoo 2015); and *Global Goes Local: Popular Culture in Asia* (King and Craig 2002). Of course, chapters on media and religion in Asia are also included in edited volumes on religion in Asia, that is, in books which do not have an explicit focus on media. An important example is the *Handbook of Religion and the Asian City: Aspiration and Urbanization in the Twenty-First Century* (Veer 2015). Last but not least, some very relevant chapters also appear in volumes concentrating on media and religion which do not necessarily have an Asia focus, such as in *Buddhism, the Internet, and Digital Media: The Pixel in the Lotus* (Grieve and Veidlinger 2015), which contains chapters on various Asian regions. This volume on *Mediatized Religion in Asia* goes one step further than all of these works, as it combines the above-mentioned three parameters (media, religion and Asia) in its approach and structure.

Not surprisingly, the study of interrelations of especially digital media and religious traditions in Asia (or Asian religious traditions located and practiced worldwide, for that matter) is continuously on the rise. Among the increasingly researched media genres are the Internet overall, social media in particular, and video games. While the scope of publications on the Internet and religion in Asia by today is much too vast to attempt even just a partial overview, I nevertheless want to point out some examples of innovative works. If we somewhat limit the scope for such exemplary studies, e.g., regarding geographical regions and religious traditions, we find that, e.g., the interrelation of Hindu traditions with the Internet in (and beyond) India has given rise to a number of studies since about 2010. Foci of research since then have been the diverse online Hindu ritual practices (Helland 2010, Karapanagiotis 2013, Mallapragada 2012), social media use around Hindu festivals (Zeiler 2018) and the overall interrelation of Hindu traditions and the Internet (Scheifinger 2015). When it comes to the study of religion and video games which touch upon Asian contexts, they span many geographical regions and religious traditions, including Buddhist (Grieve 2016), Islamic (Šisler 2014) and Hindu (Zeiler 2014) traditions.

Last but not least, I want to point to a number of studies that focus on actively reflecting their empirical material within frames of theoretical and conceptual approaches and/or relate their empirical material extensively to broader discussions of constructions and transformations of society. Exemplary studies include publications on strategic management of Israel's orthodox communities' religious websites (Golan and Campbell 2015); China's official media portrayal of religion and policy change (Yao, Stout and Liu 2011); media, citizenship and religious mobilization among Mumbai's Muslims (Eisenlohr 2015); the cultivation of the Self in Buddhist priests' personal blogs (Lee 2009); the negotiation of Islam in China's cyberspace (Ho 2010); and mediatization in relation to local rituals in the Philippines (Radde-Antweiler 2018 forthc.).

All the studies mentioned in this chapter are examples which were chosen to demonstrate the vast variety and range of existing research in the still-emerging but rapidly evolving field, as well as to point out the so far dominant, scattered nature of publication venues for this important and growing academic field. Per definition and, among other things, because of the sheer scope of the quickly expanding scholarship, especially on new media formats and religion in various Asian regions, these examples cannot be understood as constituting an exhaustive list or a classical literature review. Today, the study of religion and media in Asia is gaining increasing interest with many researchers from diverse disciplines. The constantly rising importance of media, especially digital media including social media, for the shaping of religious traditions in Asia overall and the ongoing intertwining of media and religion worldwide are certain to boost the interest in the field even more and contribute to bringing about studies with not only new case study material but also novel approaches, methods and theoretical frameworks. It is our hope to contribute to these developments by presenting this edited volume which approaches the field through the specific lens of mediatized religion.

Mediatization and Mediatized Religion

Mediatization as an approach and concept to study the interrelation of media and society first rose to prominence especially in Media and Communication Studies, but by today has gained influence in numerous disciplines which are interested in the study of media and religion overall. While as a term, and partly even already as a concept, mediatization can be traced "back to the beginnings of media and communication research in the social sciences" (Couldry and Hepp 2013, 195), specifically to 1933 (e.g., Manheim 1933), it was only at about the turn of the millennium that the two distinguishable mediatization approaches or traditions which exist today fully developed: the institutionalist and the social-constructivist traditions.

The first of these two distinguishable mediatization approaches, the institutionalist tradition, is based on the notion that the individual fields of culture and society – among them religion – are subject to an inherent media logic that is based mainly on economic interests (Altheide and Snow 1979). Out of this underlying idea and developed mainly in Journalism Studies and Political Communication, the institutionalist tradition maintains that media, first and foremost understood to be journalistic media, are an independent social institution and as such follow a specific – that is, institutionalized – set of rules. This includes the notion that "nonmedia actors have to conform to this 'media logic' if they want to be represented in the (mass) media or if they want to act successfully in a media culture and media society" (Couldry and Hepp 2013, 196).

Some scholars, such as, most prominently, Stig Hjarvard (2013), have discussed and further elaborated this institutionalist mediatization tradition specifically in relation to the field of religion. For example, Hjarvard (2008, 2013) argues that the media logic and the fact that society is increasingly mediatized have effects beyond the media, supporting, for example, an increasing secularization. Overall, the notion of a media logic that has existed since the late 1970s has since been questioned and re-discussed, especially in Communication and Media Studies. The attempts to rethink mediatization and to develop revised definitions and approaches resulted, among other things, in the full development of the social-constructivist tradition.

Established by the German communication theorist Friedrich Krotz at the beginning of the 2000s (e.g., Krotz 2001), the social-constructivist tradition highlights the interrelation of media with the construction of reality. Mediatization in this approach is defined as a meta-process which shapes modern societies alongside various other sociocultural processes such as globalization or individualization. Given these notions, this approach also necessarily means a shift from media-centered to actor-centered research. Instead of concentrating on the effect of one media genre on actors, mediatization research in the social-constructivist tradition more broadly focuses on actors in their mediatized worlds. Krotz (2008, 24) defined mediatization in this way:

> Today, we can say that mediatization means at the least the following:
>
> a   changing media environments …
> b   an increase of different media …
> c   the changing functions of old media …
> d   new and increasing functions of digital media for the people and a growth of media in general
> e   changing communication forms and relations between the people on the micro level, a changing organization of social life and changing nets of sense and meaning making on the macro level.

The social-constructivist mediatization tradition aims at comprehending everyday communication practices as a shaping factor of society and thus puts the spotlight on the changing communicative construction of culture and society. These changes currently are often, though of course not exclusively, related to digital media and communication practices (e.g., Couldry and Hepp 2016).

Today, the two mediatization traditions exist side by side. Their major difference may be seen in the way they theorize mediatization: While the institutionalist tradition so far has been largely interested in traditional mass media which were understood to adhere to a media logic, the social-constructivist tradition has laid the focus on everyday communication practices and the changing communicative construction of culture and society. But while the two traditions still diverge on certain points, more recently they also agreed more on basic aspects in the definition of mediatization (e.g., Lundby 2009). As Couldry and Hepp (2013, 197) put it:

> … the contours of a shared, basic understanding of the term have emerged. On that fundamental level the term "mediatization" does not refer to a single theory but to a more general approach within media and communications research. Generally speaking, mediatization is a concept used to analyze critically the interrelation between changes in media and communications on the one hand, and changes in culture and society on the other. At this general level, mediatization has quantitative as well as qualitative dimensions.

With regard to quantitative aspects, mediatization refers to the increasing temporal, spatial and social spread of mediated communication. ... With regard to qualitative aspects, mediatization refers to the specificity of certain media within sociocultural change: It matters what kind of media is used for what kind of communication.

Mediatization, evidently, is as relevant for the study of religion and religious practice as it is for any other field of study. The immense transformations of religion today is in large part related to mediatization processes. For example, social media in particular have contributed to an opening of debates and discussions regarding religion from the long dominant religious institutions to religious actors much more broadly. With ongoing mediatization, actors from outside institutionalized structures also have increasing opportunities to contribute their opinions and thus to shape religion and religious practice on diverse levels (e.g., Lövheim 2011). Religion as much as other fields of society today is highly mediatized (e.g., Lövheim and Lynch 2011, Lundby 2013).

Currently, the theoretical and methodical approaches of mediatization are established especially in European and North American academia and have primarily been applied to case studies from these very regions. But when it comes to geographical contexts beyond the ones mentioned, including but not limited to Asia, mediatization has yet to be applied on a broad scale. This is true for mediatized religion as much as for the mediatization of other fields of culture and society. More studies, not only for Asian contexts but for other parts of the world as well, are much needed in order to widen the scope of varied case studies and offer more diversified analyses and material which in turn allow for expanded theorizing. Mediatization may not have the same characteristics everywhere but very likely is influenced if not determined (to varying degrees) by regional cultural and social specifics. Future research needs to take such specific contexts into account. For example, it needs to verify in detail how the intensified media production, use and reception in many parts of Asia have led to transformations which, among other things, strongly influence the rearrangements of religious settings, reaching from consolidations of the existing structures in some cases to their restructuring in others.

The Approach and Chapters of This Book

In order to broaden our understanding of what constitutes mediatized religion, this edited volume goes one step beyond the so far dominant European and North American regional contexts and discusses different aspects of mediatized religion in Asia. By opening up this new field of geographical, cultural and religious contexts, it also aims at providing new material for the theoretical discussion of the pros and cons of the concept of mediatization. It asks critically if mediatization approaches are useful in non-"Western" contexts, or if it has to be verified further. In line with these aims, the individual chapters of the edited volume present different case studies from various regions and religious traditions in Asia, critically discussing the data in the light of mediatization theories and approaches and highlighting their benefits and limits for studying religion in Asia. As such, the chapters also exemplify the intensity and variety of religious constructions related to media overall, and digital media specifically, in Asia today.

This volume's structure reflects these approaches. The individual chapters cover several Asian regions ranging from the very East, namely Japan, to the very West of geographical Asia, namely Israel. The chapters are arranged in four parts which are framed by an introductory chapter at the beginning and a critical discussion at the end. The parts are arranged according to geographical parameters, proceeding from the East. Part 1 contains chapters on East Asia, namely on Japan, China and Korea; Part 2 presents case studies on Southeast Asia, namely on Malaysia, Singapore and Indonesia; Part 3 looks into case studies in India, namely India and Ladakh and Tibet; and Part 4 concludes with chapters on West Asia, namely Iran and Israel.

This volume's opening chapter provides an introduction to and overview of the study of media and religion in Asia and the mediatization and mediatized religion approaches, a contextualization of the volume's approach and an overview of the book's chapters. Part 1, East Asia, covers three geographical regions in the area: Japan, China and Korea. Birgit Staemmler in "'Does Anyone Know a Good Healer?' An Analysis of Mediatized Word-of-Mouth Advertising of Spiritual Healers in Japanese Online Question and Answer Forums" uses a Grounded Theory approach to analyze questions and answers in Japanese online forums discussing criteria for trustworthy spiritual healers. She argues that, recently, the traditional word-of-mouth propaganda related to Japanese spiritual healers is being supplemented by entries in digital and social media and discussions about healers by customers, advice seekers and skeptics in online forums which have developed into locations for mediatized word-of-mouth propaganda and communication. Wai-yip Ho in "Religious Mediatization with Chinese Characteristics: Subaltern Voices of Chinese Muslim Youths" analyzes Chinese Muslims' cyber-presence in the contexts of China's explosion of religious mediatization. Based on findings from interviews and online observations of a Chinese Muslim youth website, he argues that young Muslim leaders are forging a China Muslim network to mobilize youths and reshape the cultural image of Islam in China. In the last chapter of this part, Sam Han in "'Aren't you happy?' Healing as Mediatized Nationalism in a Compressed Modernity" critically discusses the recent boom in products and services claiming to provide "healing" in South Korean media and popular culture, focusing on televised talk shows. The chapter proposes the term "mediatized nationalism" to denote how healing media operate to promote self-recuperating subjects in service of the nation's development and, based on the empirical material from East Asia, discusses how current mediatization theory understands modernity as implicitly Western.

Part 2, on Southeast Asia, contains chapters on three regions: Malaysia, Indonesia and Singapore. Tan Meng Yoe in "Facebook and the Mediatization of Religion: Inter/Intrareligious Dialogue in Malaysia" discusses the emergence of new types of Malaysian communities through the Internet and social media platforms in relation to racial and religious relations in Malaysia and national identity. The chapter argues that online interactions allow for the observation of inter-/intrareligious engagement on a grassroots level and highlights new discourses of mediatized religion in Malaysia where the jostling for religious supremacy plays out online in a way that is reflective of the broader Malaysian community. Hew Wai Weng in "On-Offline *Dakwah*: Social Media and Islamic Preaching in Malaysia and Indonesia" explores the case studies of two popular Chinese Muslim preachers in Indonesia and how and under what conditions the intersection and mutual constituting of both online and off-line strategies contribute to a new way of Islamic preaching. Characteristic of this multi-mediated and multi-sited preaching trend is that it is led by young, media-savvy and business-minded preachers; occupies both cyberspace and urban places; and combines textual, visual and oral approaches. In her chapter "Church Digital Applications and the Communicative Meso-Micro Interplay: Building Religious Authority and Community through Everyday Organizing," Pauline Hope Cheong explains the significance of everyday communication practices for religious organizing. The chapter investigates the interactions between the work of spiritual institutions and lay followers in Singapore and thus expands the understanding of how strategic church communication works to premediate church gatherings and shape social networking to accomplish clergy authority and brand resonance. In highlighting how mediatization as a communication-centered concept can be applied to the domain of religion beyond traditional institutional and individual levels of analysis, the chapter argues that the mediatization of religion is not merely derived from a one-way, institutional directive but is contingent on the meso-micro interplay of top-down and bottom-up communication practices to build authority and community through everyday organizing.

In the volume's part 3, which focuses on South Asia, we find two chapters: one on India and the other on Ladakh and Tibet. Dhanya Fee Kirchhof in "Ravidassia: Neither Sikh nor Hindu? Mediatized Religion in Anti-Caste Contexts" concentrates on an evolving mediascape of global dimensions in the context of the Ravidassias, a socioreligious community of North Indian origin. The chapter discusses the Ravidassia mediascape as representing an upheaval emerging from mediatization processes and their complex contextual entanglements with socioreligious, political and economic changes as well as increased spatial mobility of various actors. The case study exemplifies the benefits of an ethnography-based, actor-centered mediatization perspective and of utilizing the concept of communicative figurations which considers the intertwining between various mediated communicative forms and multidirectional communication flows across borders and beyond the digital. Gregory Grieve, Christopher Helland, and Rohit Singh in "Digitalizing Tibet: A Critical Buddhist Reconditioning of Hjarvard's Mediatization Theory" analyze the digitalization of the Tibetan Buddhist ceremony of the 33rd Kalachakra. Reconditioning Hjarvard's theory through critical Buddhist communication theory, the chapter argues that Hjarvard's overemphasis on secularization occurs because of his reliance on a Protestant understanding of religion. The chapter discusses a critical Buddhist communication which theorizes mediatization not as a one-way transmission of information about an essential referent from source to destination, but as media practices that mutually condition each other.

The volume's concluding Part 4 on West Asia contains chapters on Iran and Israel. Narges Valibeigi in "Being Religious through Social Networks: Representation of Religious Identity of Shia Iranians on Instagram" focuses on how the Internet influences the process of religious identity construction for Shia Iranians, exploring the relationship between religion and media as two societal institutions that were once separated and now are intertwined. Applying mediatization as a framework suggested by Hjarvard, this chapter concludes that the concept of photo sharing on Instagram has changed Shia Iranians' experience of being religious and has individualized the process of identity formation in the Iranian community which contains nontraditional and even nonreligious elements that now symbolize ritualistic aspects of religious identity. In their chapter "Understanding Jewish Digital Media in Israel: Between Technological Affordances and Religious-Cultural Uses", Ruth Tsuria and Heidi A. Campbell offer a discussion of current studies on Israeli Judaism and digital media in light of the theoretical considerations of mediatization. Three specific case studies are highlighted: digital construction of religious terminology regarding gender and sexuality, diasporic identity and social media, and communal boundary negotiation online. The chapter suggests combining Religious Social Shaping of Technology with Mediatization of Religion to allow for a framework that considers both religious worldviews and the technological character of media. The volume concludes with a critical reflection by Kerstin Radde-Antweiler who presents the concept of communicative figuration to analyze the particular constellation of actors, the thematic action orientation and the communicative practices in relation to a changing media environment. As a case study, she uses the self-crucifixion in the Philippines.

Overall, *Mediatized Religion in Asia* presents a broad range of innovative studies on the interrelation of media and religion in Asia, specifically by applying and critically discussing the application, including advantages and limits, of mediatization. As such, this volume is informative of how and why mediatization intensely influences the construction of religious beliefs and practices in contemporary Asian societies. Bringing together recent scholarship from both leading and emerging scholars in the field in a cohesive collection, the book also allows for insights into transregional processes and interactions in Asia and beyond. As a volume in the new Routledge Research in Digital Media and Culture in Asia Series, it addresses various audiences with interests in digital culture and religion in Asia, and in communication theories and approaches – including but not limited to Media and Communication Studies, Asian Studies, Religious Studies and broadly, Culture Studies. The diversified yet systemized case studies offered in this collected volume will accordingly contribute to mapping out future research agendas in the research on media and religion, and mediatization as a theoretical and methodical approach and concept.

References

Altheide, D. L. and Snow, R. P., 1979. *Media Logic*. Beverly Hills: Sage.

Babb, L. A. and Wadley, S. S., eds., 1995. *Media and the Transformation of Religion in South Asia*. Philadelphia: University of Pennsylvania Press.

Baffelli, E., 2016. *Media and New Religions in Japan*. London: Routledge.

Baffelli, E., Reader, I. and Staemmler, B., eds., 2011. *Japanese Religions on the Internet: Innovation, Representation, and Authority*. New York: Routledge.

Black, D., Khoo, O. and Iwabuchi. K., eds., 2016. *Contemporary Culture and Media in Asia*. London: Rowman & Littlefield International.

Campbell, H., ed., 2015. *Digital Judaism: Jewish Negotiations with Digital Media and Culture*. New York: Routledge.

Couldry, N. and Hepp, A., 2013. Conceptualizing Mediatization: Contexts, Traditions, Arguments. *Communication Theory*, 23, 191–202. doi:10.1111/comt.12019.

Couldry, N. and Hepp, A., 2016. *The Mediated Construction of Reality*. Cambridge: Polity Press.

Dorman, B., 2012. *Celebrity Gods. New Religions, Media, and Authority in Occupied Japan*. Honolulu: University of Hawaii Press.

Eisenlohr, P., 2015. Media, Citizenship, and Religious Mobilization. The Muharram Awareness Campaign in Mumbai. *The Journal of Asian Studies*, 74(3), 687–710. doi:10.1017/S0021911815000534.

Golan, O. and Campbell, H., 2015. Strategic Management of Religious Websites. The Case of Israel's Orthodox Communities. *Journal of Computer-mediated Communication*, 20(4), 467–486.

Grieve, G. P., 2016. *Cyber Zen: Imagining Authentic Buddhist Identity, Community and Practices in the Virtual World of Second Life.* New York: Routledge.

Grieve, G. P. and Veidlinger, D., eds., 2015. *Buddhism, the Internet, and Digital Media: The Pixel in the Lotus.* New York: Routledge.

Helland, C., 2010. (Virtually) Been There, (Virtually) Done That. Examining the Online Religious Practices of the Hindu Tradition: Introduction. *Online – Heidelberg Journal of Religions on the Internet,* 4(1), 148–150.

Hjarvard, S., 2008. The Mediatization of Religion. A Theory of the Media as Agents of Religious Change. *Northern Lights,* 6, 9–26. Bristol: Intellect Press.

Hjarvard, S., 2013. *The Mediatization of Culture and Society.* London: Routledge.

Hjorth, L. and Khoo, O., eds., 2015. *Routledge Handbook of New Media in Asia.* Abingdon: Routledge.

Ho, W.-Y., 2010. Islam, China and the Internet. Negotiating Residual Cyberspace between Hegemonic Patriotism & Connectivity to the Ummah. *Journal of Muslim Minority Affairs,* 30(1), 63–79.

Jacobsen, K. A. and Myrvold. K., eds., 2018. *Religion and Technology in India. Spaces, Practices and Authorities.* London and New York: Routledge.

Karapanagiotis, N., 2013. Cyber Forms, Worshipable Forms. Hindu Devotional Viewpoints on the Ontology of Cyber-Gods and -Goddesses. *International Journal of Hindu Studies,* 17(1), 57–82. doi:10.1007/s11407-013-9136-4.

Keul, I., ed., 2015. *Asian Religions, Technology and Science.* London and New York: Routledge.

King, R. and Craig, T., eds., 2002. *Global Goes Local: Popular Culture in Asia.* Vancouver: University of British Columbia Press.

Krotz, F., 2001. *Die Mediatisierung kommunikativen Handelns. Der Wandel von Alltag und sozialen Beziehungen, Kultur und Gesellschaft durch die Medien.* Opladen: Westdeutscher Verlag.

Krotz, F., 2008. Media Connectivity: Concepts, Conditions and Consequences. In: Hepp, A., Krotz, F., Moores, S. and Winter, C., eds. *Connectivity, Network and Flows. Conceptualizing Contemporary Communications.* Cresskill: Hampton Press, 13–32.

Lee, J., 2009. Cultivating the Self in Cyberspace: The Use of Personal Blogs among Buddhist Priests. *Journal of Media and Religion,* 8(2), 97–114.

Lim, F. K. G., 2009. *Mediating Piety: Technology and Religion in Contemporary Asia.* Leiden: Brill.

Lövheim, M., 2011. Mediatisation of Religion: A Critical Appraisal. *Culture and Religion,* 12(2), 153–166.

Lövheim, M. and Lynch, G. (2011). The Mediatisation of Religion Debate: An Introduction. *Culture and Religion,* 12(2), 111–117. doi:10.1080/147556 10.2011.579715.

Lundby, K., ed., 2009. *Mediatization: Concept, Changes, Consequences.* New York: Peter Lang.

Lundby, K., 2013. Transformations in Religion across Media. In: Lundby, K., ed. *Religion across Media. From Early Antiquity to Late Modernity.* New York: Peter Lang.

Mallapragada, M., 2012. Desktop Deities. Hindu Temples, Online Cultures and the Politics of Remediation. In: Dudrah, R., Gopal, S., Rai, A. S. and

Basu, A., eds. *InterMedia in South Asia. The Fourth Screen*. London and New York: Routledge, 6–18.

Manheim, E., 1933. *Die Träger der öffentlichen Meinung. Studien zur Soziologie der Öffentlichkeit*. Brünn, Prag, Leipzig, Wien: Verlag Rudolf M. Rohrer.

Radde-Antweiler, K., 2018 (forthcoming). Die Mediatisierung lokaler Rituale im globalen Mediendiskurs. Darstellung und Diskussion von philippinischen Selbstkreuzigungen und -geißelungen in digitalen Medien. In: Radde-Antweiler, K. and Offerhaus, A., eds. *Multiple Media – Multiple Religions? Facetten der Transformation von Medien und Religion*. Wiesbaden: VS Verlag.

Scheifinger, H., 2015. New Technology and Change in the Hindu Tradition. The Internet in Historical Perspective. In: Keul, I., ed. *Asian Religions, Technology and Science*. London and New York: Routledge, 153–168.

Šisler, V., 2014. From Kuma\War to Quraish: Representation of Islam in Arab and American Video Games. In: Campbell, H. A. and Grieve, G. P., eds. *Playing with Religion in Digital Games*. Bloomington: Indiana University Press, 109–133.

Thomas, J. B., 2012. *Drawing on Tradition: Manga, Anime, and Religion in Contemporary Japan*. Honolulu: Hawai University Press.

Veer, P., ed., 2015. *Handbook of Religion and the Asian City: Aspiration and Urbanization in the Twenty-First Century*. Oakland: University of California Press.

Yao, Q., Stout, D. A. and Liu, Z., 2011. China's Official Media Portrayal of Religion (1996–2005): Policy Change in a Desecularizing Society. *Journal of Media and Religion*, 10, 39–50.

Zeiler, X., 2014. The Global Mediatization of Hinduism through Digital Games: Representation versus Simulation in Hanuman: Boy Warrior. In: Campbell, H. A. and Grieve, G. P., eds. *Playing with Religion in Digital Games*. Bloomington: Indiana University Press, 66–87.

Zeiler, X., 2018. Durgā Pūjā Committees: Community Origin and Transformed Mediatized Practices Employing Social Media. In: Simmons, C., Sen, M. and Rodrigues, H., eds. *Nine Nights of the Goddess. The Navaratri Festival in South Asia*. Albany: SUNY, 121–138.

Part 1
East Asia

2 "Does Anyone Know a Good Healer?" An Analysis of Mediatized Word-of-Mouth Advertising of Spiritual Healers in Japanese Online Question and Answer Forums

Birgit Staemmler

Introduction

On 19 December 2010, *mikancyu* posted the following question in one of the largest Japanese online question and answer forums (Q&A forums):

> I am looking for a diviner in the Tokyo area who hits the truth well. I live in Nerima-district. Don't you know a (reliable) diviner who lives close by and could see me maybe even tomorrow?
> Not someone like "Mother of Izumi" or "Mother of Ginza" and so on where people always wait in line hoping they may be seen,
> but I want to consult a trustworthy diviner whom I can consult properly for 30 minutes or an hour without any rush and without having to worry about what's around us.
> Isn't there anybody whom you could recommend maybe from your own experience?
> I would appreciate detailed information (telephone, address, means of reservation and so on).
> Thank you very much.[1]

There are many similar questions in Japanese online Q&A forums, some less urgent, some in more detail about the specific problem, some asking for criteria of how to identify a *good* or *reliable* healer and so on. Most questions receive a number of informative and encouraging answers reasonably quickly, and some questioners in return post replies to those who answered their questions, thanking them, asking for more details or giving more details about their situation.

In this chapter, I analyze questions and answers in Japanese Q&A forums discussing the criteria for trustworthy spiritual healers. Rather than focusing on the actual criteria for healers, which will be evaluated in a different study (e.g., Staemmler 2018), my focus here is on the meta-level of the communication process. That is, I look, on the one hand, at the difficult balance those asking questions have to maintain between retaining their privacy in a public medium and yet offering sufficient information to elicit helpful answers and, on the other hand, at the mechanisms through which those answering questions try to establish their cognitive authority while remaining anonymous. The third focus is on the bilateral form of online word-of-mouth advertising in which entries in forums are often concluded by references to healers' own websites and weblogs providing additional practical information because anonymity and the relative brevity of written entries as opposed to oral word of mouth necessitate that word of mouth be substantiated by *tangible* evidence.

Research Setting

Spiritual Healers

This chapter is based on the data of a large research project about the way in which individual Japanese spiritual healers present themselves online as trustworthy.[2] I define spiritual healers as people who trace physical or psychological problems back to supernatural causes and/ or at least semiprofessionally strive to solve the problems of their customers by not necessarily biomedically accepted religious means. These *religious means* include prayers, recitations, meditation, rituals for the deceased, charm stones, purifications and exorcisms. Spiritual healers may roughly be classified into diviners who predict the outcome of events and hence give advice for difficult decisions, and healers as such who provide help in major crises, such as continuous misfortune and obstinate illnesses.

Japan has a long tradition of various forms of faith healing deeply rooted not only in its multifarious folk religious traditions but quite often also connected to and doctrinally substantiated by institutionalized religious traditions, especially Shinto, Buddhism, Mountain Asceticism and Confucianism. Additionally, British Spiritualism and the American and European *New Age* movement have brought a multitude of alternative diagnostic and healing techniques to Japan whose medical system is otherwise dominated by Western biomedicine and, to a lesser extent, traditional Chinese medicine.[3]

Japanese spiritual healers have always relied on word-of-mouth advertising to attract new customers, on satisfied clients telling their neighbors, friends and relatives about their experiences and recommending their services, should these too suffer from physical or mental distress or need counsel concerning their love life, family or work. Additionally, some healers used print media to disseminate information about their services, such as telephone directories and individual leaflets. Recently, however, the most important source of information about religious healers – apart from word of mouth, which has lost nothing of its impact – are digital media, such as healers' websites and weblogs located via search engines as well as online Q&A forums. In these forums, people ask for concrete recommendations as well as for criteria to help distinguish *good* healers from frauds.

Online Question and Answer Forums

Online Q&A forums are often and easily used. Anyone with access to the Internet and a web browser may after registration, which usually does not require more than a handle name and an e-mail address, write and submit a question following a simple procedure. One or more other people will hopefully write useful answers within a reasonably short amount of time. Additionally, any Internet user can read any of the conveniently archived previous questions and answers. Using online Q&A forums, thus, is cheap, technically unchallenging, and may be done within the comfort and safety of one's own room. Q&A forums are consequently used very frequently. Harper, Moy and Konstan (2009) report that 90,000 questions were posted at *Yahoo Answers* every day; *gutefrage.net* states that almost 18 million questions have been asked since its start in 2006; Zhihu.com is reported to have had over 17 million users in early 2015; and Yahoo! Japan's *Chiebukuro* counted 167,296,788 questions since 2004.[4]

Because of the immense number of questions, forums provide categories with sub- and sub-sub-categories[5] into which the posters sort their questions: computers, health, hobbies, education, pets and so on. As the providers of Q&A forums sell advertisements and hence profit from traffic, many offer incentives – grades or points – to frequent users and *best answers*, arguing that high grades enhance users' reputation or may even have monetary value.[6] There is no technical way of telling which posts are genuine and which are fake – although, for example, language, contents, meta-information about posters provide cues to this. Although advertising is prohibited in Q&A forums, some recommendations of goods and services are obviously written by people with financial motivations. Additionally, users may register under several handle names and could – at least theoretically – answer their own questions.

Numerically the most important Japanese Q&A forum is Yahoo! Japan's *Chiebukuro* (literally *bag of knowledge*) founded in 2004 with currently over 34 million registered users.[7] Much smaller is *Oshiete!goo* (literally *tell/teach me!*), which was founded in 2000 by *Goo*, a branch of NTT Resonant, which is part of Japan's largest telecommunications company (Takahashi 2014). The third important forum is *Okwave* run by a small company founded in 1999 and specialized in Q&A-forum

technology. Until January 2015 *Oshiete!goo* utilized *Okwave*'s technology, that is their databases contained – and partly still contain – exactly the same question and answer threads under identical identification numbers.[8] Both, *Chiebukuro* and *Oshiete!goo/Okwave*, provide information about posters on individual profile pages, such as the number of questions asked and answered, the number and quota of answers rated *best answer* and where applicable or desired, ranks and personal information.

This chapter utilizes the data for my larger project about online self-representation of Japanese spiritual healers. It was collected through an extensive search engine search in November 2012 which resulted not only in links to websites and weblogs of spiritual healers themselves, but also to Q&A forums discussing the criteria for trustworthy healers and asking for concrete information about healers. I have started my analysis with the threads discovered in the main corpus of data extending the data to threads directly or indirectly linked to these threads. In total, I evaluated about 20 threads with over 150 posts written between 2001 and 2011.

Mediatization as Sensitizing Concept

My research uses the Grounded Theory Method initially developed by Glaser and Strauss (1967) in the form revised and refined by Charmaz (2006) and Clarke (2005). Grounded Theory Method emphasizes the primacy of the data themselves for the development of concepts and theories and hence cautions against the use of potentially biasing or misleading pre-existing (cf. note 9) theories (e.g., Charmaz 2006, 165–168). Nonetheless, it supports the reference to "sensitizing concepts" (Charmaz 2006, 16), which may be helpful as heuristic devices.[9] Given the topic of this edited volume, I employed theories of mediatization as sensitizing concepts for this analysis of the interactions within online forums. That is, I draw on theories attempting to explain the influences media have not only on communication as such, but also on societies and cultures as a whole. They contend that media influence the formation and adaptation of values, modify modes of interaction, frame certain events as meaningful and so on.

From my perspective, Hjarvard's theory of mediatization is too much focused on institutions to be applicable to individual discussions about spiritual healers in Asia or Europe. However, some aspects may be useful. Hjarvard, for instance, emphasizes that institutions, such as family, school and church, "have lost some of their former authority, and the media have to some extent taken over their role as providers of information and moral orientation" (Hjarvard 2013, 83). Although, of course, word of mouth is not an institution, it is possible that discussions in forums extend or substitute word of mouth as a source of information, especially with topics too private to talk about with friends or for questions no friends or acquaintances could answer.

Krotz on the other hand, understands mediatization as a "metaprocess of social and cultural change" not restricted to the modern area (2007, 11) and suggested that recently, its key dimensions include (a) the intertwining of media with people's everyday lives – gathering knowledge, communicating with others, living through emotions and so on; (b) the increasing routinization of mediated communication, that is the use of mediated communication anywhere, at any time and about any topic; and (c) the increasing significance of media for providing orientation and framing things one might see, hear, feel or otherwise experience (2001, 34–35). Wellman's observation that modern societies had shifted structurally from bounded local groups to networked individualism because of changes in, among others, transportation and especially communication (2002) may hence be seen as a consequence of mediatization, although Wellman himself did not use that term. The classical categories of strong and weak ties within network societies which serve different functions (famously: Granovetter 1973, 1983) are effected differently by mediatization. Text messages via mobile phones, for example, are mostly frequent short messages to close friends and family, as opposed to more formal e-mails sent to less closely linked persons (Miyata, Wellman and Boase 2005).[10] To the distinction between strong and weak ties, Caroline Haythornthwaite added "latent ties", that is ties "for which a connection is available technically but that has not yet been activated by social interaction" (2002, 389). It is these latent ties that are utilized in Q&A forums. Latent ties, hence, constitute the main difference between the *mediatized* discussions about and word of mouth for Japanese spiritual healers in online forums, and *non-mediatized* discussion and word of mouth, which depend on strong and weak ties.

Does Anyone Know a Good Healer?

Because of Grounded Theory's emphasis on data and because my data are in Japanese and hence not accessible to most people, I present a few more examples here to give an impression.

Example 2[11]: Next Week Monday

On 28 September 2002, *original-ayumi* asked:

I'd like to go as early as next week Monday,
so please tell me about a diviner who hits the truth super well.
Please ignore diviners related to religious organizations.
Also ignore those who might pressure me into buying name stamps
 or gravestones.

I'd appreciate if you could give me their times and prices of consultation if possible!
Thank you very much.[12]

This questioning person seems to be a young woman – *Ayumi* is a common girl's name, the language is very young and urgent, and she later mentions that she is working. It was posted early on a Saturday evening that is not after a night spent sleepless with worry. Although *original-ayumi* did not mention the reason for her quest, she did mention two criteria undesirable in spiritual healers: affiliation with a religious institution and spiritual sales.[13] It is also noticeable that she asked for concrete details about the diviner's services. *Original-ayumi*'s question received two answers within 24 hours. She replied to both of them and received a follow-up answer from both her respondents. One of the answers she received was the following:

I have been to the Shinjuku branch of Tōmei Tesō.[14]
A thorough reading based on my date of birth and my hand lines took 30–40 minutes and 3000 yen [approx. 25 €].
There was not talk about religion and no pressure about name stamps or gravestones at all,
I received a really detailed reading about my character, my fortune in love, in finances, my future and so on.
When she hit the truth so perfectly about something I had not yet mentioned to anybody, I was so surprised I almost asked quite stupidly how she could know.
Hotpepper, Shinjuku walking and other voucher-magazines available in the streets,
contain 1000-yen-off vouchers, I think.
I had also asked a similar question in *Oshiete!goo* and went there because of the answer I had received.
This is only my personal experience, but I would be happy if it helped you.
As reference, I give you the website of Tōmei Tesō.
www.toumei-tesou.co.jp/[15]

The time when the answer was written (2.30 a.m.) and the fact that in the second answer the author admitted that she only knew the name of one of Tōmei Tesō's practitioners are contra-indicators, but otherwise this answer may possibly have been written by a member of Tōmei Tesō because it is almost a model recommendation. It is quick, friendly and gives concrete information, such as price, methods and duration of the reading, all of which are at the usual average for this kind of divination. What is more significant, however, is that it refutes any connection with evil institutions and practices, that it describes the reading as *thorough*, that is satisfyingly in-depth, and that it recounts the author's surprise when the practitioner knew something she could not possibly have known unless she really had supernatural powers. This mention of hitting the truth (*ataru*), be it about a personal secret or a prediction, appears in all the relevant threads and is the single most important criterion for a good spiritual healer.[16] Additionally, the author mentions vouchers in two fashionable magazines thereby implying that the diviner was trendy and seeing her was not something old-fashioned. The author constructs a common identity with *original-ayumi* and defines answers in Q&A forums as trustworthy sources by reporting that she too had received helpful information about the diviner from *Oshiete!goo*. And, the answer contains the URL of Tōmei Tesō's website so that *original-ayumi* can read more for herself.

Example 3: A Real Spiritually Gifted Person

On 23 September 2001, *mondo*, about whom nothing else is known, asked:

> Is there really anything like a real spiritually gifted person? If there is one you know, I would definitely like to know. Also, I would like to hear from your experiences to what extent they might be accurate.[17]

This may be classified as a *conversational*, rather than an *informational question* (Harper, Moy and Konstan 2009). It is pivoting around the term *real* – *a real spiritually gifted person* (*honmono no reinōsha*) – which is immensely frequent and significant in these Q&A threads as it sometimes seems to be implied that *real* healers or diviners, recognizable because their statements hit the truth, would do no harm to their customers. *Mondo*'s question received 33 answers, the first one after three hours, the last one after 11 years, indicating that the threads in Q&A forums are still read – and occasionally referred and replied to – long after the question was asked. The answers were very heterogeneous, some narrating encounters with spiritually gifted people, others naming their criteria for identifying spiritually gifted people, some giving concrete recommendations, others refuting the idea that spiritually gifted people existed, yet others expounding their personal views of souls and spirits. Some answers referred to earlier answers, while *mondo* him- or herself only replied to the first four answers, that is, those that were written within days after the question was posted.

Example 4: Opinions of Independent Third Parties

Late one night in October 2009 *caramel252* posted a long question in *Oshiete!goo*, in which she asked for an independent advice on whether she should follow her relatives' recommendation and pay a significant sum to a healer for a purifying prayer because the healer had discovered a karmic hindrance to her having a healthy baby. She thus turned to the Q&A forum in a time of crisis, torn between her own doubts on the one hand and, on the other hand, the positive reputation issued by her relatives based on their own experience. The latter was reinforced by the assertive stance of the healer who urged her to have the ritual done because her future should be more precious to her than any amount of money. She concluded:

> Because those close to me whom I could ask for advice are all friends of the healer, they cannot judge objectively. So, dear all, please let me hear your opinions as independent third parties. I would very much appreciate your help.[18]

Despite having posted her question in the middle of the night, four people answered within three hours counterbalancing the advice of her relatives and the healer, discouraging her from following their advice and simultaneously encouraging her to follow her own judgment. The person answering first told her about an old lady that she knew, who only took small donations for her healing services; the second encouraged her to follow her own judgment rather than rely on others; and the third recommended consulting a traditional Buddhist temple at a much lower fee. The answer she rated the best, however, was the fourth, which revealed how its author had almost been talked into paying a lot of money for a purification by a healer who later turned out to be a fraud.

Thus, in this thread, oral and digital words of mouth are intertwining and counterbalancing: The recommendations of close, trusted relatives with good previous experience with that particular healer *versus* the advice of anonymous strangers who base their authority on their own, possibly fictitious, experiences with completely different healers. Judging from the replies, *caramel252* wrote to all answers the very next morning – the different aspects addressed by the four answers, which added up to a multifaceted argument, and the sincerity and friendliness in the language of the answers effectively supported her own sense of doubt about the trustworthiness of the healer. To put it more sociologically: The advice given by people connected to her through strong ties was counterweighed by the cumulative voices of newly awoken latent ties.

Example 5: *I'll Keep You Informed*

At five o'clock one morning, *kanaejj* seems to have needed someone to share this with and so answered a 14-month-old question:

> Having read a certain bulletin board I commissioned [a healer] last week without further ado. I had been thinking it over and over

because 300,000 yen [approx. 2,500 €] is so much money and the healer was a bit frightening, and I had to pay it all at once, but then I read in a certain blog that a religious specialist won't be any good if she's not an eccentric person, and that good religious specialists all have a crooked personality (sorry, madam). After all, I thought, the only aim was that [my wish] would be fulfilled, and I also thought that if I postponed making it up with my boyfriend even a minute longer he might start going out with someone else. It was a really important decision.

It is now early in the morning, but my boyfriend who's refused to talk to me for half a year just called in a serious voice.

He's on his way to my room now.

In the past half year he'd not been to bed with anyone and he still loved me, he said.

I'll keep you informed.[19]

Around nine o'clock the same evening, she indeed wrote a second answer happily telling readers that she had made it up with her boyfriend. Taken together, these two answers point to the communal character, however vague and anonymous, of this thread, based on the shared minority belief that most urgent wishes can sometimes be fulfilled by religious specialists. *Kanaejj* had obviously read this thread looking for a healer herself, who could reconcile her with her boyfriend. She followed one of the recommendations given in the thread, had a first meeting but initially hesitated to commission the suggested ritual because of the high fees and the healer's somewhat intimidating character. When the ritual eventually did prove successful, *kanaejj* returned to the thread whose recommendations had helped her to find this healer and communicated her happy news, much as she would have called a friend whose advice had been helpful in an important matter.

These were just a few paradigmatic examples illustrating some of the patterns as well as the heterogeneity of the voices and discussions. Again, some of these questions and answers may well be exaggerated, strongly biased or fictitious, but they nonetheless shed light on various aspects of online discourses about a disputed religious issue.

Analysis

Asking Questions Online

Although some may want to initiate discussions about controversial topics and others only post to pass their time, some people posting questions in online forums can be regarded as doing so hoping to receive helpful, informative answers. This demands a difficult balance between vagueness and conciseness, between retaining one's privacy knowing that what is posted in a forum may be read by anyone anywhere, and between the need to include a sufficient amount of concrete, and often quite personal, information to elicit useful help from those answering the question. Whereas some questions publish no or very little personal details (Examples 1–3), others disclose a lot of very private information (Example 4).

This diversity can partly be explained by the nature of the questions. Research distinguishes between *informational questions* and *conversational questions* in Q&A forums (Harper, Moy and Konstan 2009), yet I think that, at least in this context of spiritual healers, a third category of *advice-seeking questions* needs to be added. Spiritual healers in Japan offer divinations and healing, and people needing either of these may use Q&A forums to ask for a recommendation of a trustworthy healer (informational question) or for criteria with which to distinguish a trustworthy healer from a fraud (conversational question). Neither of these questions requires much personal information to answer – although some authors ask for more information about the nature of the problem in order to recommend the most suitable healer. Yet there are also questions of people needing advice on how to react to or cope with a certain situation. This situation needs to be described in some detail to receive a truly useful answer (Example 4).

Although informational questions may well be answered by healers clandestinely advertising their own services (the answer of Example 2 is possibly a case in point), advice-seeking questions tend to receive longish, sympathetic and thoughtful answers. If a reply is written by the questioner acknowledging the effort – and usefulness – of the answer or requesting or giving more details, very short dialogues occasionally evolve in the course of which more personal information may be divulged. Those who ask advice-seeking questions appear to be glad of the attention, empathy and counsel they receive from those answering. The mediatization of asking questions, therefore, significantly extends the range of those one can ask for advice to include an innumerable amount of yet unknown people (latent ties) which is especially important for people who could not ask relatives or close friends (strong ties) because they were biased, the problem was too intimate or they simply did not know either.

Additionally, there are far more silent readers following threads than people actually writing answers – the author of Example 5, for instance, had obviously read the thread looking for similar information yet only contributed herself after her quest had been successful. Mediatization of asking for recommendations and advice, thus, extends the amount of advice one may reasonably expect from friends and relatives to include answers previously given to similar questions, which Q&A forums conveniently archive online and which, hence, are more readily available than advice columns in old issues of magazines. Granovetter's theory of the strength of weak ties (1973) may thus be expanded to include the potential strength of latent ties, especially when strong or weak ties cannot be consulted or when the solution to a problem is additive, that is, consisting of many elements, so that many short answers can sum up to be very useful – or very misleading, depending on the answers (Constant, Sproull and Kiesler 1996, 120).

Giving Authoritative Answers Anonymously

Unless they merely want to provoke or be funny, people answering questions in Q&A forums will need to demonstrate that they are credible – real people seriously trying to help – and authoritative – competent to answer a particular question. Much has been written about cognitive authority[20] and web credibility, some of which is also applicable to the answers in Q&A forums. Research about cognitive authority on the Internet has shown that an author's or website's official affiliation, convincing rhetorics, references to other publications, repetition of opinions already encountered elsewhere and a lack of contradicting previous knowledge contribute to establishing an online source's cognitive authority (e.g., Fritch and Cromwell 2001, Rieh 2002, 2005, Staemmler 2011). Research about *web credibility* distinguishes between *source credibility* and *message credibility*, that is, whether the author and that which is written can be regarded as correct and reliable (e.g., Kim 2010) and hence have cognitive authority.

Answers in Q&A forums are not only anonymous, but also text-based, most often one-shot contacts and not very long – usually between four and twenty lines of text – hence they lack most cues for source credibility, such as previous contacts, expressive URLs and official titles, illustrations, layout and so on. Those answering questions, therefore, need other means of establishing their authority and their message's credibility, and Q&A forums' reputation systems and user profiles offer structures supporting this effort.

Another important mechanism is the skillful use of rhetoric (e.g., Green 2009, 45; Kim 2010). However, in my data it is not the accuracy, logic or correct language of the answer that seems to count, as some of the best-written and most logical answers were blatantly rejected because they contradicted the questioner's worldview.[21] Particularly in advice-seeking questions, it is the author's empathy, visible in friendly language, affirmative statements and expressions of encouragement that seem to render the answer convincing and useful to the questioner.

Judging from the frequency of its occurrence and the replies by the questioners, the most significant mechanism for cognitive authority is to base one's answer on personal experience. Many authors either begin their answer by stating that they themselves or one of their relatives was a spiritual healer, or they recount experiences they themselves, a close relative or friend had as the customer of a spiritual healer. They then answer the question based on these personal experiences and questioners quite frequently reply asking for more details about these experiences. Whereas answers to informational questions requesting the recommendation of a healer are only based on experiences as a customer – because forums do not permit advertising – in threads answering conversational and advice-seeking questions, advisors also establish their cognitive authority through their experience as spiritual healers who should be able to evaluate other healers' practices.

Both types of personal experiences provide the answering person with an *insider status* (Clark 2012), establishing him or her as someone who knows. What is possibly even more important, however, is the aspect of *unit grouping* McKnight, Cummings and Chervany (1998) identified as important for establishing trust in someone one has never met before: it is easier to trust someone who belongs to the same category of people as oneself and can be expected to share beliefs and values. In recounting their own experiences with spiritual healers, answerers thus indicate that they themselves, too, belong to that minority of people who believe in the possibility of spiritual healing, that they take the questioner and his or her problem seriously, that they are part of the same community.

There are four indicators, which point to an important aspect of Q&A forums especially for people with minority beliefs or interests – providing a means of communication and community with yet unknown but like-minded people: the almost total lack of abusive answers,[22] the requests by some questioners that those not believing in spirits should not bother answering, the large number of personal experiences and the empathy expressed in the answers. As in real life, contradicting voices are unwelcome, contrary to real-life communication, however, unwelcome voices can effortlessly be refuted and ignored. Also, contrary to real-life situations, like-minded people can be found and communicated with, anonymously yet emphatically, from anywhere in the world as far as language barriers will permit.

The Bi-Lateral Nature of Online Word of Mouth

Answers in Q&A forums often conclude with a link to a healer's website or weblog suggesting that the questioner should look there for more information. These links respond to many questioners' requests for detailed, practical information about prices, methods, hours of consultation and so on. Links are added because of the relative brevity of written entries in Q&A forums, as opposed to oral word of mouth. Reference to additional information to elaborate the actual answer is thus helpful for the questioner. At the same time, these links substantiate the answer's credibility (Kim 2010), and offering easy access to the healer's website, serve as an effective means of advertising. When the sources to additional information are direct links to online shops or service providers, they positively affect consumer behavior, as studies about e-commerce have shown that online recommendations, especially by people with similar interests, significantly influence customers' decisions despite their low level of source credibility (e.g., Lim et al. 2006).

For healers, thus, a link to their website in a Q&A forum is a valuable advertisement for this website. The link not only directs readers already interested in a specific topic to their site (targeted advertising), but also increases the number of links to their site which, according to the logic of search engine algorithms, will improve its ranking in the list of results (search engine optimization). A healer could easily write the answer with the advertising link herself, which would be especially convincing if she had already answered other questions and thereby gained some degree of authority. Technically, a healer could even use two handle names and write both, the question searching for a healer and the recommendation, herself mentioning all the necessary assets and adding the multipurpose link (e.g., answer in Example 2).

Links to healers' websites in answers in Q&A forums are a good example of the dissolution of boundaries and the interweaving between media Krotz identified as one aspect of mediatization (2001, 19–26). The concrete boundaries of when to use which medium are vanishing and although, for instance, reviews of films and books have been found in magazines for decades, links to healers' websites in Q&A forums *in-mediately* connect (alleged) outsiders' recommendations with the self-representations of the service providers themselves. Word of mouth interweaves with prefabricated mass media content, such as websites, more directly than traditional media could have done, creating a kind of closely interwoven bilateral advertising for the healer's services – or, in case of critical entries, moving negative word of mouth just one click away from the owner's website.

Conclusion: Extending Advice Seeking into Mediatized Communities

Q&A forums not only provide a pool of potential advisors for almost any conceivable topic, but also extend traditional word of mouth beyond the limits of acquaintances' acquaintances to include countless latent ties. Although advertising is not allowed in Q&A forums, the borderline between advice, recommendation and advertisement is fuzzy, especially when posters use pseudonyms and multiple registration is easily possible. It is difficult to judge whether someone recommending a certain washing powder is a highly satisfied user, a sales person or a complete liar, and many users and researchers have tried to identify criteria to solve this problem of credibility and authority.

Recommendations of and criteria for *good* spiritual healers are requested in this particular mediatized form for various reasons. A large number of healers exist, yet their contact data are difficult to find as many do not belong to any organization. They use word of mouth and websites/weblogs to advertise their service; hence, Q&A forums at the technical intersection of these channels are obvious sources of information. Second, spiritual healers in general have a dubious image as obviously only negative cases get reported in newspapers and television, and it is important to find a trustworthy healer if he or she is to be consulted on important matters. Thus, personal experiences of previous customers recounted in Q&A forums are useful additions to a healer's naturally positive self-representation online. Third, many of the questions indicate that the questioner turned to the latent ties of an online forum because the strong and weak ties could not answer the question or, more often, could not be asked for help because the issue was too delicate or the friend or relative too closely involved. Q&A forums, thus, to use Schulz's (2004) expression, extend and occasionally substitute real life information seeking.

Additionally however, although many questioners simply ask for recommendations of a local, reasonably priced healer who hits the truth well and will hence be able to give solid advice, others post advice-seeking questions asking how to deal with a specific healer – how much to pay, how long to wait for an answer, how to ensure that he or she is indeed trustworthy. These questions are implicitly or explicitly directed at the latent community of like-minded people. The informational medium of Q&A forums is, thus, simultaneously a social medium. This is particularly important for people with minority beliefs, such as belief in spiritual healing in Japan, who might be ridiculed for their beliefs if they talked about them openly. Thus, although the question of credibility and authority also pertains to Japanese forums about spiritual healers, other aspects, especially the advisor's empathy, appear to be more significant. It is notable that most of the answers – and certainly most of the answers with positive replies by the questioners – can be located within the same frame of reference. Questions are directed at and answered by people who generally believe that spiritual healing is possible, although they might be unsure about a specific spiritual healer.

It is difficult to generalize the significance threads in online Q&A forums have for individual decision-making processes. Whereas the absolute figures of healer-related questions and the time lag that sometimes occurs between question and answers suggests that other sources of information might be more significant, some of the replies to answers and evolving dialogues indicate that these short communications are indeed helpful and appreciated by a fair share of those asking questions.

Based on Krotz's categorization of three types of computer-mediated communication – human-to-human, human-and-machine and human reception of standardized mass-mediated contents (2001, 74–75) – Q&A forums are an extension of human-to-human communication. They extend – and occasionally substitute – word of mouth beyond the limits of acquaintances and acquaintances' acquaintances into the realm of latent ties. Yet, they do more than that: they link human-to-human communication with the reception of standardized media contents by providing hyperlinks to healers' websites and weblogs. They thereby expand the amount of concrete information beyond that which can be written in a brief answer and often beyond that which would be remembered in a classic oral communication. For Japanese spiritual healers, Q&A forums provide opportunities for advertising – as well as dangers of negative digital, and hence archived and undeletable, word of mouth – while for potential customers, the forums significantly enlarge the number of empathic people they can ask for recommendations and advice.

When, in conclusion to these observations therefore, the eight hypotheses of mediatization with which Krotz concludes his theory (2007, 114–115) are tested against the data provided by this case study, it becomes obvious that they are effortlessly applicable: (1) Media are omnipresent: People write questions and answers anywhere and anytime. (2) Media are interwoven with people's everyday life: Digital communication is used where face-to-face communication fails to provide sufficient answers. (3) Various forms of communication intermingle: Entries in Q&A forums contain links to websites so that word of mouth becomes bilateral. (4) Media-based communication is a part of everyday life: People ask questions about things relevant to their lives or answer questions of anonymous others just as emphatically as if they were present. (5) Media increasingly give orientation and meaning: People ask for advice and discuss criteria of trustworthiness in online forums. (6) Media-based communication affects everyday life and identity, culture and society: Online forums provide opportunities for communication and networking with like-minded others. (7) People with media access increasingly present themselves and give public comments: Millions of people use online Q&A forums, voluntarily answering questions of total strangers.[23]

This is a case study about one aspect within the neglected area of research about individual religious specialists and the Internet, and it is a study based on data in Japanese and hence, located in the Japanese cultural context. The data and results therefore may not seem to permit extrapolation beyond Japan and the Japanese religious world. They do, however, show that Krotz's theory of mediatization is applicable to Japanese online forums discussing spiritual healers – and possibly also to other areas of Japanese society and culture as well as to other

(East Asian) countries, with a comparably high Internet penetration rate, in which people also use Q&A forums to share concerns about minority beliefs and marginalized interests.

Notes

1 Translated from oshiete.goo.ne.jp/qa/6395078.html. All the threads I refer to were archived and last accessed online on February 26, 2017.

2 I am most grateful to the Horst- und Käthe-Eliseit-Stiftung that is generously and patiently funding my research in the wide area of Japanese *Internet-Shamanism*. Thanks also to Svenja Ojemann who helped analyze the first few Q&A threads.

3 A wealth of literature has been published about religion and healing in Japan. See, for example, Lock 1980 and Kleine and Triplett 2012 as well as Schrimpf 2018 for present-day Japan. On spiritual healers in Japan, see, for instance, Fujita 1990, Gaitanidis 2010 and Prochaska-Meyer 2014.

4 See Harper, Moy and Konstan 2009, www.gutefrage.net/, Wang and Zhang 2016 and http://chiebukuro.yahoo.co.jp/.

5 *Oshiete!goo*, for instance, has 17 main categories divided into 86 subcategories and a total of almost 700 sub-sub-categories, see http://oshiete.goo. ne.jp/category/list/ and http://oshiete.goo.ne.jp/guide/about.

6 See, for instance, http://answers.yahoo.com/info/scoring_system/ and http://oshiete.goo.ne.jp/grade/guide/. With *Oshiete!goo* points can be used as payment towards Amazon gift vouchers and so on.

7 See http://chiebukuro.yahoo.co.jp/. Takahashi reported 15 million users for 2014, stating that 65% of the users were male and 50% in their 30s and 40s (Takahashi 2014).

8 Okwave cooperates with nearly three dozen other Q&A sites, many of which have a particular focus – cars, insurances, child rearing, etc. – and hence use only parts of the database (http://okwave-faq.okbiz.okwave.jp/faq/show/1?site_domain=help).

9 There has been a long discussion and eventually a split in the endorsers of Grounded Theory about the extent to which pre-existing theories and concepts should be used as heuristic devices. Whereas Glaser vehemently argued against their use in favor on sole reliance on the data, Strauss, Corbin and their followers encouraged their use as "sensitizing concepts" albeit cautioning against their biasing potential (see, e.g., Strübing 2014, 65–78).

10 In Japan mobile phones – *i-phones* by NTT DoCoMo – started providing access to the Internet as early as 1999. Some results of this particular study may have been overtaken by technical developments and the immense increase in the use of mobile phones, but the facts that new media-mediated communication supplements rather than substitutes face-to-face communication and that different media are used for different purposes and target groups still apply.

11 Because of the introductory example, the examples here are numbered 2–5 to facilitate cross-referencing during the analysis. Also, I distinguish between *answers* given to the questioner and *replies* the questioner sends to those who posted an answer.

12 Translated from oshiete.goo.ne.jp/qa/368613.html.

13 In recent years a variety of incidents, referred to as *spiritual sales*, have been widely reported in the Japanese press, in which people have been intimidated into purchasing goods or services for very high prices to avoid alleged

misfortunes caused by supernatural agents (e.g., Sakurai 2009, 64–101). Religious institutions, especially new religious movements have been regarded with extreme scepticism in Japan since 1995 when Aum Shinrikyō attacked passengers in Tokyo's underground with poisonous gas (see, e.g., Baffelli and Reader 2012). See also Staemmler 2018.

14 Tōmeian (literally: *Eastern Light Hall*), was founded in 1992 and has currently about 400 "fate consultants" in 40 shops (www.toumei-tesou.co.jp/).

15 Translated from oshiete.goo.ne.jp/qa/368613.html.

16 Hitting the truth is also mentioned as key criterion in offline contexts (e.g., Fujita 1990, 68 and Prochaska-Meyer 2014).

17 Translated from oshiete.goo.ne.jp/qa/140042.html.

18 Summarized and translated from http://oshiete.goo.ne.jp/qa/5362983.html.

19 Translated from the ninth answer in oshiete.goo.ne.jp/qa/2106846.html.

20 Patrick Wilson's concept of *cognitive authority*, for example, explains why second-hand knowledge based on information provided by other people or external sources can be as persuasive as first-hand knowledge based on one's own experience (Wilson 1983, 14–26).

21 Answers 2 and 3 in http://oshiete.goo.ne.jp/qa/3695269.html.

22 Offensive answers deleted by administrators leave a gap in the numbering of the answers. Thus, the lack of such gaps indicates that hardly any answers have been deleted which might have been illegal or abusive.

23 The last hypothesis relates to standardized communication – television and so on – which is not addressed in my case study and hence cannot be tested.

References

Baffelli, E. and Reader, I., eds., 2012. Aftermath: The Impact and Ramifications of the Aum Affair. *Japanese Journal of Religious Studies* (Special Issue), 39(1), 1–28.

Charmaz, K., 2006. *Constructing Grounded Theory: A Practical Guide Through Qualitative Analysis*. London: Sage.

Clark, L. S., 2012. Religion and Authority in a Remix Culture: How a Late Night TV Host became an Authority on Religion. In: Lynch, G. and Mitchell, J., eds. *Religion, Media and Culture: A Reader*. London and New York: Routledge, 111–121.

Clarke, A., 2005. *Situational Analysis: Grounded Theory after the Postmodern Turn*. London: Sage.

Constant, D., Sproull, L. and Kiesler, S., 1996. The Kindness of Strangers: The Usefulness of Electronic Weak Ties for Technical Advice. *Organization Science*, 7(2), 119–135.

Fritch, J. W. and Cromwell, R. L., 2001. Evaluating Internet Resources: Identity, Affiliation, and Cognitive Authority in a Networked World. *Journal of the American Society for Information Science and Technology*, 52(6), 499–507.

Fujita, S., 1990. *Ogamiyasan: Reinō kitōshi no sekai*. Tokyo: Kōbundō.

Gaitanidis, I., 2010. *Spiritual Business? A Critical Analysis of the Spiritual Therapy Phenomenon in Contemporary Japan*. PhD thesis, School of Modern Languages and Cultures, The University of Leeds. Available at http://etheses.whiterose.ac.uk/1375/1/Gaitanidis_I_Modern_Languages_and_Cultures_PhD_2010.pdf, accessed 17 July 2014.

Glaser, B. G. and Strauss, A. L., 1967. *The Discovery of Grounded Theory: Strategies for Qualitative Research.* New York: Aldine de Gruyter.

Granovetter, M. S., 1973. The Strength of Weak Ties. *American Journal of Sociology*, 78(6), 1360–1380.

Granovetter, M. S., 1983. The Strength of Weak Ties: A Network Theory Revisited. *Sociological Theory*, 1, 201–233.

Green, M. C., 2009. Trust and Social Interaction on the Internet. In: Joinson, A. N., McKenna, K. Y. A., Postmes, T. and Reips, U. eds. *The Oxford Handbook of Internet Psychology*. New York: Oxford University Press, 43–51.

Gutefrage net GmbH, 2006. *gutefrage*. Available at www.gutefrage.net/, accessed 25 November 2016.

Harper, F. M., Moy, D. and Konstan, J. A., 2009. Facts or Friends? Distinguishing Informational and Conversational Questions in Social Q&A Sites. In: Association for Computing Machinery, ed. *Proceedings of the SIGCHI Conference on Human Factors in Computing Systems*, 759–768. Available at https://dl.acm.org/citation.cfm?id=1518819, accessed 5 June 2018.

Haythornthwaite, C., 2002. Strong, Weak, and Latent Ties and the Impact of New Media. *The Information Society*, 18, 385–401.

Hjarvard, S., 2013. *The Mediatization of Culture and Society*. London and New York: Routledge.

Kim, S., 2010. Questioners' Credibility Judgments of Answers in a Social Question and Answer Site. *Information Research*, 15(1). Available at www.informationr.net/ir/15-2/paper432.html, accessed 2 April 2017.

Kleine, C. and Triplett, K., eds., 2012. Religion and Healing in Japan. *Japanese Religions*, 37(1&2), 1–156.

Krotz, F., 2001. *Die Mediatisierung kommunikativen Handelns: Der Wandel von Alltag und sozialen Beziehungen, Kultur und Gesellschaft durch die Medien.* Wiesbaden: Westdeutscher Verlag.

Krotz, F., 2007. *Mediatisierung: Fallstudien zum Wandel von Kommunikation.* Wiesbaden: Springer VS.

Lim, K. H., Sia, C. L., Lee, M. K. O. and Benbasat, I., 2006. Do I Trust You Online, and If So, Will I Buy? An Empirical Study of Two Trust-Building Strategies. *Journal of Management Information Systems*, 23(2), 233–266.

Lock, M. M., 1980. *East Asian Medicine in Urban Japan: Varieties of Medical Experience.* Berkeley: University of California Press.

McKnight, D. H., Cummings, L. L. and Chervany, N. L., 1998. Initial Trust Formation in New Organizational Relationships. *Academy of Management Review*, 23(3), 473–490.

Miyata, K., Wellmann, B. and Boase, J., 2005. The Wired – and Wireless – Japanese: Webphones, PCs and Social Networks. In: Ling, R. and Pedersen, P. E., eds. *Mobile Communications: Re-negotiation of the Social Sphere.* London: Springer, 427–449.

Okwave, 2015. '*Pātonā saito' to wa nan desu ka?* Available at http://okwave-faq.okbiz.okwave.jp/faq/show/1?site_domain=help, accessed 19 October 2016.

Oshiete!goo, no year. *Oshiete!goo kategori ichiran.* Available at http://oshiete.goo.ne.jp/category/list/, accessed 25 November 2016.

Oshiete!goo, no year. *Oshiete!goo gurēdo.* Available at http://oshiete.goo.ne.jp/grade/guide/, accessed 25 November 2016.

Oshiete!goo, no year. *Oshiete!goo to wa?* Available at http://oshiete.goo.ne.jp/guide/about/, accessed 25 November 2016.

Oshiete!goo: Individual questions:

Q 6395078: "Tonai de yoku ataru uranaishi-san o sagashite imasu." Available at http://oshiete.goo.ne.jp/qa/6395078.html, accessed 26 February 2017.

Q 368613: "Tōkyō no yoku ataru uranaishi no kata o oshiete kudasai!" Available at http://oshiete.goo.ne.jp/qa/368613.html, accessed 26 February 2017.

Q 140042: "Honmono no reinōsha." Available at http://oshiete.goo.ne.jp/qa/140042.html, accessed 26 February 2017.

Q 5362983: "Ogamiya ni tsuite (chōbun ni otsukiai kudasai)." Available at http://oshiete.goo.ne.jp/qa/5362983.html, accessed 26 February 2017.

Q 2106846: "Ogamiyasan to iwareru katagata no jōhō onegai itashimasu." Available at http://oshiete.goo.ne.jp/qa/2106846.html, accessed 26 February 2017.

Q 3695269: "Reishi no tekichūritsu to reinōsha no nōryoku no miwake-kata" Available at http://oshiete.goo.ne.jp/qa/3695269.html, accessed 26 February 2017.

Prochaska-Meyer, I., 2014. *Kaminchu: Spirituelle Heilerinnen in Okinawa.* (Vienna Studies on East Asia 2). Wien: Praesens Verlag.

Rieh, S. Y., 2002. Judgment of Information Quality and Cognitive Authority in the Web. *Journal of the American Society for Information Science and Technology*, 53(2), 145–161.

Rieh, S. Y., 2005. Cognitive Authority. In: Fisher, K. E., Erdelez, S. and McKechnie, L., eds. *Theories of Information Behavior: A Researchers' Guide*. Medford: Information Today, 83–87.

Sakurai, Y., 2009. *Rei to kane: Supirichuaru bijinesu no kōzō.* Tokyo: Shinchōsha.

Schrimpf, M., 2018. Medical Discourses and Practices in Contemporary Japanese Religions. In: Lüddeckens, D. and Schrimpf, M., eds. *Medicine – Religion – Spirituality: Global Perspectives on Traditional, Complementary, and Alternative Healing.* Bielefeld: Transcript, 57–90.

Schulz, W., 2004. Reconstructing Mediatization as an Analytical Concept. *European Journal of Communication*, 19(1), 87–101.

Staemmler, B., 2011. Shaping Shamanism Online: Patterns of Authority in Wikipedia. In: Baffelli, E., Reader, I. and Staemmler, B., eds. *Japanese Religions on the Internet: Innovation, Representation and Authority.* New York and London: Routledge, 150–172.

Staemmler, B., 2018. Religion, Risiko und Vorurteil: Was spirituelle Heiler keinesfalls tun dürfen. Eine Analyse japanischer online Frageforen. In: Wachutka, M., Schrimpf, M. and Staemmler, B., eds. *Religion, Politik und Ideologie: Beiträge zu einer kritischen Kulturwissenschaft. Festschrift für Klaus Antoni.* Frankfurt: iudicium, 118–132.

Strübing, J., 2014. *Grounded Theory: Zur sozialtheoretischen und epistemologischen Fundierung eines pragmatistischen Forschungsstils.* 3rd ed. Wiesbaden: Springer VS.

Takahashi, A., 2014. Yahoo!Chiebukuro no amakudatta! Q&A saito-shea haya wakari, *ASCII.jp*, 30 June. Available at http://ascii.jp/elem/000/000/906/906958 and http://ascii.jp/elem/000/000/906/906958/index-2.html, accessed 13 February 2017.

Uranai no Mise: Tōmeikan, online. n.d. *Kotae wa anata no te no naka ni*. Available at www.toumei-tesou.co.jp/, accessed 4 June 2018.

Wang, Z. and Zhang, P., 2016. *Examining User Roles in Social Q&A: The Case of Health Topics in Zhihu.com*. ASIST, 14–18 October. Available at www. asist.org/files/meetings/am16/proceedings/submissions/posters/23poster.pdf, accessed 4 April 2017.

Wellman, B., 2002. Little Boxes, Glocalization, and Networked Individualism. In: Tanabe, M., van den Besselaar, P. and Ishida, P., eds. *Digital Cities II: Computational and Sociological Approaches*. Berlin: Springer, 10–25.

Wilson, P., 1983. *Second-hand Knowledge: An Inquiry into Cognitive Authority*. Westport: Greenwood Press.

Yahoo! no year. *"Points Table"*. Available at http://answers.yahoo.com/info/scoring_system/, accessed 14 June 2018.

Yahoo! Japan, 2004. *Chiebukuro*. Available at http://chiebukuro.yahoo.co.jp/, accessed 26 November 2016.

3 Religious Mediatization with Chinese Characteristics

Subaltern Voices of Chinese Muslim Youths[1]

Wai-yip Ho

Introduction

Restive Muslim populations at China's northwest border have provoked concern among authorities that separatist factions may agitate for independence, at the same time, China's Hui Muslims have gone online to create new identities. To what extent does Chinese Muslims' emerging use of new media survive under the Chinese Communist Party's censorship? Based on interviews and online observations of the reported activities and growth of a Chinese Muslim youth website since 2015, this chapter argues that young Chinese Hui Muslims have been attempting to extend their influence through online networks to mobilize Muslim youths and trying to reshape the cultural image of Islam in China. It shows the ways in which marginalized Muslim youths maintain their religious vision at the national and international level. Domestically, Chinese Muslim youths aim to construct new understandings of Islam in China as they handle issues facing Muslim youths at the societal level, while at the international level, they align with the global Muslim brotherhood (*ummah*).

In comparison with concepts such as globalization, individualization and commercialization, mediatization has been viewed as a far better narrative or alternative conceptual framework to explain the global meta-process and long-term global development (Krotz 2007). Some have even argued that mediatization has played a key role in almost all areas of social and cultural transformation in contemporary high-tech societies (e.g., Lundby 2009). There have been a number of pioneering scholarly studies on mediatization in religious life: Some have emphasized the personal use of media technologies in reconfiguring everyday religious practices (Meyer and Moors 2006), some have claimed that mediatization may result in secularization (Hjarvard 2013). As in North America and Europe, social and religious life in Asia has become rapidly and deeply mediatized. The mainstream assumption is that individual religious actors in modern Western secular society are able to actualize human agency and realize full autonomy in mediatization, immune from the imposition of state power (e.g., Hjarvard 2013, Lövheim 2011).

However, this chapter suggests that mediatization, beyond the Western context, has not become a fully autonomous institution that is independent from state power. Mediatization could fall under coercive state power that constrains religious actors' liberty. While Radde-Antweiler rightly emphasizes that contemporary "religious studies directs its focus on the discursive constructions on the levels of religious actors, groups and institutions, comparing them to one another" (Radde-Antweiler 2017, 143), this chapter suggests that China's individual religious actors are struggling to survive within state power in the process of religious mediatization. A case study of the mediatization of Islam through Chinese Hui youths shows how strong state power has suppressed the growing autonomy of mediatization that featured the power of public mobilization, which has been viewed as a potential threat to sovereign power. A longstanding homogenizing force of Han Chinese has led to the silencing of subaltern ethnic and religious subjects in China, including China's Muslims (Gladney 2004); this chapter thus seeks to give voice to the marginalized Muslims in the new realm of religious mediatization.

In the Chinese context, state power is deeply mediatized and – as this chapter makes clear – is the most decisive *media logic* acting as a driving mechanism behind and within the processes of Chinese mediatization. As religious mediatization operates within the censoring power of the state, the processes of Islamic mediatization are possible only if Chinese Muslim youths endorse the political program advocated by the People's Republic of China (PRC) and also respect traditional Islamic authorities in existing religious structures, to recover subaltern and reforming voices in Chinese "cyber-Islamic environments" (Bunt 2009, 1). These survival strategies are illustrated by the emphasis on charity work for the public good while fostering Muslim entrepreneurialism, promotion of solidarity among Muslim groups by de-emphasizing sectarian differences and encouraging inter-religious understanding in addition to the work of Islamic preaching.

Mediatized Religion: An Emerging Dimension of Chinese Media Studies

China's recent global outlook has been in full force partly due to the national strategy of *Go Global* and *One Belt, One Road*, a new Chinese foreign and global initiative reviving the concept of the ancient Silk Road. No longer insulating itself from external influence as in the Imperial period, China's re-emergence and reintegration in the international community have been greatly enhanced by the rapid development of the Internet and new social media. Among many issues of concern to scholars and policy-makers, one attracting global attention is the extent to which China's Internet and social media development are sanctioned by the power of state surveillance and censorship on the Internet. However, would the rise of new media at the same time, empower civil society to engage in social and political activism? The way that different religious groups in China appropriate the Internet and new media, and the impact of this appropriation have been generally understudied. Hence, this chapter focuses on the understanding of the mediatization of Hui Muslim youths in negotiating state power. It will ask, critically, how they take up the Internet as a media platform to reimagine Chinese Islam.

Often, government policy has been heavy-handed when new media is used as a tool of public mobilization threatening social stability and the sovereign rule of the PRC. This heavy-handedness was evident when the government shut down the Internet network to contain riots and demonstrations in Xinjiang, the Northwestern part of China, and Tibet. Several recent examples of Uyghur–Han conflicts have occurred over the past decade, and interethnic tension has been very high. Religious mediatization could be understood as marginal, private and apolitical. In sketching the contours of Internet culture in contemporary China, Yang Guobin describes it as characterized by a lightness inaugurating a new political vision (Voci 2010), multiple voices in online carnival activities (Herold and Marolt 2011), and the politics of ambivalence (Sun 2010), liveliness and entertainment (Liu 2011), and control and contention (Yang 2009, 2011a, 2011b). However, while the political lightness, heterogeneous paths, consumerism and civil activism of Chinese Internet culture have been discussed, emerging online features of religious piety and spirituality in the process of mediatization have been inadequately studied.

The Chinese government has concerns about the use of new media to incite religious sectarianism and radicalization in the form of cyber-terrorism or cyber-separatism. In line with that, this chapter focuses on how the China Muslim Youth Club (CMYC), a Beijing-based Hui Muslim group, has survived under state power and made use of an online platform, the China Muslim Youth Net (CMYN), to promote Islam as a social force forging a harmonious society, which is aligned to the government's policy of maintaining social stability. Based on interviews in Beijing and online observations of the reported activities and growth of the CMYC, this chapter suggests that Muslim youths make use of the online platform to mobilize their peers and reshape the cultural image of Islam in China. Alongside the *Chinese Dream* proposed by Chinese President Xi Jinping, Muslim youths develop a religious vision of a transformative *Qingzhen* (Halal) *Dream*. Young Chinese Muslims are fashioning innovative strategies, as is illustrated by their volunteer work for the public good in China while fostering Qingzhen Muslim entrepreneurialism, promoting the emerging China-Arab trade along *One Belt, One Road*, the new Silk Road route.

Mediatization and China: Allah Online vs. The Great Firewall?

With more than 20 million Muslims living in China, the number of non-Han Muslim minorities in China is already comparable to the total population of Saudi Arabia. Yet, a number of issues concerning Islam and its relation with contemporary China remain unobserved and unnoticed. One significant issue is the understanding of the liberating effects of the global information network in the ordinary lives of Muslims in China, and the effects of the state's restrictions on this network. The reintegration of China's Islam within the global Muslim community and its network has been accelerating and expanding through the increasing number of Chinese Muslim students in Islamic Studies at universities in Muslim-majority countries. Nonetheless, China's Muslims have been sporadically cut off from the global informational network when Beijing closed down Internet connections to contain social unrest.

Acknowledging the diversity between and within different zones in cyberspace that represent varied Muslim worldviews within the Muslim belief system, Gary R. Bunt coined the umbrella term *cyber-Islamic environment* (CIE) (Bunt 2009). Juxtaposing the globalizing development of a cyber-Islamic environment, or *Allah On-Line* (Lawrence 2002) and the state censorship system of the *Great Firewall* for defending the sovereignty of the PRC in the informational age, this chapter aims to consider neglected political constraints in the mediatization of religion. For instance, to reduce interethnic friction, the PRC had no hesitation in blocking websites during the Urumqi confrontations between Uyghurs and Han Chinese in 2009. In 2016, a popular Chinese Muslim website was forced to shut down after posting a critical letter addressed to Chinese President Xi Jinping (Reuters 2016). Subsequently, the majority of Muslim websites were suspended, according to an interview with the CEO of CMYN. The tension between connectivity and constraint is vividly shown in the readiness of China's Muslims to reconnect the global *ummah* across the Great Wall by reciting the famous Hadith of the Prophet Muhammad, "Seek Knowledge Even unto China" in the virtual realm, and overt state policing through cyber-police constraining the free expression of web portals and netizens.

Hui Muslims or Sino-Muslims are the largest of the ten official Muslim nationalities in China (the others are Uyghur, Kazakh, Dongxiang, Kyrgyz, Salar, Tajik, Uzbek, Bonan and Tatar). This chapter traces the development and features of the CMYN, a representative Hui Muslim network, before his suspension by the Chinese government in August 2015. Demonstrating political loyalty to the sovereign power of the PRC and demonstrating religious piety with global Muslim *ummah* can go hand in hand. Methodologically, the conceptual framework and data in this chapter are partly derived from my ongoing project of online participant observation and documentation of the rapidly changing Chinese Islamic new media network (Ho 2010, 2011, 2015a, 2015b, 2016). In addition, offline fieldwork interviews were conducted by contacting and interviewing the host portal organizations, executive board members and volunteers of managing websites in Beijing. Rather than a network analysis of various Chinese Muslim nodes, this study focuses on a single Muslim organization, the CMYC, and its online platform, the CMYN. The author interviewed Mr. Li Xiaolong, CEO of the CMYC, and other managing committee members of the portal in Beijing, and engaged in ongoing observation of the CMYN's development. An email interview was also conducted with Mr. Li Xiaolong before the PRC's severe censorship of all Muslim websites in 2015.

Mediatized Islam in China: A Case Study of the Chinese Muslim Youth Club

Understanding mediatization requires a critical analysis of the interrelation between changes in media and communication, and between changes in culture and society (Couldry and Hepp 2013, 197). This chapter explores these changes through interviews with Li Xiaolong about the history and recent development of the CMYC and the social and cultural transformation in China. The CMYC has a simple structure, with a Chief Executive Officer, managing editor of the webpage, art editor, marketing team and other volunteers and staff to run the website. In the past seven years, the number of visitors has increased from a few hundred to more than 200,000, with 8,000–12,000 daily page views. The CMYC has started to use the *Sina Weibo*, *Tencent Weibo* and *WeChat* platforms for people to communicate. It has 8,000, 10,000 and 100,000 followers on those platforms, respectively. Focusing on youth, the CMYC is working on events for Muslim youth, such as correspondence training and volunteer training, and providing guidance for youth in employment, dating and marriage. One key purpose of the CMYC is social networking. Outdoor activities provide opportunities to youths so that they can contribute to community services and have opportunities for dating. In the following sections, several distinctive features and themes of the CMYC are identified to illustrate the new voices of Chinese Muslim youths expressed through the online platform, the CMYN.

Revitalizing Muslim Cosmopolitanism: Progressive Islam and Innovation

In contrast to other Muslim websites in China, the CMYC emphasizes that it aims to connect Muslim youths online. Li Xiaolong illustrates the power and uniqueness of youth groups with his choice of user-name, which sets the CMYC apart from other Hui Muslim cohort groups:

> "Gather the flowers while the dew is on them" is a phrase from Mr Lu Xun's literature: "Instead of picking the morning flowers at dawn, we should gather those flowers while the dews are still on." It means that youth should seize every moment and opportunity to act, and not wait … like the saying "Gather the flower at the right time, do not wait until it dies out and leaves you only with the twig." It means whatever we do, seize the moment, and treasure what we have before we lose it. So the line "Gather the flowers while the dew is on them" encourages youth to work hard, do meaningful things whole-heartedly, and as soon as they can. This comes from Mr. Lu Xun's collection of prose works. So this is my online username; it is not the name of the website…In fact, the name of our website is "Chinese Muslim Youth Net" and we have a club, in English, known as the China Muslim Youth Club.
>
> (Li Xiaolong, interviewed by the author,
> Beijing, 10 May 2010)

In an interview, Li further elaborated that the primary target group of the CMYN is Hui Muslim youth whose mother language is Chinese. Yet unlike other Muslim webpages that only give access to Hui Muslim users, the CMYN is an open forum that can be accessed by other religious groups and nationalities. Avoiding the perils of sectarianism and exclusivity that provoke political scrutiny from the PRC, the CMYC has been attempting to increase tolerance toward the *Other*, as shown in the welcoming icon and the interview note from Mr. Li:

> The Chinese Muslim Youth Net targets youth, and was established later than Muslim Net. Muslim Net has not yet fully developed despite its earlier establishment, probably because Muslim Net mainly focuses on the Hui people. There are Han Muslims and other ethnic minorities who do not use the website because of its use of the Chinese language; therefore, we improved in this sense by allowing everyone to log in. Whether you are Christians or from other nationalities, you are welcome to log in and express your opinion through our website…so this is one important feature. Secondly, we have improved the language setting of the website so it supports the use of Arabic, English, and Chinese…
>
> (Li Xiaolong, interviewed by the author,
> Beijing, 25 October 2010)

While some scholars have emphasized that the mediatization of society involves all social spheres (Mazzoleni 2008), the embedded state power that monitors individual religious actors is often neglected or not taken into account. This section shows that liberation of hidden Muslim youth power has become possible through mediatization. Mediatization provides Muslim youths a new platform to present Islam to a wider non-Muslim Chinese public. Meanwhile, Muslim youths have a channel to express themselves, but attempt to be inclusive by not provoking the patriotic sentiments of the majority Han Chinese, and avoid igniting religious sectarianism and ethnic separatism. Muslim youths not only innovate in religious mediatization but at the same time demonstrate loyalty to state power.

Reforming Muslim Politics: Harmonious Society and Law-Abiding China

The primary target group and mission statement of the CYMC concerns youth. One year before the hosting of the Olympics in Beijing, a group of young Hui Muslim in Beijing established a social network, the CMYC, promoting interethnic solidarity among young Muslims, interreligious understanding with non-Muslims, and 'harmonious society', which echoed the PRC's political program and propaganda. Aware of the importance of recognizing the PRC's rule, the CYMC well understands the distinction between the state apparatus and nongovernmental organizations, and positions itself as a member of civil society, which is to say, under the control of the Chinese government. With this prerequisite of recognizing the PRC's legitimate rule, the CYMC, as a member of civil society, is never confrontational toward state power. In the CYMC's understanding, propagation of Islam and the development of their website have become more effective with support from the state:

> No matter what you do in China, Chinese Muslims have to follow the laws in China. The China Islamic Association is China's official Muslim association. In China, every single religious activity has to be supervised and advised. The same rule applies to our Internet site. So we are under the government's leadership as well as the China Islamic Association's. We are fulfilling this requirement and obeying the Chinese government, and in this way we can better combine the power of citizens and the government and promote Islamic culture effectively. I am not saying whether one party is leading the other, but a website that promotes Islamic culture has to be under the management of the government.
>
> (Li Xiaolong, interviewed by the author,
> Beijing, 25 October 2010)

The CYMC understands the thorny issues of ethnic and religious sectarianism. By making an Internet platform for both Muslim and non-Muslim youth, the CYMC is not only a law-abiding civil organization, but it also operates parallel to the state program of creating a harmonious society:

> The China Muslim Youth Club aims at promoting the sense of Islamic identity among Muslim youth in the aspects of spirit, emotion, and thought, through diversified activities and programs for young Muslims and working together with different Muslim groups. We are also concerned about the common interest of Muslim youth groups and actively foster and strengthen contact and communication with non-Muslim youth groups...to build a harmonious community... By bringing together many outstanding young people who are Muslim and non-Muslim, we make an integral virtual platform for all netizens to engage in social life, spiritual life, literature, charity, entertainment, dating, chatting, and social activities, therefore forming a concrete and harmonious social community on the Internet.[2]

Scholars of mediatization rightly suggest that everyday life and operations of society depend on the media, arguing the impossibility of relating to one's world without accessing the news through suitable media (Lundby 2009), and some have even claimed that through mediatization the media become an independent institution within society (Hjarvard 2008). Nevertheless, the case of Chinese mediatization suggests that the everyday life of the Muslim community, the sustainability of Muslim networks and the operations of society do not depend on media, but mediatization in some countries is only possible with the permission of state power. While Habermas famously contended that the media power of instrumental reason may *colonize* the lifeworld (Habermas 1987), this case study suggests that the media network in China could be suspended and mediatization discontinued by state power. In short, state power can colonize media. As a result, mediatization in the Chinese context is far from forming an autonomous institution that is independent from legal institutions and government control.

Resocializing Muslim Youths: Social Philanthropy and Public Good

Interviews and ongoing observations of the CMYC reveal that its primary vision and its portal is to revive the true spirit of Islam by youths, by repackaging Islam as a progressive religion for the non-Muslim community in China. When organizing philanthropic activities in public spaces, the club members always display a banner showing the club's four watchwords: *Traditional, Rational, Tolerant, Fun*; these are well-integrated themes and complement each other. By bringing Islam into everyday life, the CMYC is attempting to revive Islam from its present stagnancy. It aims to rebrand Islam as a progressive social force and help non-Muslims to understand Islam as a peaceful way of life. The CMYC is attempting to demonstrate that Islam is not merely an unrestrained external force alienated from Chinese social and political life; young Muslim Chinese can be viewed positively and accommodated perfectly in the Chinese polity:

> Islam in China in recent years has been waning...compared to its development back in Ming and Qing Dynasty. Islamic development is strong outside the country...but in China it is in decline. So how Islam should develop under China's culture of acceptance becomes an issue for us, and this drives us to revive Islamic culture in China. We strive to help Islam to find its way out in China through different means such as the Internet, by gathering young Muslim elites on-line who are open-minded in accepting new thinking and changes, and using their knowledge to navigate a new direction and pathway for Islam to revive its influence in China. This is what we will be doing in China in the near future. Some activities we do, such as visiting the elderly and children, we do so that those who share the same faith can actually put their faith into practice, to let these values live not only in the Mosque and Qur'an, but also in our daily lives. I think this is the path we have to take for reviving Islam, the path of transforming the value and knowledge conveyed by the Qur'an into actions that Muslims around the world can perform. We want to make use of such characteristics of youth to assist in the restoration of Islam in contemporary China; at least we are trying to make this happen... Furthermore, we want to lead the Chinese in a better direction in their journey to understand Islam. We want to shape and build up the image of Islam, so that people will not simply associate Islam with terrorism. I think this is really crucial because an image can help clearing a lot of problems that have been mixed up with Islam.
>
> (Li Xiaolong, interviewed by the author,
> Beijing, 10 May 2010)

In playing a positive social role amid the millions of unmarried single Chinese men and women, the CMYC also provides an online forum for social networking among Muslim youths to use their own methods to meet potential partners for dating. Members normally use an eye-catching topic to attract others to click on their post, and in the posts they explain what kind of friends they are looking for and introduce themselves. Interested members can either leave private messages or open comments so they can contact each other. There are also posts relating success stories. They share their experience and their happiness in finding a suitable person and even announce marriages. They also thank the CMYC for providing them this platform, which gives them the chance to get to know more people:

> There are ten couples get married in these two to three years. In fact some of them still dating and those focus in going to office, included youth that go to university. There are less in the village (...) (b)ut our activities still continue there may be more and more people find their partner through this website, why? You may understand this, because Muslim should find their partner in the same religion, different in ethnicity [is fine] but should be same in faith.
>
> (Li Xiaolong, interviewed by the author, Beijing, 25 October 2010)

The key feature of the CYMC is that it mobilizes Muslim youths to engage in offline volunteer work – building orphanages in various regions of China, helping disadvantaged children and visiting elderly Muslims. Through volunteer work in supporting the elderly and supporting youth, the CYMC has been resocializing Muslim youths in the public good of practicing familial piety and paying respect to elders, when some believe that postsocialist Chinese society is losing such traditional values. In the midst of growing inequality between rural and urban life, a program of bringing talented children to big cities has been launched. In this program, talented children from Ningxia, who live in a rural area, are sent to major cities like Beijing for experience and to encourage them to study.

Social networking thus helps Muslim youth to find personal intimacy and involves them in charity work, which suggests that religious mediatization does not stay in the culture of individualization and consumerism, but resocializes online young Muslims back into offline social networks for the public good.

Rewiring Muslim Ummah: The New Silk Road and Global Halal Market

While the CMYC identifies itself as fully Chinese and has a strong sense of patriotism, Muslim youths have been developing transnational bonding with the global Muslim brotherhood. Aside from translating news of the Muslim world and reporting on the Arab world, the CMYC forges closer connections and friendship with the expatriate community of Arab Muslims in China. My observations and interviews revealed that genuine concern for China's Arab expatriate community is one key feature distinguishing the CMYC from other religious online groups in China. As one example of relieving needy foreigners living in China, in 2009 the CMYC used the online platform to mobilize donations to a Yemeni doctoral student who had leukemia. While President Xi Jinping proposed the *Chinese Dream* (*Zhongguo Meng*) as an official discourse to revive the glorious past of Chinese civilization, there are divergent views of *Chinese Dreams* emerging in civil society. It is quite common for many Chinese to dream of having human rights and a clean environment. Yet unlike environmentalists' understanding, the CMYC joins many Muslims in imagining a *Green China*, developing the everyday concern for health and food safety according to Islamic principles:

> Chinese General Secretary, Xi Jinping, has named three necessary ways to fulfill the "Chinese Dream," that is, we must walk in China's own pathway, promote China's own spirit, and gather up China's own strength. The only thing that Chinese people lack is the key to cohesion, but not strength. Today, we are together in the China International Halal Industry Summit Forum to find the key for unlocking this great power. However, even as the halal industry has expanded each year, a number of unscrupulous companies that call themselves halal have also entered the market. They are producing and selling fake halal products to gain benefits and save costs. At the worst, they also use other meat to substitute for beef and mutton. That totally subverts the main idea of halal companies, which require absolute cleanliness and zero tolerance for fakeness. We must confront this problem by joining together and boycotting those companies.[3]

From the bottom-up, the CMYC redefines the *Chinese Dream* into the *Halal Dream* (*Qingzhen Meng*) in terms of healthy lifestyle and food safety. With reference to the Islamic way of life, the reimagining of the *Chinese Dream* as the *Qingzhen Dream* provides a powerful alternative developmental path for China's future. It pinpoints corrupt practices of food treatment and addresses the crisis of trust in food made in China. By highlighting the problem of food safety in China, the CMYC suggests that fulfilling *Qingzhen* standards will be the key factor in unifying China, and will help China to target new global halal markets in the Muslim world. Since its inception, the CMYC has regularly promoted Arabic language training through the Internet, holding it in Beijing. When the Arab Spring started in 2011, the Arab world market did not improve; the training continued but did not expand. However, Arab-China ties have been strengthening cooperation with the embassies of the Kingdom of Saudi Arabia, Islamic Republic of Iran, Turkey and Malaysia. Around the globe, a quarter of the world population is Muslim; the halal food industry is thus worth approximately two trillion US dollars annually. In China, the plentiful supply of livestock and twenty-three million Muslims make the development of the halal food industry promising in domestic and foreign markets. Northwest China, especially Ningxia Hui Autonomous Region, Qinghai, Gansu, Shanxi and Inner Mongolia Autonomous Region, with substantial Muslim populations and supply of halal food, reconnect the Silk Road economy between the Muslim world and China. Muslim Hui entrepreneurialism has been one of the major areas that the CYMC is working on, especially in promoting halal food inside China and exporting Chinese halal food to Muslim countries.

The CYMC has redefined the *Chinese Dream* in the Islamic framework plus promoting halal food to reconnect with the Muslim world. It suggests that Chinese Islamic mediatization should closely follow the PRC's foreign initiative of building a new Silk Road, namely *One Belt, One Road*, in which the Chinese government has been realigning itself with Muslim nations from Eurasia to the Middle East. Unlike the existing literature of mediatization in relation to sovereign states' international relations, the chapter argues that religious mediatization in the Chinese case reflects the development of the sovereign power's transnational network and endeavors.

Conclusion: Muslim Mediatization, State Power in China

Muslim forms of mediatization, such as the CMYC, enjoyed unprecedented alternatives and critical space to innovate until the sovereign state clamped down on most Muslim networks in August 2015. Through the appropriation of this online platform, a young Muslim voice was emerging to rebrand Chinese Hui Muslims as a reforming force characterized as progressive, young, smart and even fun, using social networking to find other Hui Muslims for marriage. Muslim mediatization is not, however, an extension of egoistic desire and individualism; rather, the CMYC's vision and mission is to retrieve or revive the genuine spirit of Islam by resocializing Hui Muslims to engage in charity and volunteering activities for the public good. The CMYC also utilizes its online platform for patriotic purposes to reimagine their transnational Muslim identity by forging closer Arab-China ties and reconnecting the Silk Road economy, such as the halal food business.

The chapter discussed the case study of the CMYC as a representative example of mediatized Islam, innovated by a young Hui Muslim generation in China. Rather than arguing that mediatization has appeared more and more as an independent institution within society (Hjarvard 2008), this chapter illuminates how state power has been deeply embedded with Islamic mediatization, and how religious mediatization is far from becoming an autonomous institution. As religion itself is already mediatized (Radde-Antweiler 2017), the Chinese case study of Islamic mediatization in this chapter confirms the global trend of religious mediatization. While acknowledging that religious mediatization is going global, this chapter highlights the sanctioning state power of the PRC, as the *media logic*, in silencing the voice of religious actors in the process of mediatization. Other versions of *media logic* have been largely neglected by the West (e.g., Hjarvard 2008, Lövheim 2011). This case study of Muslim mediatization in China, among a growing field of non-Western contexts, illustrates the *subalternity* of religious mediatization, as state power has been centrally embedded as the *media logic* in regulating mediatization. In defending Chinese sovereign power from alleged threats, sanctioning state powers can deactivate religious mediatization and nullify the agency of religious actors by ruthlessly closing media portals. In this sense, how sovereign state power functions as another *media logic* in a non-Western context deserves further research.

Notes

1 The chapter was revised from my previous presented paper in the panel of "China's Religions Online: The Politics of Buddhism, Protestant Christianity, and Islam in Cyberspace", Association for Asian Studies (AAS) 2014 Annual Conference, Philadelphia, US. The author thanks the very friendly invitation from Stefania Travagnin, Andrè Lalibertè and Carsten Vala for the opportunity to attend and present my paper in the panel in 2014 AAS Conference.
2 http://baike.baidu.com/view/6066124.htm#1 (accessed on 24 February 2015).
3 http://bbs.tianya.cn/post-worldlook-1202687-1.shtml (accessed on 14 May 2018).

References

Baidu Baike. Available at http://baike.baidu.com/view/6066124.htm#1, accessed 24 February 2015.

Bbs Tianya. Available at http://bbs.tianya.cn/post-worldlook-1202687-1.shtml, accessed 14 May 2018.

Bunt, G. R., 2009. *iMuslims: Rewriting the House of Islam.* London: Hurst.

Couldry, N. and Hepp, A., 2013. Conceptualizing Mediatization: Contexts, Traditions, Arguments. *Communication Theory,* 23, 191–202.

Gladney, D. C., 2004. *Dislocating China: Reflections on Muslims, Minorities and Other Subaltern Subjects.* London: Hurst.

Habermas, J., 1987. *The Theory of Communication Action: Lifeworld and System, A Critique of Functionalist Reason.* Cambridge: Polity Press.

Herold, D. K. and Marolt, P., eds., 2011. *Online Society in China: Creating, Celebrating, and Instrumentalising the Online Carnival.* Abingdon: Routledge.

Hjarvard, S., 2008. The Mediatization of Society: A Theory of the Media as Agents of Social and Cultural Change. *Nordicom Review,* 29(2), 105–134.

Hjarvard, S., 2013. *The Mediatization of Culture and Society.* London: Routledge.

Ho, W.-Y., 2010. Islam, China and the Internet: Negotiating Residual Cyberspace between Hegemonic Patriotism & Connectivity to the *Ummah. Journal of Muslim Minority Affairs,* 30(1), 63–79.

Ho, W.-Y., 2011. Emerging Islamic-Confucian Axis in the Virtual Ummah: Connectivity and Constraints in the Contemporary China. *Comparative Islamic Studies,* 7(1–2), 137–155.

Ho, W. Y., 2015a. Islam in Hong Kong. In: Esposito, J. L., ed. *Oxford Islamic Studies Online*. New York: Oxford University Press. Available at www.oxford islamicstudies.com/article/opr/t343/e0156, accessed 03 Nov 2018.

Ho, W.-Y., 2015b. *Islam and China's Hong Kong: Ethnic Identity, Muslim Networks and the New Silk Road*. London: Routledge.

Ho, W.-Y., 2016. Digital Islam across the Greater China: Connecting Virtual Ummah to the Chinese-Speaking Muslim Netizens. In: Travagnin, S., ed. *Religion and the Media in China*. London: Routledge, 187–202.

Krotz, F., 2007. The Meta-Process of 'Mediatization' as a Conceptual Frame. *Global Media and Communication*, 3(3), 256–260.

Lawrence, B. B., 2002. Allah On-Line: The Practice of Global Islam in the Information Age. In: Hoover, S. M. and Schofield Clark, L., eds. *Practicing Religion in the Age of the Media*. New York: Columbia University Press, 237–253.

Liu, F., 2011. *Urban Youth in China: Modernity, the Internet and the Self*. Abingdon: Routledge.

Lövheim, M., 2011. Mediatisation of Religion: A Critical Appraisal. *Culture and Religion*, 12(2), 153–166.

Lundby, K., ed., 2009. *Mediatization: Concept, Changes, Consequences*. New York: Peter Lang.

Mazzoleni, G., 2008. Mediatization of Society. In: Donbach, W., ed. *The International Encyclopedia of Communication* (Vol. VII). Malden: Blackwell, 3025–3055.

Meyer, B. and Moors, A., 2006. *Religion, Media and the Public Sphere*. Bloomington: Indiana University Press.

Radde-Antweiler, K., 2017. Digital Religion? Media Studies from a Religious Studies Perspective. In: Nord, I. and Zipernovszky, H., eds. *Religious Education in a Mediatized World*. Stuttgart: Kohlhammer, 138–150.

Shepherd, C., 2016. Popular Chinese Muslim website down after posting letter critical of Xi. *Reuters*, 14 December. Available at www.reuters.com/article/uk-china-censorship-islam/popular-chinese-muslim-website-down-after-posting-letter-critical-of-xi-idUSKBN1431LC, accessed 22 May 2018.

Sun, H., 2010. *Internet Policy in China: A Field Study of Internet Cafes*. Lanham: Lexington Books.

Voci, P., 2010. *China on Video: Smaller-Screen Realities*. New York: Routledge.

Yang, G., 2009. *The Power of the Internet in China*. New York: Columbia University Press.

Yang, G., 2011a. Lightness, Wildness and Ambivalence: China and New Media Studies. *New Media and Society*, 14(1), 170–179.

Yang, G., 2011b. Technology and Its Contents: Issues in the Study of Chinese Internet. *The Journal of Asian Studies*, 70(4), 1043–1050.

4 "Aren't you happy?" Healing as Mediatized Nationalism in a Compressed Modernity

Sam Han

Introduction

While mediatization as a theoretical analytic and research agenda has made its presence felt in scholarship across many disciplines and regions, there has been, as Nie et al. have argued, a dearth of mediatization research in an Asian context. This is especially curious, since, as they correctly note, Asia is now full of "superpowers such as China, Japan and Korea" (Nie, Kee and Ahmad 2014, 366). Although their characterization as 'superpowers' is arguable, it is still an important point. Moreover, it is especially striking since the recent proponents of mediatization, including Hjarvard (2013) and Krotz (2014), speak of it as a concurrent, or at least one aspect of modernization without necessarily specifying its implication globally. Drawing in large part from the social theory of Anthony Giddens, Hjarvard specifically suggests that mediatization is on par with developments, such as globalization, urbanization and individualization. The question, then, is whether *modernization* or *modernity* is the same everywhere, particularly in East Asia. If indeed, modernization and globalization go hand in hand, we can, in turn, ask whether there are aspects of modernity in Asia that are unique, thus necessitating a shift in perspective from (the largely European) mediatization research as presently constructed.

This chapter, therefore, stands as a way to not only extend but also critically discuss mediatization approaches. This position is largely inspired by the work of Kuan-Hsing Chen (2010), who offers an approach to *decolonizing* mediatization theory and research. Like Chen, the point here is not to reject mediatization as entirely Western, and thus, inapplicable to non-European sociocultural contexts, but to "multiply frames of reference" (Chen 2010, 23). While this cannot be done in full within the confines of this chapter, the basic purpose here is to scrutinize an aspect of mediatization in South Korea – to offer juxtaposing ideas to some of the core tenets of mediatization so as to refine and clarify them. First, the chapter examines *mediatization* as an analytical concept for case studies in a context whereby modernity is somewhat different from the West, specifically northern Europe. Second, the chapter also examines a phenomenon called *healing*, which sits at the margins of the current institutionalist orientation of mediatization theory as represented by Hjarvard and Krotz. In particular, it examines an instance of mediatization of religion and politics within a social theoretical backdrop unique to East Asia called *compressed modernity*. Within this context, I specifically look at the recent boom in products and services claiming to provide *healing* in South Korean media and popular culture, including televised talk shows based on *healing*. Of these, I critically explore the most popular – *Healing Camp, Aren't You Happy?* (SBS) – primarily through a form of interpretive, critical media content analysis, whereby I detail the way in which the television show operates in terms of theme as well as format (Gurevitch et al. 1982). I argue that healing *smuggles in* more accurately, ideas and values about how to live and survive in a *compressed modern* context, amounting to a mediatization of religion and politics, which I dub *mediatized nationalism*.

In so doing, I begin with a reading of the Giddensian social theory at the heart of mediatization, while putting forth the argument that by relying on a slightly different version of modernity theory, it could be opened up to new possibilities. I then move on to detailing the *healing* phenomenon in South Korean television programming, providing a content and discourse analysis of two specific programs. I demonstrate that there is a clear *media format* detectable in the work that draws from the spiritual/religious history of Korea, which overlaps with the *sociobiographical* and narrative techniques in *healing*. Finally, I provide a critique of these developments based on the kind of subjectivities produced by this sort of programming, mainly the self-recuperating citizen that heals for the nation – not the self.

Mediatization's Social Theory: Late Modernity and Compressed Modernity

While there have been many different definitions of *mediatization*, perhaps the one that has gained the most traction across bodies of scholarship has been Krotz's assertion that it is a "meta-process" (Hepp and Krotz 2014, 68). By this, Krotz clearly tries to link together two distinct traditions of mediatization research. On the one hand, there is the institutionalist tradition, which sees media as a separate institution with its own set of rules that have begun to inflect its logic onto other social institutions. On the other hand, there is the social-constructivist tradition which evaluates media as now having a bigger part (perhaps the biggest part) in the process of producing and constructing reality (Hepp and Krotz 2014, 3). By suggesting that mediatization is a meta-process, Krotz is attempting to highlight the "duality of this structural relationship" (2013, 3) of being both inside other institutions and being a standalone provider of a common perspective on society, as Hjarvard describes it (2013, 4). Hjarvard himself endorses such a view, describing mediatization as "[moving] the focus from particular instances of mediation to the structural transformations of the media in contemporary culture and society" (Hjarvard 2013).

However, as critics of mediatization have noted, mediatization scholars need to be clearer on the social ontology from which they operate. In particular, Couldry argues that claiming that media has changed the social world "without producing an explicit account of the understanding of the wider social world on which that claim, even its very possibility, relies" limits the usefulness of mediatization (Couldry 2014, 67).

Indeed, to take Couldry's point further, I would suggest that mediatization does have a social ontology, one that adheres closely to that of Anthony Giddens. In fact, Hjarvard's work explicitly draws upon Giddens' structuration theory as well as adopts the latter's language of "high modernity" (Hjarvard 2013, 13). Furthermore, in tracing the concept of mediatization, he points to the work of sociologist John B. Thompson, who early on used the term *mediatization* and linked it with the "development of modernity" (Hjarvard 2013, 11). Thompson, a well-known proponent of Giddensian social theory, can hardly be seen to provide diversity in mediatization's social-theoretical approach, at least with respect to its perspective on modernity. Therefore, I take Couldry's critique not to imply that mediatization does not specify a *social ontology* but rather that it is unsatisfactory. While Couldry's grievances involve numerous areas, in his most conciliatory moments, Couldry stresses upon the importance of studying the "local nature of transformations" (Couldry 2014, 58) that mediatization rightly points out.

It is my contention here that in order to be more sensitive to the local forms of mediatization, we must pay attention to the larger "framing culture," as Krotz calls it (Krotz 2014, 75). Put otherwise, to make mediatization more *local*, we must reconsider the fundamental social-theoretical basis upon which it makes claims. Here, I wish to put forward a line of social theory that has gained traction in East Asia called *compressed modernity* (Chang 2010). Stemming in large part from the work of Ulrich Beck, the concept of compressed modernity, like Giddens' notion of late or high modernity, is understood as a complex of major institutional changes relating to changes in various spheres, including labor, family relations and politics. However, uniquely rapid modernization of East Asia has wrought certain kinds of consequences specific to East Asia. The term *unintended consequences* is one that has been associated with Beck since the publication and the subsequent widespread discussion of *Risk Society: Towards a New Modernity* in 1992 (Beck 1992). *Risk* in Beck's influential theory emerges from what Giddens had previously called a *runaway world* (Giddens 2003). As a result of some of the *successes* of modernity, by which Beck means the accomplishments of the stated principles of modernity *as a project*, so to speak, some developments have emerged that are now reflecting back onto modernity in negative ways.

For instance, climate change can be seen to be a result of a century plus worth of industrialization and urbanization in a capitalist mode of production, beginning in Western Europe and extending now to nearly every corner of the globe. With such unpredictability in weather patterns, even manufacturing – arguably one of the chief drivers of air pollution – is experiencing a negative impact from climate change. One example is the air pollution crisis in China, which has plagued Beijing and other cities. Due to the severity of the smog, the mayor of Beijing has had to place stop-work orders and curb activities such as outdoor barbecues. For Beck, the irony is not lost on some of the very causes of air pollution being shut down because of air pollution. This feedback loop exemplifies a phrase that Beck deploys quite often when describing the world today: "all in the same boat" (Beck 2009, 37). In other words, the effects of modernization cannot be contained in any meaningful way by national borders. Although its impact may be differential, what happens in one part of the world always affects others. *Action at a distance* is not a problem solely for theoretical physics. What we have then is a world connected by common risk, which Beck dubs a "world risk society" (Beck 1999). In this manner, the foregrounding of risk begets a new sort of modernity – one whereby modernity reflects back onto itself, and is able to acknowledge, if it is to survive, its limitations and missteps. This is why Beck sometimes calls this "second modernity" *reflexive* modernity, where there is recognition of its internal discontinuity (Beck 1999).

In this vein, East Asian scholars have drawn upon Beck in order to address some of the major consequences of what they view to be historically unprecedented rapid modernization. Scholars like Sang-jin Han, Young-Hee Shim, Chang Kyung-Sup, Emiko Ochiai (Chang 1999, Han and Shim 2010, Ochiai 2011) and others have pursued research that takes stock of the unique consequences of modernization, which in the West, took at least 150 years and in the East, took half a century. Ochiai in Japan, for instance, has written extensively of the specific burden that Japan's Lost Decade (which has spilled over into two decades) has placed on families (Ochiai 2011). With privatization, corporate downsizing and the increasing strain on the welfare state due to the aging population and negative birthright, the financial responsibility of families has undoubtedly increased. In East Asia, the *sandwich generation*, a term describing middle-aged adults who take care of their elderly parents as well as their children, has become a worry since the job prospects of their grown children seem grim while life expectancy has risen (Parker and Patten 2013). This has placed a particular economic burden on families, who can rely neither on the state for entitlements of a safety net nor on the private sector to provide pay raises for individual members. Families are the only institution that individuals on the short end of the neoliberal stick can rely on for any sort of social support.

For Chang, compressed modernity is a "peculiar ideological constellation" (Chang 1999, 46). Specifically, capitalism in South Korea since the Korean War had featured a close relationship between *chaebol*, large family-owned conglomerates, similar to *zaibatsu* in Japan, and politicians. Today, many analysts see the economic growth of South Korea as overly reliant on these "megaconglomerates," the most globally recognized of which is Samsung (Albert 2018). As Chang describes, the "compressed transition" (Chang 1999, 46) from military rule to civilian democracy was predicated on growth above democracy, which was fortified by a succession of military dictators that forged ties with the economic elite. To a large extent, this has *worked* – at least in terms of economic growth.

However, according to Chang, beginning with the Asian Financial Crisis of the 1990s, which resulted in South Korea taking on massive loans from the International Monetary Fund, this arrangement's unsustainability had reared its head. The economic miracle that so many Koreans still feel as a point of pride, Chang argues, was actually a product of awkward fits, in comparison to Western modernity.

In the West, risks are mitigated somewhat by social development. In Korea, however, that has not been the case. Chang offers the example of the various accidents that have plagued Korea, including department buildings, bridges and most recently, the ferry holding many young students (Chang 1999, 49). This sort of growth-first, safety-later approach embodies the very essence of *compressed modernization*. With the increased frequency of these risks, there is growing disenchantment toward this form of modernity. There is ambivalence toward whether to be proud to have achieved what took Western societies far longer to achieve, since Koreans are not sure about the values underlying those achievements. This ambivalence has resulted in phenomena such as "nationalism without historical consciousness" and "individualization without individualism" (Chang 1999, 51). These did not cause much consternation until these risks became bigger. Chang writes:

Regardless of their own material conditions, the sheer tempo and amount of unprecedented economic and social transformations so amazed people as to create a hypnotic state, in which various serious problems and costs accruing to such transformations did not immediately irritate their sense. *But, what if economic and social development slows down or even comes to a halt?*
(Chang 1999, 51. Emphasis added)

Today, not only is there evidence of such a slowdown, there are actual consequences. South Korea has some of the highest suicide rates in the world, not to mention the highest *youth* suicide rate in the OECD (Organization for Economic Cooperation and Development) (cf. Han and Hussain 2016). Korean students are some of the most stressed out in the world (Phillips 2013). The ultracompetitive education system in Korea has been linked to not only the high suicide rate but also the low fertility rate. Korea has tried to pass legislation to curb the booming private tutoring industry but has been met with pushback from various sectors, including not only the shadow education industry (rather expectedly) but also parents. The capital city of Seoul tried instituting a curfew of 10 p.m. for cram schools (Chandler 2011). Korea has the second longest working hours in the OECD and a labor productivity rating lower than the average of 49 US dollars as of 2015 (Ock 2015).

Healing in Korean Television Programming

Amid these realities, there has been, as a backlash, a turn toward finding a salve for these troubles under the heading of *healing*. *Healing* is a term that is now used with relative ease and frequency, which emerged around 2010 (Park 2016). The term, while uttered in English, has not quite the same meaning as its original English definition. In contemporary Korea, healing refers to any sort of "physical wellness, mental health, freedom from anxiety and life satisfaction" (Lee 2013). Going to the sauna counts as healing. So does going on a hike in the woods. While these are somewhat translatable to non-Korean audiences, *healing* has now taken such commercial appeal to the point of scholars evoking a *healing wave* in Korea with cafes, self-help books and television programs bearing the term. In 2013, a report by the Ministry of Culture, Sports and Tourism stated that *healing* would be the new trend in cultural and artistic industries in 2013 (Yoon 2013). Another report from the Samsung Economic Research Institute noted that the reason behind

> the popularity of healing products is the prolonged economic recession coupled with a variety of other factors: high youth unemployment, weak income growth, lack of communication with friends and family, increasing distrust of the government and pessimistic views about society.
>
> (Lee 2013)

With the preponderance of *healing* in popular culture, there has been, as just mentioned, a rise of television programs premised entirely on healing.

One of the first programs to title itself with the term was *Healing Camp*, which aired on Seoul Broadcasting System (SBS), starting in 2011.

Two comedians, Lee Kyung-kyu and Kim Je-dong, as well as the actress Han Hye-jin share the show's hosting duties. The format is rather simple. As a talk show, each episode has a celebrity guest, who sits with the three hosts in the first segment, while they go through various questions about the guest's life. Unlike talk-show formats in the USA or the UK, *Healing Camp, Aren't You Happy?* spends the entirety of the episode with that guest (although for special episodes, there would be multiple guests). While there were over 200 episodes of the show that aired before it was canceled, each episode operated in a similar manner. The core, and major draw, of the show is the intimate conversation between the guest and the hosts and the rather emotional tenor of the conversation, which usually centers on the life of the guest and the struggles and hardships along the journey.

As an illustration, we can look at one particular episode with the guest Lee Hyori, a former member of a girl group who later had major success as a solo artist in the early 2000s, and became a successful television host in the late 2000s (Jo 2012). When she appeared on *Healing Camp*, she had overcome a few high-profile scandals: She had just ended her contract with Lotte liquors and had stopped being the spokesperson for the Korean beef industry as she had just become a vegetarian. She was also becoming a leading animal activist, who in Korea are labeled with the term *social-tainer* to describe entertainers or celebrities who are active in social causes. The episode falls, at least it is presented in this way, at the turning point of Lee's career – from the nation's *sexy diva* to its leading social activist from the entertainment world (Ock 2014).

The conversation begins with discussing her childhood such as growing up in poverty and reaching levels of stardom and wealth she could not imagine. However, it turns more serious when Lee Kyung-kyu, one of the hosts, turns to a plagiarism issue that she had been embroiled in a few years prior, when a producer had plagiarized songs from the USA and simply reused them without any permission from the original artists. After suspending broadcasting activities, Lee admits that she had a psychological evaluation spurred by not only the stress surrounding the scandal but also being sued for breach of contract by companies for which she was the spokesperson. In the wake of this, she sold her house and car, and had a spiritual experience. She drastically transformed herself, giving up meat, alcohol, coffee, carbonated drinks and developed an interest in animal activism.

She details the depression she had suffered after this fall from grace. She could not leave her house. During this time, she watched a television program about abandoned dogs in the streets of Seoul and decided to get involved. She was reminded of how she grew up with a dog and when her family's financial situation got bad, her father had sold her dog to a dog soup restaurant. During this difficult time, she decided get involved by volunteering at the animal shelter. It is through this initial foray into animal shelters that she became a vegetarian and then a leading spokesperson for other causes, including taking care of former *comfort women*, who were now elderly.

The mention of the comfort women issue is not accidental here. The acknowledgment of sexual slavery during the Imperial period has long been a point of contention in East Asian diplomatic relations. With China and South Korea on one side, and Japan on the other, the comfort women issue has resulted in many spats, which has involved a range of tactics including the placement of statues in front of embassy buildings as well as wholesale erasure in textbooks. When Lee mentions that she volunteers by spending time with comfort women, the implication is that she is doing a work of *national* importance. In fact, other celebrities who have appeared on *Healing Camp* have named comfort women as one of the issues that they support with either their time, money or both.[1] She goes on to say that now she has reevaluated her life, looking to simplify it so that she can start using her celebrity for good. In the closing sequence of the episode, she brings the hosts to tour a large facility that she helped found which is no-kill, meaning that the animals there are taken care of for life.

Throughout the conversation, it is clear that there is linear trajectory to Lee's story. The narrative, which basically embodies the classical definition of tragedy, ends with a calm. When asked whether she has "fulfilled her dreams," she replies that she has, by focusing her efforts on others (Jo 2012). To illustrate this, she tells the hosts that her boyfriend summarized her situation prior to the scandal: she was rich in gold but was poor in rice. In other words, she had many useless things but very little of the necessities of life. In very last segment, the hosts gift her what they call a *healing surprise*, which is a bag of organic rice and grains. At the end, during a period where the hosts thank her for her time and exchange pleasantries, Lee thanks them in return stating, "I couldn't say all the things that I said here before this" (Jo 2012).

Surely, this particular episode contains certain features that are unique to the guest and the dynamics between her and the hosts. In spite of this, we can view this episode as typical regarding the flow of conversation and its emotional overtones. *Healing Camp*, as one of the advertisements for it stated, is the "show that comforts our tired hearts." It "charges [as in a mobile phone] your hearts" (Bark 2012). Its draw for audiences is the intimacy, and even "para-sociality," that an extended conversation can provide (see Rojek 2015). Compared to Western talk shows, *Healing Camp* and similar shows are long. The pace is deliberate. The late night shows in the USA are not quite equivalents since they are a hybrid of interviews and other segments that are in the tradition of variety shows, which of course South Korea is full of, and is quite famous for in Southeast Asia with shows such as *Running Man* and *Infinite Challenge*. Thus, a show focused on healing is unique when compared to other shows on Korean television although since *Healing Camp*, there have been many others, including one hosted by Kim Je-dong, one of the co-hosts, called *Kim Je-dong's Talk to You: Don't You Worry* (JTBC).

Healing as Mediatized Religion and Politics

In the healing phenomenon, we see that there is mediatization in a general sense, but by engaging more fully, with the work of Hjarvard specifically, we see that there is more specifically, a mediatization of religion and politics. Moreover, in using Hjarvard's work in this way, I argue that we can reveal something at the core of his specific argument regarding the mediatization of religion, with implications for understanding it in less institutional terms.

It is my contention to this point that healing programs on South Korean television embody mediatization at a general level due to a specific *media logic* centered on emotionality and constant reference to the nation. Although the term has been met with some trepidation, especially by the more critically oriented scholars (Couldry 2014, Couldry and Hepp 2013, Hepp and Krotz 2014), Hjarvard (2013) provides a defense of the term which has clarified that the idea of *media logic* is hardly meant to be a singular or unified logic behind all forms of media. In fact, *media logic*, as inherited from the mediatization researchers from a generation ago, including Mazzoleni, Schulz and Altheide (Altheide and Schneider 2013, Mazzoleni and Schulz 1999), he suggests, was a conceptual shorthand for "the institutional aesthetic and technological modus operandi of media, including the ways in which media distribute material and symbolic resources" (Hjarvard 2013, 126). He insists that the purpose of the concept was not so much to identify a singular logic of all media but to point out that the lines between what was properly media and what was playing by the rules of media were being blurred. The media is both "out-there," meaning it comprises an institution on its own, and "in-here," as part of the various parts of the lifeworld (Hjarvard 2013, 126).

The spiritual orientation underlying the media phenomenon of healing is one that stands in line with the longer religious history of Korea. As the historian of Korean religion Baker has shown, *healing* was one of the major expectations for religion ever since the introduction of Buddhism to the peninsula in the 4th century. In fact, the native shamanism of the peninsula had prioritized healing power. As Baker argues, religion had "to promise to explain the unexplainable, control the uncontrollable and predict the unpredictable" in order to maintain interest in South Korea (Baker 1994, 71). He shows in his work that Buddhism was able to become state religion in the Koryo period not in small part due to its bringing together of Indian and Chinese medical theory.

Later on, this proved to be true for Christianity as well, which is a major force in contemporary South Korean society. While many view Korean Christianity as overwhelmingly evangelical in style, what remains unclear is how this sort of style came to dominate even in mainline Christian denominations such as Presbyterianism and Methodism. Sangyil Park, among others, has argued that Korean preaching, characterized by its storytelling has always worked "to deal with the *han* of the Korean *minjung*" (Park 2008, 14). *Han* here refers to feelings of resentment that emerge as a product of injustice. *Minjung* refers to *the masses* but with clear implications of marginalization and oppression. Some have even tried to make links with the Marxian notion of the *proletariat*. *Mindam* is the language of the *minjung*, their stories of suffering and hope, where "they find comfort in one another as a community." Park describes them as "social biographies" (Park 2008, 20). Preaching that incorporates *mindam* acts as *hanpuri* – the act of resolving *han* that goes back to shamanism. The sermon in a Christian context, according to Park, acts in a similar manner. In effect, the healing of today can be traced back to foundational expectations for religiosity in Korea.

By generating a media logic based on emotionality, community, shared suffering and hope, these healing programs are tapping into what may be called the spiritual infrastructure of Korea. The format itself, most significantly with its inclusion of biography, does this most obviously. This is evidence of what Hjarvard has famously described as banal religion. Constituting one of the three types of mediatization, banal religion, for Hjarvard, is how "religious imaginations" enter into the "cultural realm" (Hjarvard 2013, 90). Mediatization subjects religion to a process of banalization whereby its theological and institutional aspects are disembedded from their original contexts and juxtaposed with symbols and ideas from general culture. In other words, religious representations when mediatized "may have no, or only a limited, relationship with the institutionalized religions" (Hjarvard 2013, 91). Examples of this include the use of Christian imagery in high fashion as when fashion house Dolce & Gabbanna's Autumn/Winter 2013–2014 women's ready-to-wear collection featured images of mosaics from Sicilian cathedrals. Hjarvard's description of this as banal speaks to the fact that religious content, including symbols and images, may travel unnoticed or be invoked independently from their institutional or theological bases.

Rather overlooked in the critical discussions of this particular aspect of Hjarvard's theory is where he derives the idea of banal religion. As he acknowledges, it is the work of Michael Billig on *banal nationalism*. Banal nationalism is connected to cultural identity.

Nationalism, which is buttressed by identity, is created and maintained through not only explicit symbolism of the nation – be it the flag, the logo of the ruling party, the national anthem and so on – but also everyday phenomena, which "constantly remind the individual of his or her belonging to the nation and the national culture" (Hjarvard 2013, 90).

We can see an example of banal nationalism in the videos that circulated in Switzerland during the infamous minaret referendum of 2009. The right-wing coalition political parties called *the Egerkinger committee* took advantage of an aspect of Swiss law that allows for "federal popular initiatives" to become constitutional amendments if passed by a certain percentage of the population (Mayer 2011b). This coalition of right-wing parties pushed for the ban of the construction of minarets with a campaign full of videos and posters that juxtaposed pan-Islamic imagery (e.g., women in niqabs) with *native* Swiss images (e.g., the Swiss flag or the Alps). In one particularly striking video, the adhan, the Islamic call to worship, which traditionally does emanate from minarets, can be heard. While the audience is listening to this, the video features scenes from the bucolic Swiss countryside, including grassy green valleys, snow-capped mountains of the Alps, cows and people donned in Swiss traditional costumes. The idea is rather clear. It is to *offend* the sensibility of non-Muslim Swiss. To see quintessentially *Swiss* scenes with the audio backdrop of what is meant to be quintessentially *un-Swiss* – the adhan is clearly trying to stir up Islamophobia, setting a clash of Swiss-ness and Islam (Mayer 2011a, 2011b). The national symbols deployed here are as much implicitly *religious* as they are explicitly so. They are everyday symbols, which now function in a *religious manner.*

While a rather lengthy detour, when returning to the issue at hand, we see that within the mediatization of religion and politics as exemplified in the *healing* phenomena in South Korean media culture, the media logic consists of incorporating techniques and cultural tropes from the spiritual history of Korea. In so doing, it acts as the primary mechanism that allows media, in this case television programming, to provide both moral and spiritual guidance, as well a sense of community (Hjarvard 2013, 102).

Healing the Self, Healing the Nation

Healing as represented by these shows stands as a strategy for coping with the perils of contemporary life under compressed modernity. However, these hardships, whether material or psychological, are to be solved, for the most part, by the individuals themselves and not by the societies as a whole. The self becomes the center of healing. In addition to this instance of *individualization*, there is also the emergence of the purpose of healing, that is to say, to what end this healing is encouraged. In compressed modernity, the self's healing serves a higher purpose – the nation. The nation becomes the calling of the burned out self's regeneration and resilience.

The self is not simply inner-directed in the compressed modern situation of South Korea. Rather it is oriented toward the nation and its development. Yet, healing is decidedly not couched within a language of sacrifice. Healing is a process, therefore, of spiritualization not sublimation, to borrow the language of Phillip Rieff (1987). By spiritualization, Rieff distinguishes it from the process of sublimation inherent to culture proper. Sublimation requires renunciations of some kind for some greater good, and a commitment to that good. To the contrary, spiritualization is the morality of the self. It is the pursuit of the therapeutic, which he describes as the respite from the everyday, without guilt or a higher purpose. Thus, Rieff refers to the therapeutic as "un-religion" or "anti-religion" since it offers no transcendence (Rieff 1987, 10–13). However, the presented case study made clear that *healing* is a way of surviving the changes within the confines of the nation. Certainly, the lessons of *Healing Camp* and *Talk to You* are not so much about changing the social and political conditions of compressed modernity but rather changing ourselves. The self must *heal* him- or herself since the nation itself cannot be transformed. Healing, as a media and cultural phenomenon, can be understood as capitulation to a fixed reality where a new world cannot be imagined. This is because the self is always conflated with the *we* and *us* of the nation. The most that we, as individuals, can do is to offer comfort to one another with narrative. Recall the words of Lee Hyori, who stated on *Healing Camp* that a nation that can keep its animals safe is one that can keep its citizens safe (Jo 2012).

By healing oneself, he or she is healing the collective, which in this case, is the nation as per the developmentalist logic of compressed modernity. Moreover, by *mediatizing* both religion and politics in this manner, healing television programs allow viewers to identify others in similar positions as them. What mediatization of both religion and politics has facilitated is a process of subjectivization. Viewers are able to see that there are others like them, who struggle too. Facilitated by the formal and substantive structures – the *media logic* of these programs – viewers undergo what is effectively a "catechism of the citizen" as Simon Critchley has described (Critchley 2012).

Conclusion

In this chapter, I offered an analysis of the *healing* phenomena in South Korea as manifested in television. I argued that doing so occasions a revisit of the foundational social theoretical assumptions of mediatization, especially the interpretation of modernity. By using a *compressed modern* backdrop, I have illustrated how mediatization can also be seen not only within distinct institutions (e.g., religion, politics) but also across so-called institution, entangling them. In particular, this chapter has highlighted the unique role of mediatization in what may be called the collective individualization of compressed modernity, a dynamic that I have dubbed *mediatized nationalism*.

Healing is but one of the many ways, which help to understand the consequences of compressed modernity. While this chapter has viewed it as a cultural *response* to the rapidly changing conditions of the particular form of modernity experienced by South Koreans, there clearly seems to be movement in the realm of politics, particularly in the wake of what has been called the Candlelight Revolution of 2016–2017, where South Korean citizens came out in crowds totaling a million, with candles demanding that then-President Park steps down. These protests have been widely commented on as a point of national pride – with almost no violence reported and spontaneously organized trash pickups afterwards – even by politicians who sit in office currently. The then-speaker of the National Assembly Chung Sye-kyun is quoted as saying:

> I take pride in what our citizens have accomplished and I feel like boasting about it to our friends elsewhere in Asia, or around the world. That is how great the historical significance of these protests is for us… We must put to good use the stunning energy, the enthusiasm unleashed at those demonstrations so as to *solve the many problems that we face and there are many from youth unemployment to growing income disparity.* We can turn this movement of the citizens into the engine that will drive reform in Korea and give our people hope for the future.
>
> (Pastreich 2017. Emphasis added)

While the newly elected President Moon Jae-in has declared that his election "completes" the Candlelight Revolution (Shorrock 2017), it remains to be seen whether *healing* will continue in the form described above or whether there will be sustainable change in the social conditions that wrought *healing* in the first place.

Note

1 A case in point is actor Cha In Pyo, a previous guest on the program, who is widely recognized for his work with comfort women charities. See Chung (2009).

References

Altheide, D. and Schneider, C. J., 2013. *Qualitative Media Analysis*. Los Angeles: SAGE.

Baker, D., 1994. Monks, Medicine, and Miracles: Health and Healing in the History of Korean Buddhism. *Korean Studies*, 18, 50–75.

Bark, J., 2012. Big Bang's G-Dragon and Daesung to Appear on SBS "Healing Camp." *Soompi* [blog]. Available at www.soompi.com/2012/02/10/big-bangs-gdragon-and-daesung-to-appear-on-sbs-healing-camp/, accessed 10 February 2012.

Beck, U., 1992. *Risk Society: Towards a New Modernity*. London: SAGE Publications Ltd.

Beck, U., 1999. *World Risk Society*. Cambridge: Polity.

Beck, U., 2009. *World at Risk*. Cambridge: Polity.

Chandler, M., 2011. S. Korea Tries to Wrest Control from Booming Private Tutoring Industry. *Washington Post*, 3 April. Available at www.washingtonpost.com/world/s-korea-tries-to-wrest-control-from-booming-private-tutoring-industry/2011/01/12/AFNXQfXC_story.html, accessed 16 January 2017.

Chang, K.-S., 1999. Compressed Modernity and its Discontents: South Korean Society in Transition. *Economy and Society*, 28(1), 30–55.

Chang, K.-S., 2010. *South Korea under Compressed Modernity: Familial Political Economy in Transition*. Abingdon: Routledge.

Chen, K.-H., 2010. *Asia as Method: Toward Deimperialization*. Durham: Duke University Press.

Chung, A., 2009. Actor Touches Comfort Women in Novel. *The Korea Times*, 3 April 2009. Available at www.koreatimes.co.kr/www/culture/2018/05/142_42516.html, accessed 12 May 2018.

Couldry, N., 2014. When Mediatization Hits the Ground. In: Hepp, A. and Krotz, F., eds. *Mediatized Worlds*. London: Palgrave Macmillan, 54–71. doi:10.1057/9781137300355_4.

Couldry, N. and Hepp, A., 2013. Conceptualizing Mediatization: Contexts, Traditions, Arguments. *Communication Theory*, 23(3), 191–202.

Critchley, S., 2012. *The Faith of the Faithless: Experiments in Political Theology*. London: Verso.

Giddens, A., 2003. *Runaway World: How Globalization is Reshaping Our Lives*. London: Routledge.

Gurevitch, M., Bennett, T., Curran, J. and Woollacott, J., eds., 1982. *Culture, Society and the Media*. London: Methuen.

Han, S.-J., 2016. The Legacy of Ulrich Beck in Asia: Introduction. *Theory, Culture & Society*, 33(7–8), 253–256. doi:10.1177/0263276416678049.

Han, S. and Hussain, N. A., 2016. Death and Disaster: The Catastrophe of Suicide in Japan. In: Elliott, A. and Hsu, E. L., eds. *The Consequences of Global Disasters*. London: Routledge, 34–49.

Han, S.-J. and Shim, Y.-H., 2010. Redefining Second Modernity for East Asia: A Critical Assessment. *The British Journal of Sociology*, 61(3), 465–488. doi:10.1111/j.1468-4446.2010.01322.

Hepp, A. and Krotz, F., 2014. *Mediatized Worlds: Culture and Society in a Media Age*. New York: Springer.

Hjarvard, S., 2013. *The Mediatization of Culture and Society*. Abingdon: Routledge.

Jo, M., 2012. "Lee Hyori." *Healing Camp: Aren't You Happy.* Seoul Broadcasting System (SBS).

Krotz, F., 2014. Media, Mediatization and Mediatized Worlds: A Discussion of the Basic Concepts. In: Hepp, A. and Krotz, F., eds. *Mediatized Worlds.* London: Palgrave Macmillan, 72–87. doi:10.1057/9781137300355_5.

Lathion, S., 2011. In the Shadow of the Minaret: Origins and Implications of a Citizens' Initiative. In: Haenni, P. and Lathion, S., eds. *The Swiss Minaret Ban: Islam in Question.* Translated from French by T. Genrich. Fribourg: Religioscope, 17–18.

Lee, S., 2013. Can "Healing" Marketing Cure Korea? freshtrax, [blog] 12 November. Available at http://blog.btrax.com/en/2013/11/12/can-healing-marketing-cure-korea/, accessed 16 January 2017.

Mayer, J.-F., 2011a. A Country without Minarets: Analysis of the Background and Meaning of the Swiss Vote of 29 November 2009. *Religion*, 41(1), 11–28. doi:10.1080/0048721X.2011.553140.

Mayer, J.-F., 2011b. In the Shadow of the Minaret: Origins and Implications of a Citizens' Initiative. In: Haenni, P. and Lathion, S., eds. *The Swiss Minaret Ban: Islam in Question.* Translated from French by T. Genrich. Fribourg: Religioscope, 10–16.

Mazzoleni, G. and Schulz, W., 1999. 'Mediatization' of Politics: A Challenge for Democracy? *Political Communication*, 16(3), 247–261. doi:10.1080/105846099198613.

Nie, K. S., Kee, C. P. and Ahmad, A. L., 2014. Mediatization: A Grand Concept or Contemporary Approach? *Procedia – Social and Behavioral Sciences*, 155, 362–367. doi:10.1016/j.sbspro.2014.10.306.

Ochiai, E., 2011. Unsustainable Societies: The Failure of Familialism in East Asia's Compressed Modernity. *Historical Social Research / Historische Sozialforschung*, 36(2), 219–245.

Ock, H., 2014. Sexy Icons Son Dambi and Lee Hyori Show off Friendship. *The Korea Herald*, 31 August. Available at www.koreaherald.com/view.php?ud=20140831000256, accessed 12 May 2018.

Ock, H., 2015. Koreans' Average Work Hours Still Second-Longest in OECD. *The Korea Herald*, 2 November. Available at www.koreaherald.com/view.php?ud=20151102001240, accessed 16 January 2017.

Park, J. K., 2016. 'Healed to Imagine': Healing Discourse in Korean Popular Culture and Its Politics. *Culture and Religion*, 17(4), 375–391.

Park, S., 2008. *Korean Preaching, Han, and Narrative.* New York: Peter Lang.

Parker, K. and Patten, E., 2013. *The Sandwich Generation.* Pew Research Center's Social & Demographic Trends Project, 30 January. Available at www.pewsocialtrends.org/2013/01/30/the-sandwich-generation/, accessed 14 January 2017.

Pastreich, E., 2017. "The Greatest asset of Korea is our people", Speaker Chung Sye-kyun on Impeachment and Korea's Future. *Huffpost*, 3 January. Available at www.huffingtonpost.com/emanuel-pastreich/-the-greatest-asset-of-ko_b_13934432.html, accessed 19 January 2017.

Phillips, M., 2013. Korea Is the World's Top Producer of Unhappy School Children. *Quartz*, [blog] 3 December. Available at https://qz.com/153380/korea-is-the-worlds-top-producer-of-unhappy-school-children/, accessed 12 May 2018.

Rieff, P., 1987. *The Triumph of the Therapeutic: Uses of Faith after Freud*. Chicago: University of Chicago Press.

Rojek, C., 2015. *Presumed Intimacy: Parasocial Interaction in Media, Society and Celebrity Culture*. New York: John Wiley & Sons.

Shorrock, T., 2017. South Korea's New President Says His Election Completes the 'Candlelight Revolution.' *The Nation*, 10 May. Available at www.thenation.com/article/south-koreas-new-president-says-his-election-completes-the-candlelight-revolution/, accessed 7 September 2017.

Weissmann, J., 2012. Whoa: Samsung Is Responsible for 20% (!?) of South Korea's Economy. *The Atlantic*, 31 July. Available at www.theatlantic.com/business/archive/2012/07/whoa-samsung-is-responsible-for-20-of-south-koreas-economy/260552/, accessed 15 January 2017.

Yoon, S., 2013. *"Healing" Rises as New Trend of Korean Culture: Report*. Korea.net: The Official Website of the Republic of Korea, 4 January. Available at www.korea.net/NewsFocus/Society/view?articleId=104566, accessed 16 January 2017.

Part 2
Southeast Asia

5 Facebook and the Mediatization of Religion

Inter-/Intrareligious Dialogue in Malaysia[1]

Tan Meng Yoe

As media technologies develop over time, it is possible to suggest that media, as "something that modifies and transforms communication" (Krotz and Hepp 2011, 143), will inadvertently play an important part in how people experience and express religion in their everyday lives. For example, with the Internet, a change that is evident is the availability and accessibility of alternative knowledge and freedom to engage with more people in the religious discourse. This has led to the emergence of new religious discourses on the internet, both in interreligious and intrareligious contexts (Pons-de Wit, Versteeg and Roeland 2015, 90). This emerging discourse is explored in the Malaysian online context in this chapter, with particular focus on a public Facebook group called *Project Engage*.[2] The group aims to foster interreligious dialogue among Malaysians, *and* is independently managed by a small team of like-minded individuals. It is neither owned nor supported by political parties, unlike traditional mainstream media in Malaysia, which are largely controlled by the Malaysian government or other political parties directly and indirectly (Randhawa and Venkiteswaran 2010, 86). As this is an independently run group, the interactions that take place on this Facebook page can serve as a snapshot of how mediatized religion on an everyday level in Malaysia looks like.

The description of the Facebook page will show how in a largely unmoderated setting, *Project Engage*'s attempt to reinforce particular religious ideals and engage their members with alternative and sometimes controversial views of how religion should be practiced in Malaysia, and how these attempts are responded to. The subsequent theoretical discussion will show how *Project Engage* can shed light on some of the debates surrounding the theory of mediatization, such as banal religion, determinism and the need to take a broader approach to what every day represents.

As *Project Engage*'s content is largely situated within the context of broader Malaysian inter-/intrareligious narratives, it is necessary to provide a background to the Malaysian ethno-religious context. This context will in turn provide the basis on which *Project Engage* is analyzed in the subsequent sections.

Malaysia is often promoted as a multicultural country. This notion of *multicultural* is packaged with positive connotations both locally and internationally. When advertised internationally, a multicultural Malaysia represents a beautiful form of societal diversity.[3] For potential tourists, this evokes the allure of experiencing a harmonious collection of various exotic cultures in a single locality (Webster 2010). For the international political community, Malaysia is often portrayed by official representatives as a Muslim majority country that harmoniously integrates other ethnic and religious minorities (Ariff 2017).

The idea of harmony in diversity is also frequently used in local propaganda, mainly for maintaining peaceful relations between various ethnic communities. Since the independence of Malaya in 1957 from the British Empire, and subsequently the formation of Malaysia in 1963,[4] Malaysians are repeatedly inundated with messages reminding them of the importance of multicultural unity (Osman 2011, 626). A recent prominent example is the *1Malaysia* campaign launched by then-Prime Minister Najib Razak in 2010. The campaign promoted and emphasized the "importance of national unity regardless of race, background or religious belief for a better tomorrow" (1Malaysia 2014). The campaign was designed to inform the various policies and public service initiatives undertaken by the government.

However, the very existence of such measures to promote intercultural peace domestically points to the reality that not all is as rosy as advertised. A general reading of Malaysian history shows that multiethnic and religious issues dominated much of the proceedings in the formation of the country (Kua 2015, 99–133). Until today, most political parties in Malaysia are either ethnic-based or religion-centric. Major incidents of ethnic dispute such as the 1969 ethnic/political riots which led to the suspension of parliament for two years (Lee 2010, 40–42) and the 2001 clash between Hindus and Muslims in a local village, Taman Medan, serve as reminders that ethno-religious tensions are real and can be very violent. In the past decade, the more liberal and inclusive political parties gained prominence in the country. However, highly active and vocal far-right Malay-Muslim supremacist organizations, such as *Persatuan Pribumi Perkasa* (Perkasa)[5] and *Ikatan Muslimim Malaysia* (ISMA)[6] also emerged, which champion a hardline stance on affirmative action policies favoring the Malay-Muslim community. In addition, they assert that the other ethnic groups, such as the Chinese and Indians, are merely *pendatangs* (foreigners), and are to be denied equal rights despite being citizens of Malaysia. Examples include ISMA president Abdullah Zaik. Abdul Rahman stated in 2014 that Chinese "entered this country together with the British invaders as intruders" (Anonymous 2014); and Perkasa president Ibrahim Ali, who on another occasion in 2011, threatened a crusade against Christians after alleging that Malaysian Christians were conspiring with opposition politicians to Christianize Malaysia (Chooi 2011).

Significant tension was raised with the government's ban on the use of the term *Allah* (Arabic for *God)* in a Malay-Language Christian publication. It was a long-running legal battle which ended when the Federal Court of Malaysia upheld the ban in June 2014 (Brown 2014) and the Islamic authorities seized Malay-language Bibles in 2009 (Koswanage 2014) and 2014 (Fisher 2009). With regard to the *Allah* controversy, Neo comments that the "contrasting reactions to the judgments reflect a distrust between the Malay-Muslim community and religious minorities in Malaysia" (Neo 2014, 767). She points out the competing arguments: a judge's comment that "the Christians' insistence on using *Allah* was a strategy to confuse and convince Muslims in Sabah and Sarawak to convert to Christianity" (Neo 2014, 767) and the Christians' assertion that their rights were infringed on, as a sharp point of religious contention in Malaysia. Many of these court decisions and incidences were justified on the premise of protecting the Muslims from converting to Christianity. The fear of conversion to Christianity is a well-known one, and is an issue that has representatives of both sides repeatedly trading barbs.

In 2005, the Malaysian parliament grappled with the looming threat of a bill to amend the existing Syariah law in the country since 2015.[7] The proposed amendment to loosen existing limits of punishment of the *Syariah* courts and replace it with significantly harsher punishments generated hostile political posturing from every party on both sides of the aisle. Although the bill began as a Private Member's bill proposed by an opposition lawmaker from a conservative Islamist party, it garnered support from the United Malay National Organization (UMNO), the majority party within the government coalition. UMNO subsequently lobbied aggressively to have the bill tabled and passed (R. Ahmad et al. 2016). After months of political mudslinging, UMNO announced that they would no longer table the bill (Razak 2017). The concern raised by several politicians, religious institutions and public commentators was that such a move would eventually pave the way for *hudud*[8] law to be introduced to Malaysia, and that it would inevitably affect the non-Muslim population of the country.[9] The aftermath of the political posturing came in the following forms: supporters of the bill threatened non-Muslims from interfering in Islamic affairs, and attempted to remind the dissenting Muslims regarding their responsibility to support Muslims in the matter. Non-Muslims contend that matters of national significance should not exclude their input and that their concerns must be addressed too. This is an example of how a single issue can generate interreligious an intrareligious dialogue, and that the harmonious *1Malaysia* narrative is far from a reality on the metapolitical realm.

The interreligious context presented above are mediated narratives that are accessed primarily through mainstream and alternative news portals, or on a secondary level, through social networking sites of politicians. This narrative is limited because, as stated earlier, the limited freedom accorded to mainstream media channels has led to accusations of framing bias. It is crucial, then, to move beyond interreligious engagement, beyond institutional mass media representations of national level interreligious engagement in Malaysia and explore the everyday forms of interreligious and intrareligious dynamics in Malaysia. The issues that appear are not wholly representative of all forms of media content related to religion in the country. For this chapter, I specifically refer to a Malaysian Facebook group, *Project Engage* that exclusively discusses religious issues and attempts to create a platform for religious harmony. I will analyze the interactions in these groups as a form of religious mediatization that is more closely connected to grassroots sentiments of everyday Malaysians, and ask how these mediatized inter-/intrareligious occurrences can be situated in the evolving religious narrative of Malaysia.

The online ethnographic description and analysis of this Facebook group will take the socio-constructivist approach to mediatization theory, which refers to "the process of a communicative construction of socio cultural reality and analyzes the status of various media within that process" (Couldry and Hepp 2013, 196). The initial inquiry on what forms of interreligious engagement takes place on an everyday level is understandably too broad as it takes place on too many avenues. Thus, the focus is narrowed down to a mediatized world, defined as "structured fragments of life-worlds with a certain binding intersubjective knowledge inventory, with specific social practices and cultural thickenings" (Krotz and Hepp 2011, 146), which in turn allows for a concretization of accessible and analyzable data. As such, the field chosen for observation and analysis is an online one. The Internet is a useful site for research because of the affordances accorded by it for both the user and the researcher. Users experience it differently due to affordances such as interactivity, access, anonymity and more. Researchers access it as a research site differently as the user-centric and archival nature of online communities, namely that "individual expressions of opinion can be made visible, and therefore more tangible and academically determinable" (Radde-Antweiler 2017, 140). This combination of affordances yields rich data that can provide a snapshot of what transpires in interreligious communication on the ground.

An Introduction to *Project Engage*

Project Engage is a content portal that is overseen by a group of scholars, activists and artists who started what they describe as a project for social development, with the purpose of promoting healthy debate and understanding in the diverse Malaysian community. Currently, they publish on two platforms, a blog and a Facebook page. The blog features commentaries and updates regarding various sociopolitical events in Malaysia: Its writings resemble that of opinion pieces, and while there is no public information regarding its traffic, most posts do not generate any comments. The Facebook page, however, serves as a public forum for sociopolitical issues (a majority is relating to religion). In the *About* section of the Facebook page, the aim of the group is described as a desire to "empower moderate voices" through intellectual discourse. The Facebook page is more frequently updated than the blog, and experiences high activity. Although it is difficult to get demographic data of the members of Project Dialog, it is linguistically possible to generalize that a majority of the commenters are Malaysian, as the Malaysian-Malay language is the primary language used.[10] The commenters also demonstrate a general awareness of the Malaysian religious environment in their comments.

From a statistical point of view, the Facebook page has been very successful. As of October 2016, the group has 24,489 members subscribed to the group, which means, their updates on the page are easily noticeable. The group is also highly active. Over the three-month period from April 2015 to June 2015 that the group was observed, it averaged 149 status updates a month, which translates to five a day. The reception toward these posts is equally high, with an average of 41 *likes* and 5 comments per status. The actual distribution is much more varied, with the highest activity recorded at 415 *likes*, and 115 comments, and no response at the lowest.

The group posts a wide variety of content relating to religious issues and a significant subset of it, religious issues within Malaysia. Its usual format of a status update involves either posting a link to an external site about a current issue, be it news, third-party commentary, or an article on their own blog. This shared link is accompanied by a short statement of the group's official stance on the subject matter. An example of this would be in the case of the group resharing a third-party post regarding a person's eye-witness account of an elderly Malay man publicly scolding a pregnant Malay-Muslim woman who discreetly ate at a corner of a mall during the fasting month of Ramadan, and this same person's attempt to defend the pregnant lady. The link to the story was accompanied by a short statement by *Project Engage* that translates to:

Sigh, I don't know what to say anymore. When it comes to women, people think they can scold them as they like. I wonder, if it was a strong young man, whether an attempt to scold him would be made?[11]

Apart from current social issues, the group also actively posts content giving people information about the basics of Buddhism, Hinduism, as part of their effort to create understanding among religions. Like the make-up of content, the readers and commenters are also very diverse, based on the type of comments that appear. This can be seen in the following case study.

The Case of the Protest outside a Church

To make it directly relevant to religious engagement within Malaysia, here is a description of a status update regarding an incident on 19 April 2015, where a group of fifty Malay-Muslim protesters gathered outside a newly set-up church in Taman Medan to pressure them to remove the cross as the church was located in a Muslim-majority township (Cheng 2015). The incident received widespread media attention, with many calling for the arrest of the protestors for criminal intimidation. The incident escalated further when it was reported that the person heading the protest is the brother of the Inspector-General of Police (Zolkepli, Meikeng and Cheng 2017), further fueling conspiracy theories that the protest was engineered for political purposes. The matter was largely settled when the church agreed to remove the cross despite receiving authorization from the state government of Selangor to restore the sign of the cross on the building (Lee 2015). In response to this, *Project Engage* published an article called *What's with the Cross?* on their blog, and as per the group's modus operandi, the blog post was shared on the Facebook timeline, accompanied by the following text:

> Rationally, when (a cross) is taken down or removed, it is because there is a group of people who are frustrated with it, for whatever reason. The cross is only plastic structure, a piece of metal or wood that's in a shape of a cross. However, for the Christians, they are not simply denied the right to put up a piece of decoration to beautify their place of worship. They are denied their rights to interpret and practice their own religion. They are denied their identity as they were unable to express themselves as a Christian in their own birthplace.[12]

The reception for this post was quick and high. It has since generated 386 *likes*, the second highest number in the three-month period, and drew 114 comments. Two threads of comments in particular were particularly active. The first one, a comment by *Yusuf*, is as follows:

> The statement above is wrong. While the way the sentiment was expressed by the protesters is not right, the protest was only to stop the Christians from erecting the cross in that place. There is no objection to them adopting Christianity or worshipping their god.

Disagreements in such public postings are not uncommon. *Yusuf*'s post was not hostile in nature. Rather, he criticized *Project Engage*'s opinion on the matter by offering his personal viewpoint. *Project Engage* responded to *Yusuf*'s comment two hours later, writing that "freedom of religion encompasses many dimensions, not just in the matter of the cross, but also the freedom to worship without fear". This was followed by a comment by *Chong*, who offered a commentary about the Muslim populace in general, arguing that through this protest the Muslims have shown themselves to be a community that rejects ethnic and religious diversity, as well as freedom of religion. He continues by saying that the "Christians have not fought back because of Jesus's teachings of forgiveness, and that Christians will forgive this trespass".

Chong's comment sparked off a series of responses. This is likely because *Chong*'s comment was a two-edged sword – it criticized the Muslim community at large, and insinuated the superiority of Christian forgiveness, which directly addressed neither the original post, nor *Yusuf*'s opinion. The comments that followed mostly asserted the superiority of the commenters' respective religions, such as *Michael*'s short rebuttal that "Jesus was a man, not god. Just like other prophets. The issue now is about the erecting of a cross. We have laws, please follow them". This was followed by another comment by *Zul*, who simply told *Chong* to be quiet, and not raise the matter of race and religion. As the argument ensued, there were attempts to diffuse the quarrel by drawing attention back to the initial topic, even by Muslims. *Fikri* pleaded thread, "we have our religion, they have theirs. Islam does not instruct us to take down the religious symbols of others. How would you feel if others did that to us? How would we feel?" Based on *Fikri*'s comment, it is probable that he is a Muslim who agrees with *Project Engage*'s approach to the matter. He received some support in the subsequent comments, but the conversation largely degenerated into a back and forth of members ridiculing or talking down those who disagreed with them.

The second thread that generated many comments under this status update is more pertinent in its critique. While *Yusuf*'s comment was contained within the current issue of the cross being displayed by a church, this second post by *Hamid* invoked a broader issue in Malaysia:

> The writer states that opposing the cross is a form of denying the Christians the right to practice their faith and worship their god. If so, then the protest is not right. I agree. Then how about those who insult and oppose the implementation of hudud when it is a requirement in Islam? Aren't they opposing Muslims from practicing their faith?

While it is easy to categorize the first comment by *Yusuf*'s as an attempt to engage *Project Engage*'s argument, this comment by *Hamid* switches the focus of the discussion entirely. His comment led to a thread of 35 more comments – entirely on the subject of *hudud*. If this thread is read in isolation from the original post, it would have been difficult to situate it within the larger discussion of the protest outside the church in Taman Medan. However, as presented in an earlier section, the subject of *hudud* is a hot-button issue in Malaysia, and under this thread, a debate about *hudud* developed quickly. The response initially centered on the point that Muslims themselves opposed the *hudud* issue. *Project Engage* commented that the issue of *hudud* is different because there remains "a great debate within the Muslim community, before we can even discuss implementing it", followed by *Remy*'s comment that "the main bloc of people who reject *hudud* are the Muslims in West Malaysia."

The discussion then evolved to the subject of whether *hudud* would involve non-Muslims, with the first commenter himself asking "Does *hudud* involve non-Muslims?" in response to a comment by *Michael* that "while Christians don't oppose *hudud* implementation in any state, can we really believe that it won't affect Christians?" With no resolution to that discussion, the conversation took another turn when *Winnie* made the following comment:

> Actually, "hudud" is in the Bible but after Jesus came, it was no longer practiced, because Jesus fulfilled the law. Hudud was adopted by the early Jews but since Jesus' birth it has changed. That's why Christians today reject hudud.

An observation in this group is that once an issue pertaining to a religion (in this case, *hudud* and Islam) is responded to from the perspective of another religion (in this case, Christianity), the argument degenerates into name-calling and self-defense. *Winnie*'s comment drew a response saying:

> "you're stupid... You don't know anything about *hudud*, but talk as if you do. Go learn about it before commenting. Stupid". This was followed by *Hamid*, who asked, "Did Jesus abolish hudud, or did Christians today distort the Bible to not mention it? Why don't Christians follow the Bible?"

Mediatization and *Project Engage*

With the above description of *Project Engage*'s Facebook page and the specific case study of the protest outside the church, it is now possible to discuss religious mediatization more productively. Mediatization, as noted by Lundby, is not a new term, with various scholars such as Mazzoleni, Habermas, and more having tackled this term from different angles (Lundby 2009, 4). He suggested that mediatization "points to societal changes in contemporary high modern societies and the role of media and mediated communication in these transformations" (Lundby 2009, 1). In order to make sense of these societal changes, Krotz and Hepp called for a more comprehensive presentation and analysis of different *mediatized worlds* in order to more effectively develop new theories of mediatization (Krotz and Hepp 2011). Furthermore, Clark proposed that notions of mediatization could benefit from embracing "emergent theories of cybernetics as a means of understanding the relationships between communication technologies, humans, and social change" (Clark 2011, 180).

Following this, *Project Engage* can be discussed in relation to existing mediatization theory in three ways: *Project Engage* as a site of religious education; a site for self-affirmation; and a site of everyday religion. Mediatization of religion cannot be fully grasped without first acknowledging the mediatization of behaviors. Krotz and Hepp rightly stated that mediatized worlds are structured fragments of lifeworlds that contain "specific social practices and cultural thickenings" (Krotz and Hepp 2011, 146). This means that it is important not only to describe religion or religious practices in isolation, but its broader network of sociocultural contexts and interactions.

Project Engage as a Site of Religious Education

Firstly, *Project Engage* can be characterized as a platform where a type of religious education takes place. Here, I approach the term *education* broadly. The content creators are attempting to assert their brand of faith, and create an inter-/intrareligious awareness of different ways to interpret the faith. Although many of their posts primarily target issues pertaining to Islam, they make significant effort to provide information on other faiths. For example, over the course of a few weeks, they documented a travel series where they featured places of worship in Malaysia, and posted introductory articles about the basics of various major faiths in Malaysia. These largely take a documentary form. Then, there are direct engagements of social issues in Malaysia, such as the incident described above – that of a group of Muslims protesting the public display of a cross on a church – and abroad, where they have, on numerous occasions, provided arguments for the tolerance and acceptance of the LGBT community. In these issues, it is evident they are proactive in reinforcing their preferred doctrine or religious ideals – in principle, educating their audience.

When Malaysian politicians attempt to either stir up or diffuse religious issues, it is a direct form of political leaders engaging with the public on how to interpret their faith, and since much of these political communication is reproduced, disseminated, consumed and negotiated through the media, one can argue that mediatization of religion is expressed on that front. This is quite usual since one of the key features of the media, the Internet in particular, is that religious knowledge is no longer limited to the one source, such as the pulpit and/or a preacher. Rather, religious knowledge has become readily available on all major media platforms. In fact, the Internet has become so cluttered with information that it would take some discernment on the part of the reader to process.

With the Internet allowing for the simultaneous presentation of multiple sources of knowledge, the question of authority arises. Who owns religious knowledge? Hjarvard argues, in his notion of *banal religion*, that pop-culture's uses and representations of various religious elements in its content has made it the dominant representation of religion in society, and thus a major authority in religion (Hjarvard 2011). This is also Jin's argument in his process of inference of mediatized Buddhism in the film *Avatar.*, where he provides a comprehensive overview of the Hwaom-Buddhist faith and how it can be inferred in the movie Avatar – e.g., in its title and elements in film (Jin 2015). The analysis serves as the author's personal projection and inference of religious meaning in the film, rather than an active charting of possible social change through this particular expression of religious mediatization. As Clark points out regarding this approach to mediatization, it can be a stretch to consider how pop-culture movies (such as *Constantine* or *Indiana Jones*) can take over the role of the religious institution, as the primary educator of religious matters (Clark 2011, 169). Although mediatization seems to pay attention to the interaction and transaction between actors and structures, these interactions are not apparent. Furthermore, Hjarvard asserts that mediatization is nondeterministic, yet he contextualizes religion as a cultural institution that has "in various ways become influenced by the media" (Hjarvard 2011, 119). The problem with the concept of banal religion, then, is that it presupposes mediatization of religion as a linear process of communication, and that religious institutions and individuals passively allow mass media to become conduits of religious education.

Banal religion, then, can be problematized by user engagement of media technologies. Its media/medium-deterministic limitations are made apparent by *Project Engage*'s inability to *banalize* religion, because anyone can assert their religious authority on the Internet, thus making educating audiences a convoluted battleground of ideas. The significant resistance that *Project Engage* faces regularly in their posted content is itself a form of resistance to the notion of banal religion. Audiences also serve as content creators, and actively reject *Project Engage*'s liberal media content, and take the initiative to educate others in their personal capacities – even in the comments section. This is seen in the example above, where *hudud* was discussed out of context. Multiple individuals attempt to clarify and assert their views to those whom they consider to be ignorant of issues surrounding *hudud* and *Syariah* law in Malaysia, and affirm the dominance of the majority (in this case, Malay-Muslims in Malaysia). The subsequent dialogue that emerged descended into a long series of individuals reinforcing their existing ideological positions, with an ascending incivility. Analyzing the development of the two major threads, it seems that *Project Engage*, through its use of the media platform called Facebook, was unable to effectively engage the participants on these threads about the politics of placing a cross on a church in a predominantly Muslim neighborhood.

Project Engage as a Site for Self-Affirmation

Going online to assert and reinforce existing ideological positions online may sound like an oxymoron. After all, the Internet, as the largest repository of information, should make it the ideal vehicle for education and change. However, once we consider that the online experience is rooted and symbiotic with the offline experience, the idealistic view of the Internet dissipates. In Baum's analysis of Barack Obama's 2008 presidential campaign, he notes that Obama's use of the media can be broken down to "preaching to the choir" and "converting the flock" (Baum 2012, 185). Using different communication styles for different media is not a new idea, but he points out interestingly that Obama's online content – through emails and social media, was primarily for the purpose of reinforcing his base's support, thus using the Internet to preach to the choir – people who already support him. Baum states that the "political blogosphere functions primarily as an arena for partisan and ideological self-selection" (Baum 2012, 192).

Furthermore, Larsen provided five things that *religion surfers* look for online: information for reference and study, social activities for fellowship, advice and support, and membership, providing credible evidence for each of these (Larsen 2003). These factors suggest that religion surfers go online primarily to advance their personal spirituality, as none of it necessarily includes engaging with other religions in any way.

If so, we have to ask critically: If it is true that people have the habit of tailoring their online experience to reinforce their preexisting beliefs, what are the regular dissenters doing on *Project Engage*, and where do they fit into Larsen's model? After all, it is a public group that people voluntarily subscribe to. Why not unsubscribe from *Project Engage* and have nothing to do with it? There are many viewers who air their dislike of the group regularly in the comments section, with some coming on regularly to simply say "the admin is provoking again," "stupid admin" or something else in a similar vein, sometimes with profanity.

Based on that observation, I propose a new category of social-media users, called *hate-browsers*. This term is adopted from the New Yorker description of television audiences who regularly watch certain TV shows so that they could talk about how much they hate it. The article called this practice "hate-watching," and it was used widely during the run of Aaron Sorkin's TV series, *Studio 60 on the Sunset Strip*, and later on, *The Newsroom* (Nussbaum 2012). Both TV series contained strong political slants on various issues, and many viewers watched the show in order to express their disagreement with the writers. In the case of the Internet and religion, there is a similar phenomenon that I term as *hate-browsing*. I characterize them as people who have zealous belief in their own views, and that within this zealotry, lies a certain militancy to not just resist content of popular culture, mass media or popular social media groups, but to actively and regularly participate in various platforms in order to project their own authority over any given issue. Applied to religion, this would mean adopting a superiority complex when it comes to engaging with others who disagree with their views. This behavior is performed through predictable forms of argumentation. Drawing from my observations in *Project Engage*, these forms include, but are not limited to, blaming other religions, use of profanity, discrediting the original poster, name calling, labeling the group as liberal, refusal to engage the topic even if called out by others to. Although there are some attempts at rationalization, most of the comments are argumentative, condescending and disruptive. In short, they appear to browse *Project Engage* for the sole purpose of expressing their hatred for it.

Project Engage is simultaneously attempting to convert the flock and preach to the choir, but what is expressed most often is affirmation of preexisting beliefs on the part of the readers. This is reflected in the quantity of *likes* clicked and quality of comments expressed. There is a clear division between the *choir*, who already agrees with the ideological opinion of the site and affirms their agreeing through their *likes* and comments, in contrast to those who see this site as an avenue to hate-browse. As such, the engagement between religions is superficial and hostile in most cases.

Project Engage as a Site of Everyday Religion

The above leads to the third observation, that the community on *Project Engage* is representative of the everyday religiosity and spirituality of some Malaysians. Krotz and Hepp's approach is an important one because it addresses a recurring concern in the study of mediatization: Instead of considering how new technologies are shaping society as they are developed – a process known as media logic – they stress on the necessity to look how technology and society are in the "constant process of changing everyday life, of changing identity constructions and social relations, of a changing economy, democracy and leisure, of a changing culture and society as a whole" (Krotz and Hepp 2011, 139). In other words, they shift the perspective of research from media-logic frameworks into a description of mediatized worlds, where one considers how "various contexts of present, everyday life are marked by media communication" (Krotz and Hepp 2011, 146). When applied to online religion, this approach resonates with Lövheim's assertion that studies on the mediatized religion should not be confined to "how religion is transformed through the media, but how religions transform in the modern world in interaction with the media" (Lövheim 2011, 164).

In this sense, Radde-Antweiler posits *"digital religion* is nothing that can be thought of independently from an *offline religion.* In the sense of communicative constructivism, it becomes clear that religious identity is produced communicatively, and that communication can make use of different media" (Radde-Antweiler 2017, 148). This means that the Internet "is not only textual" (MacWilliams 2002, 322), but in the analysis of it, it should be "situated within the larger environment of everyday religion" (Tan 2014, 144). Howard, in his description of vernacular religion, suggests "the web exists alongside institutional discourse, but is embodied only in the aggregate personal choices to communicate made by many different individuals over time" (Howard 2009, 732).

Theoretically, this, along with the observations of *Project Engage*, raises a new consideration. A lot of the discussion of mediatization has so far revolved around the mediatization of meta-elements of society, such as religion, education, politics and more, and on the meso-level, we see discussion on (in the case of religion), the mediatization of religious imagery, text, knowledge and even institutional structure. It is hard to gauge the impact of any phenomenon in *Project Engage* without including a deeper discussion about how behavior and etiquette is mediatized. If we accept the argument that the dichotomy between the online and the off-line is an imaginary one, and that the self is ultimately projected in both realms, then in addition to religious and spiritual characteristics, one must consider the broader social logic of individuals and communities. For example, in *Project Engage,* the mediatization of behavior takes the form of the inability to engage difference in opinion, a problem that is evident even in the highest level of government. This is also applicable to the category of people I described as hate-browsers, who mediatize their preexisting attitudes toward their beliefs into a more varied community.

There are evident similarities between the online and off-line worlds presented in the group, such as the divisions of ethnicity and religion, and how issues are debated publicly, such as name-calling, asserting one's own position without regard for the perspective others and more. It can also be considered that the commenters approach is not unlike the approach taken by leaders that is presented in mainstream media, where leaders are eager to assert to their views more than rationally debated issues. So, if the Internet is perceived as a platform for a positive evolution of everyday social engagement, that space has yet to be broached in this context. The media lifeworlds that are recreated in the everyday expressions on *Project Engage* show that the things that divide opinion in the mainstream media are the same things that divide audiences on Facebook.

Conclusion: Mediatized Religion and Interreligious Engagement in Malaysia

The case study demonstrates that by describing a fragment of an everyday mediatized lifeworld, one can gain valuable insights into the broader societal narrative that forms a larger part in how religion is consumed and articulated on various platforms in Malaysia. The interreligious media environment in Malaysia is at times a convoluted environment to navigate. Yet it also serves as a good example of how the context is too broad to generalize, and Krotz and Hepp warns against oversimplifying media worlds (Krotz and Hepp 2011, 146). To borrow Latour's methodological approach to describe data, he says that it is crucial to allow "the complexities of collectives to be deployed, rather than fit them in frameworks of existing theory" (Latour 2007, 57). This philosophy pairs well with the call to "identify different grounded theories of how media communicative change and socio cultural change are interlaced with each other" (Krotz and Hepp 2011, 148). The mediatized world of *Project Engage* described and discussed above has already engaged with various approaches to the theory of mediatization. It has considered how the media-deterministic approach is difficult to apply in a highly interactive mass media technology like Facebook, and how it is pertinent to describe the off-line (and by extension the non-media) aspects of everyday life in the description of a mediatized world. It also reveals that specifically when analyzing religious expression, the element of how individual behavior is mediatized should also be considered. Perhaps future research that combines media studies and psychology studies may prove fruitful in this regard.

Returning to the aforementioned parliamentary debate of the *hudud* bill in Malaysia, the aftermath saw a local daily newspaper, *The Star*, publish an article *entitled Tech-savvy Malaysians Still Lack Knowledge of Religions, Say Academicians*. The author of this article states "despite rapid technological advances, Malaysians are still lagging behind in terms of religious tolerance and understanding" (Ghazali 2017). The statement infers an expectation that technological advancement should have been a vehicle in improving religious engagement. While that is a logical ideal due to the potential of the Internet, the analysis above paints a different picture: It is misinformed. At present, the online is merely an extension of the off-line. It states what is already so. After all, militancy, reinforcing of one's existing belief, contesting of authority and vulgar disagreements with people with different beliefs are common even in the off-line. In *Project Engage*, they mainly publish what can be considered a more *moderate* or *liberal* brand of Islam, and while there are many comments, there is very little engagement. The lines of divide are clearly drawn, and religious engagement is limited.

The case study as a form of mediatized religion allows researchers and the public a window into a vibrant grassroots community interested in matters of religion, beyond the headlines of mainstream politics and media messages. Ahmad et.al state that in Malaysia, "all citizens should have the right to engage on religious issues", and that "society must debate openly and rationally to be able to decide what is in the best interest of the people" (N. Ahmad, Masum and Ayus 2016, 750). *Project Engage* has certainly provided such a space for engagement, but only time will tell if the online religious community in Malaysia will develop into a space where rational discussions can take place. One possible way to further this research and discussion is to explore further the mediatization of religion and behavior in parallel in the constantly evolving *media lifeworld* of Malaysian online religion.

Notes

1 The author would like to express gratitude to the Global Asia in the 21st-century research platform at Monash University Malaysia for the support given in this research. Thanks also to Tham Yee Quan and Koh Chien Aun for their research assistance, as well as colleagues Dr Sandra Ng Siow San and Adrian Yao for their valuable editorial feedback.
2 This is a pseudonym. Although the Facebook group is a public group with many members, a pseudonym is used for both the group and the commenters featured in this article as the subject matter may be deemed sensitive in the Malaysian context.
3 See www.malaysia.travel/en/au/about-malaysia for the official description by the Tourism Ministry of Malaysia.
4 In 1957, the nation was called Malaya. When Sabah, Sarawak, and Singapore joined the federation in 1963, it became known as Malaysia. Singapore became an independent state in 1965.
5 Loosely translated as *The Mighty Natives Organization.*
6 Its English name is *Malaysian Muslim Solidarity.*
7 In Malaysia, the *Syariah* court serves as a special court that handles cases pertaining to Islam. The civil court remains the highest court of the land.
8 In Malaysia, *hudud* is generally defined as Islamic punishments based on literal adoption of Quranic instruction.
9 See FTM Reporters, 2017.Christian group says Hadi's Bill will have grave consequences. Available at www.freemalaysiatoday.com/category/nation/2017/03/03/christian-group-says-hadis-bill-will-have-grave-consequences/ and Anonymous 2016.Sarawak and Sabah BN opposition to Hudud commendable. Available at www.theborneopost.com/2016/09/29/sarawak-and-sabah-bn-opposition-to-hudud-bill-commendable/.
10 The Malay language is widely used only in Malaysia, Singapore, Indonesia, and Brunei. The variations of the Malay language is distinct enough to be

identified by the author, apart from Malaysia/Singapore. However, there is little indication that Singaporeans actively engaged in the discussion.

11 As almost all of the status updates, and most of the comments, in *Project Engage* are written in Malay, all quotes used in this article are translations.

12 As mentioned earlier, Project Engage is a pseudonym. As such, all commenters are given pseudonyms as well, and quotes attributed to them are not directly linked to the Facebook page to minimize potential tracking.

References

1Malaysia, n.d. *The Story of 1Malaysia*. Available at www.1malaysia.com.my/en/the-story-of-1malaysia, accessed 15 May 2018.

About Malaysia, n.d. Available at www.malaysia.travel/en/au/about-malaysia, accessed 15 May 2018.

Ahmad, N., Masum, A. and Ayus, A. M., 2016. Freedom of Religion and Apostasy: The Malaysian Experience. *Human Rights Quarterly*, 38(3), 736–753. doi:10.1353/hrq.2016.0038.

Ahmad, R., Anis, M. N., Carvalho, M., Hamdan, N., Rahim, R., Sivanandam, H., Shagar, L. K., Yi, T. X., Ghazali, R., Yunus, A., Murad, D., Bedi, R. S. and Zainal, F., 2016. Federal Govt to Take over Hadi's Bill. *The Star Online*, Nation, 2 December. Available at www.thestar.com.my/news/nation/2016/12/02/federal-govt-to-take-over-hadis-bill-for-other-party-leaders-reactions-najib-nonmuslims-need-not-fea/, accessed 31 March 2017.

Anonymous, 2014. Isma: Chinese Migration into Tanah Melayu 'a Mistake' Which Must Be Rectified. *The Malay Mail online*, 6 May. Available at www.themalaymailonline.com/malaysia/article/isma-chinese-migration-into-tanah-melayu-a-mistake-which-must-be-rectified, accessed 31 March 2017.

Anonymous, 2016. Sarawak and Sabah BN opposition to *Hudud* commendable. *Borneo Post*, September 29. Available at www.theborneopost.com/2016/09/29/sarawak-and-sabah-bn-opposition-to-hudud-bill-commendable, accessed 15 May 2018.

Ariff, S. U., 2017. The Malaysian Example: 'A Beautiful Image of Islam'. *NST Online*, 13 July. Available at www.nst.com.my/node/256945, accessed 1 August 2017.

Baum, M. A., 2012. Preaching to the Choir or Converting the Flock: Presidential Communication Strategies in the Age of Three Medias. In: Fox, R. L. and Ramos, J. M., eds. *iPolitics: Citizens, Elections, and Governing in the New Media Era* (1st ed.). New York: Cambridge University Press, 183–205.

Brown, S., 2014. Malaysian Court to Christians: You Can't Say 'Allah'. *CNN*, 24 June. Available at www.cnn.com/2014/06/24/world/asia/malaysia-allah-ban/index.html, accessed 31 March 2017.

Cheng, N., 2015. Group Stages Protest over Cross on Church Building. *The Star Online*, Nation, 19 April. Available at www.thestar.com.my/news/nation/2015/04/19/protest-agaist-church/, accessed 30 March 2017.

Chooi, C., 2011. As Police Probe, Ibrahim Ali Threatens Crusade against Christians. *Malaysia Today*, 15 May. Available at www.malaysia-today.net/as-police-probe-ibrahim-ali-threatens-crusade-against-christians/, accessed 7 April 2011.

Clark, L. S., 2011. Considering Religion and Mediatisation through a Case Study of J+K's Big Day (The J K Wedding Entrance Dance): A Response to Stig Hjarvard. *Culture and Religion*, 12(2), 167–184. doi:10.1080/14755610. 2011.579717.

Couldry, N. and Hepp, A., 2013. Conceptualizing Mediatization: Contexts, Traditions, Arguments. *Communication Theory*, 23(3), 191–202. doi:10.1111/ comt.12019.

Fisher, D., 2009. Seizure of 15,000 Bibles in Malaysia Stuns Christians. *Christian Headlines.com*, 10 November. Available at www.christianheadlines.com/ news/seizure-of-15-000-bibles-in-malaysia-stuns-christians-11616546.html, accessed 10 November 2017.

FMT Reporters, 2017. Christian group says Hadi's Bill will have grave consequences. *Free Malaysia Today*, 3 March. Available at www.freemalaysiatoday. com/category/nation/2017/03/03/christian-group-says-hadis-bill-will-have-grave-consequences/, accessed 30 March 2018.

Ghazali, R., 2017. Tech-Savvy Malaysians Still Lack Knowledge of Religions, Say Academicians. *The Star Online*, Nation. 29 March. Available at www. thestar.com.my/news/nation/2017/03/29/academicians-malaysians-tech-savvy-but-lack-knowledge-of-religions/, accessed 30 March 2017.

Hjarvard, S., 2011. The Mediatisation of Religion: Theorising Religion, Media and Social Change. *Culture and Religion*, 12(2), 119–135. doi:10.1080/1475 5610.2011.579719.

Howard, R. G., 2009. Enacting a Virtual 'Ekklesia': Online Christian Fundamentalism as Vernacular Religion. *New Media & Society*, November, 729–744. doi:10.1177/1461444809342765.

Jin, D. Y., 2015. The Mediatization of Buddhism in Digital Media: The Contemporary Reflection of Uisang's Hwaom Thought. *Journal of Media and Religion*, 14(4), 196–210. doi:10.1080/15348423.2015.1116265.

Koswanage, N., 2014. Malaysia's Islamic Authorities Seize Bibles as Allah Row Deepens. *Reuters*, 2 January. Available at www.reuters.com/article/us-malaysia-religion-idUSBREA010C120140102, accessed 31 March 2017.

Krotz, F. and Hepp, A., 2011. A Concretization of Mediatization: How 'Mediatization Works' and Why Mediatized Worlds Are a Helpful Concept for Empirical Mediatization Research. *Empedocles: European Journal for the Philosophy of Communication*, 3(2), 137–152.

Kua, K. S., 2015. *Racism & Racial Discrimination in Malaysia*. Petaling Jaya: SUARA INISIATIF SDN BHD.

Larsen, E., 2003. Deeper Understanding, Deeper Ties: Taking Faith Online. In: Howard, S. and Jones, S., eds. *Society Online: The Internet in Context* (1st ed.). Thousand Oaks: SAGE, 43–56.

Latour, B., 2007. *Reassembling the Social: An Introduction to Actor-Network-Theory* (New ed.). Oxford: Oxford University Press.

Lee, J. C. H., 2010. *Islamization and Activism in Malaysia*. Singapore: Institute of Southeast Asian Studies.

Lee, L. H., 2015. PJ Church Forgives, Awaits 'God's Order'. *Malaysiakini*, 26 April. Available at www.malaysiakini.com/news/296436, accessed 31 March 2017.

Lövheim, M., 2011. Mediatisation of Religion: A Critical Appraisal. *Culture and Religion*, 12(2), 153–166. doi:10.1080/14755610.2011.579738.

Lundby, K., 2009. *Mediatization: Concept, Changes, Consequences.* First printing ed. New York: Peter Lang.

MacWilliams, M. W., 2002. Virtual Pilgrimages on the Internet. *Religion,* 32(4), 315–335. doi:10.1006/reli.2002.0408.

Neo, J. L., 2014. What's in a Name? Malaysia's 'Allah' Controversy and the Judicial Intertwining of Islam with Ethnic Identity. *International Journal of Constitutional Law,* 12(3), 751–768. doi:10.1093/icon/mou050.

Nussbaum, E., 2012. Hate-Watching 'Smash.' *The New Yorker,* 27 April. Available at www.newyorker.com/culture/culture-desk/hate-watching-smash, accessed 30 March 2017.

Osman, B., 2011. The Evolving Face of Religious Tolerance in Post-Colonial Malaysia: Understanding Its Shaping Factors. *Islam and Civilisational Renewal,* 2(4), 621–638.

Pons-de Wit, A., Versteeg, P. and Roeland, J., 2015. Contextual Responses to Interreligious Encounters Online. *Social Compass,* 62(1), 89–104. doi: 10.1177/0037768614560977.

Radde-Antweiler, K., 2017. Digital Religion? Media Studies from a Religious Studies Perspective. In: Nord, I. and Zipernovszky, H., eds. *Religious Education in a Mediatized World.* Stuttgart: Kohlhammer, 138–146.

Randhawa, S. and Venkiteswaran, G., 2010. Civil Society Use of the SOS Selangor: A Case Study of the SOS Selangor Campaign. In: Guan, Y. S., ed. *Media, Culture and Society in Malaysia.* Oxon: Routledge, 85–95.

Razak, A., 2017. Govt Will Not Table RUU355 Bill. *The Star Online,* Nation, 27 March. Available at www.thestar.com.my/news/nation/2017/03/29/govt-will-not-table-bill-to-amend-syariah-courts-powers/, 31 March 2017.

Tan, M. Y., 2014. Malaysian Christians Online: Online/Offline Networks of Everyday Religion. In: Maj, A., ed. *Post-Privacy Culture: Gaining Social Power in Cyber-Democracy.* Oxford: Inter-Disciplinary Press, 177–201.

Webster, G., 2010. Malaysia: Asia's Cultural Melting Pot. *CNN,* 26 October. Available at www.cnn.com/2010/WORLD/asiapcf/10/22/malaysia.country.profile/index.html, accessed 15 May 2018.

Zolkepli, F., Meikeng, Y. and Cheng, N., 2017. IGP's Brother Gets Statement Recorded over Cross Protest. *The Star Online,* Nation, 23 April. Available at www.thestar.com.my/news/nation/2015/04/23/igps-brother-gets-statement-recorded-over-cross-protest/, accessed 31 March 2017.

6 On-Offline *Dakwah*

Social Media and Islamic Preaching in Malaysia and Indonesia[1]

Hew Wai Weng

Introduction

Tapping into the growth of popular Islamic preaching, an increasing number of Chinese converts-turned-preachers have emerged, such as Lim Jooi Soon and Firdaus Wong Wai Hung in Malaysia, as well as Tan Mei Hwa, Koko Liem, Syafii Antonio and Felix Siauw in Indonesia. They are popular religious figures, not only among Chinese converts, but also non-Chinese Muslims. They appear regularly in religious programs on television, are active on social media and give public talks. Chinese preachers appear to have a special marketing pull, because of their ethnicity and their status as converts. Their Chinese appearances stand out as exotic trademarks in the crowded preaching market. At the same time, many Muslims think that having experienced the spiritual journey towards piety, these *converts-turned-preachers* can provide a persuasive role model for non-practicing Muslims. Many Chinese Muslim preachers are aware of their distinctive qualities and thus, they strategically use their differences to augment their popularity (Hew 2012, 2018a). This chapter focuses on two of these popular Chinese Muslim preachers – Felix Siauw and Firdaus Wong – who are active in both online and off-line *dakwah* (Islamic preaching),[2] to examine how social media, together with other social processes, are shaping and being shaped by contemporary Islamic discourses and practices in Malaysia and Indonesia.

On 5 November 2016, thousands of young female Muslims attended the *Festival Sahabat Taat* (Festival of Devout Friendship) in an Islamic Center in North Jakarta, featuring the popular yet conservative social media preacher Felix Siauw and his *dakwah* team. They have used various social media platforms to promote the event. The festival provided opportunities for Felix's social media followers to socialize and build off-line friendships and face-to-face interactions. At the event, participants had opportunities to take photos in front of Islamic-inflected photo booths provided by his *dakwah* team. They were then able to upload these photos to social media accounts such as Instagram. The entire event was also creatively designed so that it could be recorded and shared on YouTube and Facebook Live, thus displaying how Felix Siauw skillfully maneuvres both online and off-line spaces in maximizing his *dakwah* efforts (Hew 2018b, 69).

In the early afternoon of a hot Sunday in 2014, in the heart of Kuala Lumpur's shopping district, a group of Muslim volunteers preached Islamic messages to non-Muslim pedestrians on busy streets. This street *dakwah* was led by an evangelical-minded Chinese Muslim preacher, Firdaus Wong. Firdaus Wong and his preaching team recruited volunteers through Facebook event pages and then broadcast the event on YouTube. They spread Islam through a variety of media – banners, Islamic-themed T-shirts, religious-themed books and the Quran (in Malay, English and Chinese). From cyberspace to urban places, from new media to existing media, Firdaus believes his multilingual and multi-mediated *dakwah* activities help him disseminate Islam to a broader audience (Hew 2015, 199).

Felix Siauw from Indonesia and Firdaus Wong from Malaysia share several similarities – "both are Chinese converts, in their mid-30s, hold conservative religious values, are media savvy, have marketing experience and are eager to spread 'true Islam' as they understand it" (Hew 2018b, 66). They have different foci in their preaching – whereas Firdaus is enthusiastic in communicating Islamic messages to non-Muslims, Felix spends most of his time trying to convince nonpracticing Muslims to become a pious one. Firdaus often compares Islam with other religions, while Felix tends to view Islam not only as a religious belief, but also as a political system, in which he juxtaposes Islam with ideologies such as secularism, communism and capitalism. Despite these differences of targeted audiences and preaching contents, their *dakwah* strategies show that digital and nondigital sites are not only complementing each other, but they are also mutually constitutive. Because of rapid urbanization and the increasing popularity of social media in many Muslim-majority societies, such creative combination of cyber activities and urban events exemplifies a new trend of Islamic preaching in contemporary Indonesia and Malaysia, as I will illustrate in this chapter. Many studies have examined how various digital media inform Islamic discourses, religious practices and *dakwah* activities (Barendregt 2009, Bunt 2009, Campbell 2013, Hosen 2008, Nef Saluz 2011), yet these have only been considered to a much lesser extent the interplay between online and off-line religious activities, as well as the varying forms of mediation across different online realms. This chapter aims to fill in this gap.

Mediatization, Social Media and Islamic Preaching

Using the term mediatization, there are various theoretical propositions in studying the connections between religion and media. Hjarvard (2008) proposes a strong claim that the logic of media plays a determining role in reshaping social domains such as religion, as he says, "religion is increasingly subsumed under the logic of media" (Hjarvard 2008, 11). He goes further to argue that increasing mediatization of society contributes to secularization (Hjarvard 2013). In contrast, Krotz (2009) suggests that media transformations are connected to broader structural changes, social processes and interpersonal interaction in multidirectional ways, a theme that can be extended to communication in religious settings. In other words, he suggests a shift of research on mediatization of social and religious processes from being media-centered to being actor-centered. Such a position shares similarity with the paradigm of mediation of religion. Meyer and Moors (2005) indicated that religious processes are always mediated, and thus, it is important to "explore how the transition from one mode of mediation to another, implying the adoption of new mass media technologies, re-configures a particular practice of religious mediation" (Meyer and Moors 2005, 7).

Informed by such conceptual debates on mediatization and mediation, while acknowledging the role of new and social media in shaping Islamic practices and discourses, this chapter is not intended to view digital media as the sole driving force behind the current trend of Islamic preaching. Instead, it explores how social media, together with other social processes, such as the expanding of Muslim middle classes, rapid urbanization, contestation of political Islam and diversification of Muslim authorities, shape and are shaped by Islamic discourses and practices. It acknowledges the entanglements between online and off-line forms of Islamic sociality (Slama 2017b), the interconnection between cyberspace and urban space (Hew 2015) and the agency of religious actors to take part in the shaping of media (Lövheim 2011). In other words, the aim of this chapter is "not to explore how religion is transformed through the media, but how religions transform in the modern world in interaction with the media" (Lövheim 2011, 164). As a result of various entanglements between Islamic practices, media forms and social processes, different types and styles of Islamic preaching, authority and sociality have emerged, allowing various religious discourses ranging from progressive to conservative, from moderate to radical, to compete in various online and off-line spaces (Hew 2018b).

In Indonesia and in Malaysia, many of the Muslim youth are frequent social media users, and spend a lot of their time in following, liking and sharing posts on Facebook, Twitter and Instagram. To engage with these youth, many media-savvy preachers have creatively used such social media platforms to disseminate various Islamic messages, a trend called digital or online *dakwah*. Such popularity of social media and the rise of digital *dakwah* have significant impacts on the practices of Islamic preaching today. Arguably, a certain logic of social media, or the ways how social media work, transform contemporary Islamic preaching. Yet, various social processes, political dynamics, religious interpretations and individual actors have also, in different ways, shaped the usage of social media in Islamic preaching. Here, I highlight three key features on how social media change the dynamics of Islamic preaching and their limitations.

First, social media platforms allow Muslims from diverse backgrounds to freely disseminate their ideas, bypassing editorial interventions and government censorship. Traditional media owners and editors could exclude controversial Muslim preachers who they view as not suitable for public promotion. In contrast to that, various social media platforms provide these preachers with cost-free channels to increase their public visibilities. In other words, radio and television stations might refuse to feature preachers who have radical political stands or religious viewpoints, yet social media platforms might allow these preachers to propagate their ideas. One prominent example is the emergence of Felix Siauw, who is a staunch supporter of hardliner Hizbut Tahrir Indonesia (HTI),[3] a transnational Islamist movement. This does not mean that social media preachers are free from state interventions, online regulations and social pressures. According to the community standards of various social media platforms, social media managements have the rights to delete postings that violate the guidelines, as well as to suspend or to terminate certain accounts.

Second, to establish popularity online, preachers not only have to master Islamic knowledge, but also need to equip him or herself with communication skills and media strategies. Both the appearance and form of the message, as well as the substance and knowledge of the preacher are integral parts of Islamic preaching market. This *dakwah* trend allows young Muslims without formal and strong religious qualifications to get involved in preaching activities. Everyone can be a preacher, if he or she manages certain visual skills, marketing knowledge and communication strategies. As Felix Siauw put it, "Everyone can conduct *dakwah*. It is as easy as you only need to 'give a thumb' (liking on Facebook)". Many scholars have argued that the rise of new and social media has led to the fragmentation of Islamic authority (Eickelman and Anderson 2003, Hoesterey 2016, Hosen 2008) that is often more dialogically constructed today (Slama 2017a). However, as I observe, such fragmentation does not necessarily undermine or bypass (in some cases, even strengthen or popularize) certain existing religious ideologies, organizations and institutions (2018b).

Third, following the logic of social media, especially Instagram and Facebook, images, photos, videos, colors and infographics play important roles in contemporary Islamic preaching. For many preachers, such *beautification* and *visualization* of *dakwah* are crucial for their preaching, not only to increase visibilities and draw attentions, but also to convince their audience and followers to believe in the messages they are delivering (Hew 2018b). However, this does not mean that the preachers are passive recipients, as they also exercise their agency. For example,

Felix Siauw claims that he does not only follow the logic of social media, but also seeks to "Islamize these platforms" (Interview, Felix Siauw, 8 September 2016). Moreover, there is a limitation to digital *dakwah* activities, as they cannot reach people who do not follow them online. Therefore, off-line *dakwah* activities are important to complement online preaching strategies. For example, in addition to online video *dakwah*, Firdaus Wong has run off-line street *dakwah* to spread Islamic messages to non-Muslims. Indeed, both Felix Siauw and Firdaus Wong carry out their *dakwah* in almost every possible online space and off-line place. They are not only active on almost all social media platforms, but also involve themselves in various off-line programs, such as Islamic study groups, mosque activities, street *dakwah* and religious retreats. Often, such off-line events are staged, captured and recorded for online sharing. By illustrating the preaching activities of Felix Siauw, Firdaus Wong and their *dakwah* teams, the following sections further examine these three features that influence contemporary Islamic preaching.

Felix Siauw, Visual Dakwah and Islamic Hangout

"He is not only famous in the real world (*dunia nyata*), but also in cyberspace (*dunia maya*)" – this was how the host of a religious talk introduced Felix Siauw in front of thousands of Muslims in a mosque in Central Jakarta (Field note, 8 September 2016). Indeed, to optimize his *dakwah*, Felix Siauw combines online and off-line activities, as he puts it, "online is important for spreading Islamic messages (*syiar*), offline is crucial for strengthening Islamic faith (*pembinaan*)... hopefully, online discussions will lead to offline activities... these activities will then be reported on social media..." (Interview, Felix Siauw, 9 September 2016).

Felix Yanwar Siauw (Siauw Chen Kwok), best known as Felix Siauw, was born in 1984 in Palembang, South Sumatra. He was a Catholic before converting to Islam in 2002, after learning about Islam through his friends who are HTI activists in the Faculty of Agriculture, Bogor Agriculture Institute (IPB, Institut Pertanian Bogor) in West Java. Since his conversion, he has been active in *dakwah* activities. Felix Siauw worked in an agrochemical industry, Biotis Agrindo after finishing his studies. He was the marketing manager of the company until he quit the position to become a full-time preacher in 2012. Like many other youths, Felix Siauw is interested in activities, such as gaming, comics, traveling and photography. Considering this combination of marketing experience, IT awareness and visual interest, it does not come as a surprise that Felix Siauw becomes a successful market-conscious, digital-savvy and visual-oriented preacher (Hew 2018b).

When I first met him in 2008, Felix Siauw was running a blog. Since 2012, he switched his focus to social media platforms. As of January 2018, he has more than four million followers on Facebook, two million followers on Twitter, one million followers on Instagram and 15,000 subscribers on YouTube, making him one of the leading social media preachers in Indonesia today. Just as the easing of media restrictions after the fall of the New Order regime and the proliferation of television stations are important developments that enabled the rise of celebrity preachers such as Aa Gym (Hoesterey 2016), the increase of internet access and the popularity of social media are crucial for allowing digital-savvy figures such as Felix Siauw to establish themselves. Social media preachers have more freedom in their preaching styles and content, as they are not only free from government censorship, but also free from the interventions and preferences of television producers and news editors. Social media platforms provide spaces for nonviolent yet radical figures such as Felix Siauw to express and propagate their viewpoints. Felix Siauw differs from many popular preachers in that he does not refrain from commenting on contentious political issues – instead, he is committed to the establishment of an Islamic Caliphate, in solidarity with HTI. Seeing democracy, nationalism, capitalism, socialism, feminism and secularism as *secular* inventions, in his talks and social media postings, he often subtly points out the *weaknesses* of such ideologies and suggests that Islam is the best solution to various problems faced by Indonesia today. By labelling non-Muslims as *kafir* (infidel), he disapproves of them leading Muslim societies.

The rise of social media preachers has been criticized by learned Muslim scholars for undermining traditional Islamic authorities, challenging proper ways of Islamic learning and promoting superficial Islamic interpretations. In some ways, to be a popular social media preacher, quite often, marketing skills and multimedia technologies are more important than proper Islamic qualification. Felix made a Facebook post on 22 May 2017 proposing that Muslims should view *dakwah* as an art of transmitting the truth, and that it should be made *keren* (cool). It is not just the content of Felix's messages that contribute to his popularity, but also the mode of display and delivery. Felix's team contributes to this; although many are lacking in formal theological education, they make up for it with their communication, visual and IT skills. Felix Siauw stands out for his attention-grabbing combination of *bahasa gaul* (casual language) and colorful imagery – whilst crowd-pleasing, this has been criticized by some Muslim scholars for being "superficial, ahistorical, uncritical and ill-informed" (Hew 2018b, 71). He also operates various businesses to promote and sustain his *dakwah* activities. With his wife, he runs Hijab Alila, an Islamic fashion brand and has his own publishing house, AlFatih Press (Hew 2018b).

Central to social media marketing is making the posted messages *go viral*. As a former marketing director, Felix Siauw masters such logic: "It is good if someone likes my postings and follow my page. It is even better if many people are sharing my postings..." (Interview, Felix Siauw, 9 September 2016). He does not only have accounts on various social media platforms but is also part of a network of persons and groups who share similar content on those platforms. On his Facebook account, he posts messages almost daily, often together with images, and sometimes video clips. He writes on diverse topics, ranging from giving tips on how to practice Islam in daily life, sharing stories of his traveling, commenting on current affairs and religious debates in Indonesia, promoting religious talks and Islamic study events to endorsing commercial products of his HTI friends (Hew 2018b).

Felix has been active on Twitter and Instagram since 2010 and 2013, respectively. He has commented upon the demographics of his Twitter and Instagram followers, saying that he notices more male followers in the former and more female followers in the latter. He noted that

> Twitter is text-based, while Instagram is a visual medium. Men tend to engage more with texts, and women like images...Hence, the discussions on Twitter is often rougher (*kasar*) and the interaction on Instagram is softer (*lembut*). ... Now I prefer to use Instagram. It is a good medium to engage with young female followers... Women are more communicative and play an important role in *dakwah*.
> (Interview, Felix Siauw, 9 September 2016)

Furthermore, his hobbies, photography, comics and animations, have also driven him to conduct 'visual dakwah' – preaching Islam using visual approaches (Hew 2018b).

Yet, in his perspective, the visual images on social media platforms have to be in accordance with Islamic guidelines. In this sense, improper ways of using visual images or exhibiting body beauty to attract attention are deemed as *"pelacuran visual"* (visual prostitution) (Siauw and Noor Achni 2015, 21). Therefore, his visual *dakwah* is not only about using visual methods to promote Islamic agenda, but also about infusing his religious thoughts into visual practices (Hew 2018b). Since Felix Siauw was a marketing manager in a company before he became a full-time preacher, it seems that his *dakwah* strategy is influenced by contemporary trends and techniques in marketing, such as visual marketing, placement promotion and embedded marketing – emphasizing visual communication as well as subtly generating a positive feeling toward a certain brand. In other words, for Felix Siauw, Islam, or more specifically HTI ideology, is a product to be sold creatively and in a subtle way to the Muslim youth (Hew 2018b).

Additionally, Felix encourages his online followers to attend his offline events as well, finding encouragement that "If my online followers attend my talks, it means they are interested in what I am preaching. It is a sign showing that my social media preaching is effective"

(Interview, Felix Siauw, 9 September 2016). Indeed, visual images on Instagram, brief messages on Twitter and short videos on Facebook are effective ways to capture attention, yet they do not provide sufficient space for more in-depth engagement. To complement the short social media communication, Felix's *dakwah* team's YukNgaji (literally meaning *Let's study*) organizes various online religious classes, as well as off-line Islamic talks and hangout. In an Instagram post of YukNgaji, to attract the participation of Muslim youth, it proposes various fun ways of learning Islam in various locations, from cafés to parks, from beaches to futsal courts. Although being promoted as fun and interactive, such hangout events are regulated by their understanding of strict Islamic guidelines, such as separation of genders and wearing of Islamic attires. The ultimate goal of these preaching activities is to convince people to participate in HTI religious study groups (*halaqah*) which require personal long-term commitment (Hew 2018b).

While social media platforms provide Felix Siauw and his team members freedom to preach, this does not mean that they are totally free from various online and off-line regulations, as well as state interventions and social pressures. Felix has been under fire for his radical political and religious propaganda – his talk in Malang on 30 April 2017 was dissolved by local police, which resulted in his followers taking to Twitter to launch the #*Savefelixsiauw* campaign. After the government ban of HTI in July 2017, more than ten of his scheduled talks have been banned or disrupted. However, this does not reduce his popularity. There has been an increase in the number of his Facebook followers – as I observed, his Facebook followers were nearly four million in March 2017 and the number had increased to 4,277,817 in June 2018.

Besides off-line pressures, Felix Siauw has also faced challenges online. In December 2017, his Facebook account had been suspended for a few days after having two postings criticizing LGBT (Lesbian, Gay, Bisexual and Transgender) groups – *Anti LGBT itu Alami* [Anti LGBT is natural] (Facebook, UstadzFelixSiauw, 20 December 2017) and *LGBT itu Penyimpangan Fitrah* [LGBT is against human nature] (Facebook, UstadzFelixSiauw, 21 December 2017). As many netizens as well as opponents of Felix Siauw had reported these postings to the Facebook management for promoting hate speech and violating the Facebook community guidelines, these two posts were deleted. Yet, he reposted them and after this, his Facebook account had been suspended for a number of days. These two postings did not totally disappear on Facebook, as some of his followers had reposted them. Felix Siauw made a comeback on 26 December 2017 and since then, he has been more careful in his postings. Indeed, he has been very strategic in finding a balance between promoting radical messages and obeying Facebook community standards. This case shows that while the guidelines of various social media platforms are crucial in regulating religious discussions, various actors – such as Felix Siauw, his followers and his opponents – also exercise their agencies to reshape the debates.

Firdaus Wong, Video Dakwah and Street Dakwah

The second case study in this chapter deals with Firdaus Wong Wai Hung, a Chinese Muslim preacher in Malaysia. I first met him at a Chinese New Year open house in 2013, which was held in a Chinese halal restaurant in Kuala Lumpur. Dressed in traditional Chinese clothing, he was one of the guest speakers. He spoke in Malay, English and Cantonese. In the conversation, Firdaus explained to me why he supported *dakwah* activities in restaurants:

> In the past, Muslims only conducted *dakwah* in seminars and on TV. Muslims only preach to Malay Muslims. This is a mistake. We should share the beauty of Islam with ethnic Chinese, who are mostly non-Muslim. Non-Muslims also have the right to learn about Islam. As Muslims, we should be more proactive, yet in a friendly manner. We should share Islam with non-Muslims, in the restaurants, in the mosques, on the streets, on Facebook....
>
> (Field note, 23 February 2013)

I met Firdaus Wong again in 2014 for an interview in his new office building – MRM (Multiracial Reverted Muslim)'s Islamic Guidance and Dakwah Centre, a three-storey shop-house building in Kuala Lumpur, testimony to his successful career as a respectable Muslim preacher. Having grown up in a Buddhist family, Firdaus Wong, born in 1973, became a Muslim in 2005 after searching for God and the meaning of life. He was once a footballer, and subsequently worked in marketing and advertising before becoming a preacher. He dedicated himself to studying Islam and spreading its message in 2011 after attending a talk by Hussein Yee, a renowned salafist-oriented Chinese Muslim preacher. He has been a full-time preacher since 2013. He believes every Muslim has the responsibility to conduct *dakwah*, either by inviting a non-Muslim to become a Muslim or encouraging a nonpracticing Muslim to become a better Muslim. He strives to increase the effectiveness of *dakwah* efforts by exploring new methods. He also claims to be a protégé of Zakir Naik, an internationally renowned yet controversial Indian preacher. He has joined Zakir Naik's *dakwah* training program overseas. Inspired by Zakir Naik, the usage of social media, video materials, English terminologies, rhetorical languages and *comparative religion* are important elements of Firdaus Wong's preaching.

MRM, founded and chaired by Firdaus Wong, is his main *dakwah* platform. MRM began as a Facebook page in 2011, under the name

Malaysia Chinese Muslim, then *Malaysia Reverted Muslim* and subsequently it was renamed *Multiracial Reverted Muslim* in 2014 to place even greater emphasis on its inclusiveness. Initially, MRM was merely a virtual space where converts could interact and support each other. In early 2018, not only has its Facebook page been liked by more than 68,000 netizens, but MRM now occupies a three-storey building that organizes a range of religious activities. With the tagline *Empowering People, Changing Lives*, MRM identifies itself as a nongovernmental organization that conducts *dakwah* aimed at non-Muslims, supports new converts and helps the needy. MRM also has its own multimedia and IT team that maintains its website, monitors its Facebook page, creates *dakwah* videos and produces various *dakwah* materials. From virtual space to physical place, from YouTube to the street, Firdaus Wong's preaching activities are multi-mediated and multi-sited.

Since August 2013, Firdaus Wong has posted, on YouTube and several Facebook groups, a series of videos in which he preaches Islam in Cantonese (a Chinese dialect which is widely spoken in Kuala Lumpur and the surrounding areas), with titles, such as *What is Islam?*, *Does God Exist?* and *In Search of God.*[4] In these videos, Firdaus Wong is sometimes dressed in traditional Chinese costumes and uses examples from everyday life to explain the existence of God and the teaching of Islam. He always uses a *Q&A* method and rhetorical messages in his presentations. Videos are also the means through which Firdaus Wong manifests his Chineseness and emphasizes that one can maintain one's Chinese cultural identity after becoming a Muslim. Inspired by the successful yet controversial Peace TV channel run by Zakir Naik, Firdaus Wong is currently establishing his own online TV channel, Ask TV, to further promote his multi-mediated *dakwah*, especially among non-Muslims and new converts.

His video *dakwah* is different from traditionally established forms of *dakwah* in at least three ways. First, he is a lay preacher with no formal Islamic education, thus differing from other well-trained *ulama* (Islamic scholars) and *ustadz* (religious teachers). Instead of challenging existing religious authorities and figures, he often makes references to popular preachers and established scholars, such as Hussein Yee, Zakir Naik, Mohammad Asri Zainal Abidin (Dr MAZA, a well-known Islamic scholar in Malaysia) and Yusuf al-Qaradawi (a famous Islamic scholar based in Qatar). Second, he uses social media creatively to facilitate his *dakwah* activities. Instead of giving religious lectures in mosques, he prefers to preach Islam through interactive methods and carries out *dakwah* on social media and on the streets. Third, unlike most of the *dakwah* activities in Malaysia which are conducted in the Malay language (and sometimes in English), he also speaks in Cantonese and other Chinese dialects. In order to promote Islam as a universal religion, his *dakwah* materials are also multilingual.

As in January 2018, his official Facebook page had attracted more than 110,000 followers. He posts messages on his Facebook page almost every day, commenting on various issues related to Islam, mostly inspired by his daily life experiences and social activities, current affairs and Islamic debates in Malaysia, and recent developments involving Chinese Muslims in Malaysia. One example of his postings is "Facebook is a platform to remind our friends to follow Allah's advice and let us use Facebook as Faithbook" (Facebook, FirdausWongMRM, 30 October 2013). While Firdaus is creatively constructing new *dakwah* spaces, he is also happy to appear in mainstream newspapers and other conventional media. For example, he has been interviewed by *Utusan Melayu* (a government-controlled Malay-language daily), *Malaysiakini TV* (an independent multi-lingual online news portal) and *TV Al-Hijrah* (an Islamic-themed TV channel).

However, there is a limitation to such online *dakwah* activities, as most of the visitors, friends and followers of *dakwah*-oriented blogs and Facebook pages are Malay Muslims, Chinese converts and those who have an interest in Islam. Ordinary non-Muslim Malaysians (the target of such preaching activities) have less opportunity to encounter such information. Acknowledging the limits of digital *dakwah*, Firdaus also pursues a more proactive approach by taking his preaching mission onto the streets, to reach out to broader audiences (Hew 2015).

Street dakwah is a new trend in Malaysia. Since 2010, a series of street *dakwah* has been conducted by various *dakwah* organizations, mainly in various city centers where Chinese non-Muslims live, work and shop. On 29 and 30 March 2014, I attended a street *dakwah* session in Kuala Lumpur organized by MRM and sponsored by the state-controlled Islamic Council of Selangor (MAIS, Majlis Agama Islam Selangor). On 29 March, Firdaus Wong held a full-day training workshop at the MRM building. About 50 volunteers attended, most of them young Malay Muslims and a few Chinese converts. The training modules included topics such as *What is a street dakwah? How to be a dai (preacher), dakwah ethics, Target audiences and coping strategies*, and *Frequently-asked questions and answering techniques*. Assisted by a PowerPoint presentation, Firdaus interspersed his talk with many jokes, stories and practical tips. Instead of focusing on religious knowledge, his training focused on communication skills and practical techniques for disseminating Islamic messages to non-Muslims. He openly acknowledged that his experience in the marketing business is important to his *dakwah* activities. He told the volunteers, "Let's have fun and gain *pahala* (a reward from Allah for good deeds)" and "We have the best product in this world (Islam) and we have to train ourselves to be good salespersons to promote Islam" (field note, 29 March 2014).

In the late morning of 30 March 2014, Firdaus Wong and his preaching team took their religion onto the busy streets of Kuala Lumpur with great enthusiasm. The volunteers were split into two groups. One preached in Bukit Bintang and the other in Petaling Street, also known as China Town in Kuala Lumpur. I attended the event in Bukit Bintang led by Firdaus. This street *dakwah* was broadcast live by *Sunnah TV* (a *dakwah*-oriented online TV channel). It started at eleven in the morning and ended at about three in the afternoon with a prayer. In Bukit Bintang, in front of a monorail station and next to several large shopping malls, Firdaus and his volunteers set up a booth adorned with two banners referring to Islam (in Chinese and English). The Quran and booklets about Islam (also in Chinese and English) were available for free. All female Muslim volunteers wore headscarves and a couple of them also wore face veils, a practice not common among Malaysian Muslim women. Most male volunteers wore black T-shirts bearing the slogan *Islam: Way of Life for Mankind* on the front and *Muslim: One God, Many Prophets* on the back. Like the banners and booklets, these Islamic-themed T-shirts are part of MRM's *dakwah* medium (Hew 2015).

The volunteers handed out a leaflet entitled *Allah, Your God and My God* to non-Muslim pedestrians to initiate dialogue. Interestingly, foreign tourists (mostly whites) were more responsive than local Chinese residents. This comes as no surprise: Tourists are keen to have an *exotic* experience in a foreign land, while local non-Muslims are afraid to engage in a conversation about sensitive Islamic matters. Firdaus Wong was arguably the most passionate and successful preacher on this occasion. After an hour-long conversation he managed to convince an Australian tourist in his early 1940s to recite *shahada* (an Islamic creed declaring belief in the oneness of God and the acceptance of Muhammad as God's Prophet). Following his verbal testimony of Islamic conversion, the volunteers chanted *Allahu akbar* (Allah is Great), with tears of joy running down some of their cheeks. Unsurprisingly, his multi-media crews recorded the conversion and uploaded it on YouTube for sharing. While this conversion may be suspicious (the *converted* tourist may not practice Islam in his home country), it motivated Firdaus and his *dakwah* team to continue their street *dakwah*. On 16 December 2017, MRM organized a *Mega street dakwah* not only in six cities in Malaysia, but also in cities in neighboring Thailand and Indonesia. From YouTube to street, the combination of online and off-line strategies is crucial to Firdaus Wong's dakwah.

Conclusion

Social media platforms, such as Twitter, Facebook and Instagram, play an increasingly significant role in shaping Islamic preaching activities, especially among the Muslim youth. Yet, instead of being passive users, many young Muslim preachers creatively *islamize* online spaces according to their understanding of Islamic teachings. Furthermore, online and off-line activities are not only complementing each other, but are also mutually constitutive in contemporary Islamic preaching (Hew 2015, 2018b). In the case of Firdaus Wong, the limitations of digital *dakwah* lead him to bring his preaching activities onto the streets. Yet, such street *dakwah* events are highly-mediated and tailored to online audiences, as well, in the hope to persuade more Muslims to join street *dakwah*, pointing to a circular intersection between online and off-line realms.

A short video posting entitled *Dakwah Dengan Cinta* (*Dakwah* with Love) on the Facebook page of *FAST Training Center* clearly exemplifies the intersections between Facebook postings and Hangout events, between social media logic and Islamic sociality (Facebook, FAST Training Center, 9 November 2016). The video features scenes of twelve young female Muslims in strict Islamic dresses, hanging out on the beach and ended with a caption *Yuk, Hijrah bareng* (*Let's withdraw from the sinful world together*). This hangout event was coordinated by Felix Siauw's *dakwah* team, YukNgaji. This video vividly reflects Felix Siauw's preaching style – a combination of beautiful images and simple languages, a blend of online postings and off-line activities, yet encompassed with conservative religious values and social codes. On the one hand, Felix Siauw and his teams follow the logic of social media marketing such as using many images to attract audiences; on the other hand, they subtly infiltrate ultra-conservative religious worldviews among the young Muslim social media users.

From Instagram visual *dakwah* to off-line hangout events, from Facebook postings to talk show persuasions, from YouTube video *dakwah* to street evangelical-type activities, this article has sought to describe and analyze the intersecting roles of social media and urban places in contemporary Islamic preaching. The preaching of Felix Siauw and Firdaus Wong is distinguished by a creative combination of online and off-line strategies intended to reach out to more audiences. They use social media (Facebook, Instagram and YouTube), other media formats (talk shows, books and, of course, religious texts) and urban places (mosques, shopping malls, restaurants and streets) to spread Islamic messages. Therefore, in order to understand how the growing popularity of social media shape and are shaped by contemporary Muslim discourses and practices, we must take into account the interdependencies between off-line and online domains.

Visual aesthetics, communication skills and marketing strategies are key elements in their multi-mediated and multi-sited preaching activities. The success of Firdaus's street *dakwah* depends not only on how he conducts them but also on how he promotes them. Similarly, Siauw and Noor Achni (2017) suggest that "*dakwah* is not only about what should be communicated, but also about how to communicate and who is communicating" (Hew 2018b, 71). Such *dakwah* trends empower young Muslims without formal religious education to get involved in *dakwah* activities, as long as they manage certain visual skills and communication strategies. Yet, such visual and market-friendly Islamic expressions might carry dogmatic and conservative viewpoints. While such *dakwah* activities help to establish new forms of Islamic preaching and may endow it with new contents and attract new audiences, they do not necessarily challenge (sometimes, popularize) conservative interpretations of religious texts. Social media platforms allow Muslims from diverse backgrounds to freely disseminate their ideas, bypassing traditional editorial interventions and government censorship. However, their postings are still regulated by the community guidelines of various social media allowing netizens to dispute and to report their preaching contents. Indeed, while the formats of social media play an important role in shaping contemporary Islamic preaching, just as in shaping religious content in general, as Krotz (2009) and Lövheim (2011) have reminded us, media transformations are always connected to broader social processes and various actors can and do contribute to reshape social media practices.

Acknowledgement

The author acknowledges the financial support of this research by Universiti Kebangsaan Malaysia (the National University of Malaysia) through Geran Galakan Penyelidik Muda (Young Researcher Encouragement Grant). The granted project is entitled 'On-offline Dakwah: Piety, Politics and Popularity of Chinese Muslim Preachers in Indonesia and Malaysia' [GGPM-2018-027].

Notes

1 Parts of this chapter have been published in Hew (2015) and Hew (2018b).
2 *Dakwah*, a term commonly used in Indonesia and Malaysia, originates from the Arabic term da'wa, literally meaning *call* or *invitation*. It has a broader meaning than proselytizing. *Dakwah* can be aimed at both Muslims and non-Muslims and may involve consolidating the faith of Muslims as well as inviting non-Muslims to embrace Islam. The *dakwah* of many Chinese Muslim preachers include both preaching Islamic messages to non-Muslim Chinese, strengthening converts' commitment to Islam, as well as providing a persuasive role model for non-practicing Muslims to become pious.
3 Hizbut Tahrir Indonesia (HTI) is the Indonesian branch of Hizbut Tahrir (HT, literally means Party of Liberation) – a transnational, anti-democratic yet non-violent Islamist political organization whose goal is for all Muslim countries to unify as an Islamic state or caliphate ruled by Islamic law. Compared to NU and Muhammadiyah, Indonesia's biggest Islamic organizations with tens of millions of members, HTI is much smaller, but it has been gaining ground in Indonesia since a decade ago. In July 2017, HTI was banned by the Indonesian government. For discussion of HT in Indonesia, see Njoto-Feillard (2015), Ahnaf (2017), Mohamed Osman (2010), and Burhanuddin (2009).

4 To view Firdaus Wong's series of *dakwah* videos on YouTube, see www.youtube. com/channel/UCurR3-mfR4ITrlVwhc26MUQ, accessed 15 January 2018.

References

Ahnaf, M. I., 2017. Haruskah HTI Dibubarkan (Should HTI be banned)? *CRCS Perspektif*, 6 May. Available at http://crcs.ugm.ac.id/news/10864/haruskah-hti-dibubarkan.html, accessed 9 June 2017.

Barendregt, B., 2009. Mobile Religiosity in Indonesia: Mobilized Islam, Islamized Mobility and the Potential of Islamic Techno Nationalism. In: Alampay, E., ed. *Living the Information Society in Asia*. Singapore: ISEAS, 73–92.

Bunt, G. R., 2009. *iMuslims: Rewiring the House of Islam*. London: Hurst & Company.

Burhanuddin, M., 2009. The Quest for Hizbut Tahrir in Indonesia. *Asian Journal of Social Science*, 37(4), 623–645.

Campbell, H., ed., 2013. Digital Religion: Understanding Religious Practice in New Media World. London: Routledge.

Eickelman, D. F. and Anderson, J. W., 2003. Redefining Muslim Publics. In: Eickelman, D. F. and Anderson, J. W., eds. *New Media in the Muslim World: The Emerging Public Sphere*. Bloomington: Indiana University Press, 1–18.

Hew, W. W., 2012. Expressing Chineseness, Marketing Islam: Hybrid Performance of Chinese Muslim Preachers. In: Hoon, C.-Y. and Sai, S.-M., eds. *Chinese Indonesians Reassessed: History, Religion and Belonging*. London and New York: Routledge, 179–199.

Hew, W. W., 2015. Dakwah 2.0: Digital Dakwah, Street Dakwah and Cyber-Urban Activism of Chinese Muslims in Malaysia and Indonesia. In: Schneider, N.-C. and Richter, C., eds. *New Media Configurations and Socio-Cultural Dynamics in Asia and the Arab World – Changing Societies?* Baden: Nomos Publishers, 198–221.

Hew, W. W., 2018a. Chinese Ways of Being Muslim: Negotiating Ethnicity and Religiosity in Indonesia. Copenhagen: NIAS Press.

Hew, W. W., 2018b. The Art of Dakwah: Social Media, Visual Persuasion and Islamist Propagation of Felix Siauw. *Indonesia and Malay World*, 46(134), 61–79.

Hjarvard, S., 2008. The Mediatization or Religion: A Theory of the Media as Agents of Religious Change. *Northern Lights*, 6, 9–26.

Hjarvard, S., 2013. *The Mediatization of Culture and Society*. London and New York: Routledge.

Hoesterey, J. B., 2016. *Rebranding Islam: Piety, Prosperity and a Self-Help Guru*. Palo Alto: Stanford University Press.

Hosen, N., 2008. Online Fatwa in Indonesia: From Fatwa Shopping to Googling a Kiai. In: Fealy, G. and White, S., eds. *Expressing Islam: Religious Life and Politics in Indonesia*. Singapore: ISEAS, 159–173.

Krotz, F., 2009. Mediatization: A Concept with Which to Grasp Media and Societal Change. In: Lundby, K., ed. *Mediatization: Concept, Changes, Consequences*. New York: Peter Lang, 21–40.

Lövheim, M., 2011. Mediatisation of Religion: A Critical Appraisal. *Culture and Religion*, 12(2), 153–166.

Meyer, B. and Moors, A., 2005. *Religion, Media and the Public Sphere.* Bloomington: Indiana University Press.

Mohamed Osman, M. N., 2010. Reviving the Caliphate in the Nusantara: Hizbut Tahrir Indonesia's Mobilization Strategy and Its Impact in Indonesia. *Terrorism and Political Violence*, 22(4), 601–622.

Nef Saluz, C., 2011. Dakwahkampus.com as Informal Student Web Portal of Hizbut Tahrir Indonesia. In: Schneider, N.-C. and Graf, B., eds. *Social Dynamics 2.0: Researching Change in Times of Media Convergence.* Berlin: Frank and Timme, 67–84.

Njoto-Feillard, G., 2015. Hizbut Tahrir Indonesia in 2014: The Political Economy of Discontent. *Trends in Southeast Asia*, 19(15), Singapore: ISEAS.

Siauw, F. and Noor Achni, E., 2015. *Yuk berhijab* [Let's Wear Hijab]. Jakarta: AlFatih Press.

Siauw, F. and Noor Achni, E., 2017. *The Art of Dakwah.* Jakarta: AlFatih Press.

Slama, M., 2017a. Subtle Economy of Time: Social Media and the Transformation of Indonesia's Islamic Preacher Economy. *Economic Anthropology*, 4, 94–106.

Slama, M., 2017b. Social Media and Islamic Practice: Indonesian Ways of being Digitally Pious. In: Jurriens, E. and Tapsell, R., eds. *Digital Indonesia: Connectivity and Divergence.* Singapore: ISEAS, 146–162.

7 Church Digital Applications and the Communicative Meso-Micro Interplay

Building Religious Authority and Community through Everyday Organizing

Pauline Hope Cheong

While mediatization has emerged as an influential theory in recent years, the notion is not without contestations. Various commentators have called for a critical assessment and extensions of the theory, including the need to pay heightened attention to the agency of religious actors to shape the meanings and practices within situated cultural contexts (e.g., Krotz 2009, Lövheim 2011, Lynch 2011). This chapter addresses a research gap in the mediatization of religion by discussing the interactions between religious organizations and individual followers, and focuses on the communicative interplay between meso and micro religious agents to build authority and community through everyday religious organizing.

Drawing upon prior research on the communicative constitution of religious authority and community (Cheong 2017), I explicate the significance of everyday communication practices for religious organizing by investigating the interactions between the work of spiritual institutions and lay followers as the latter are primed to engage via church digital applications, and called to act as strategic religious agents in branded church campaigns. In addition, this chapter contributes empirically to the globalization of religion and media research by examining the case of the internationally renowned New Creation Church (NCC hereafter) in Singapore; a context of intense mediatization and a highly developed telecommunication infrastructure. In doing so, this article expands the understanding of how strategic church communication works to premediate church gatherings and shape social networking to accomplish clergy authority and brand resonance. In turn, this analysis highlights how mediatization as a communication-centered concept can be applied to the domain of religion beyond traditional institutional and individual levels of analysis.

Mediatization and the Communicative Meso-Micro Interplay

Though the study of mediatization considers the long-term transformations associated with new media's role in society, varied approaches have emphasized the importance of non-media-centric analyses in order to explicate a holistic understanding of sociocultural change (Krotz 2007, 2009). In congruence with these views, a communication-centered approach can inform how more complex and concrete understandings of the mediatization of religion as a *meta-process* can be achieved through the social construction of everyday life, particularly digital and social media communication practices that help enact the micro processes of everyday spiritual organizing. Contemporary digital and social media communication is constitutive of religious organization when different stakeholders interact to compose and sustain distinct symbolic acts that form representations of human and ecclesiastical relations in order to orient themselves to physical and supranatural realities (Cheong 2017). Accordingly, an examination of the routine mesh of mediated communication practices helps to illuminate the "autopoietic co-constitution" of a spiritual organization whereby leaders, members and non-members discursively (re)produce a global entity with distinctive symbolic and material characteristics (Cheong, Hwang and Brummans 2014, 19–20).

Attention to and appreciation of the agency of religious actors, including clergy and laity in their day-to-day communication, fill a research gap identified in preceding discussions on the mediatization of religion (Lövheim 2011) and in organizations where media work shapes and is shaped by institutional properties and norms (Pallas, Strannegård and Jonsson 2014). Since daily life in the religious milieu progressively bears the indelible marks of digital media, it is important to observe the relations between media adoption and concurrent processes of societal change, including globalization and individualization (Radde-Antweiler 2017). As Lövheim's review of research on mediatization points out, "the role played by religious actors (institutions, groups, individuals, narratives and symbols) in the process [of mediatization of religion] needs to be recognized and analyzed to understand how this process takes form, as well as its outcomes" (2011, 164).

Specifically, the contention here is that we observe how mediatized religion is enacted by multiple religious agents in multilevel communication that is mediated and on-ground, and jointly generated by the work of faith organizations, leaders and members. Although Hjarvard's (2008) foundational conceptualization of the mediatization of religion broadly focuses on mass media as agents of social change in the Nordic context, nonetheless, examinations of mediatization can proceed on multiple levels and dimensions with broad and intricate consequences for everyday life in diverse contexts (Couldry and Hepp 2013, Lundby 2014), including spiritual life and organization.

For instance, in explicating the importance of observing structured communication phenomena across different levels and media, Hepp and Hasebrink (2014) outlined how particular *communicative figurations* constructed from a media matrix enacted by a group of actors under the auspices of a specific framework of understanding can shed light on social ties, power, inequalities and protocol. In addition, through a case study of a viral wedding video, Clark (2011) examined how a network of private and corporate actors in varied organizations and media industries, with different goals and economic motives, interact to spur action and remediation of religiously related content.

Furthermore, research studies in Asian settings have shown how religious leaders of various faiths can utilize multiple digital platforms and practice forms of strategic communication to elicit cross-level interactions with their adherents to build their organizational life. This includes strategic arbitration between competing online and traditional sacred texts such that newer digital media use facilitates the co-creation of knowledge with members, and stimulates behaviors that preserve congregational participation in prevailing church practices, including attendance in physical gatherings and rituals at local houses of worship (Cheong, Huang and Poon 2011a, 2011b). More recently with the rise in microblogging, it has been documented that religious leaders are developing novel conventions of social media interactions on Twitter to establish their authority (Cheong 2014). Clergy have also used social media platforms to share faith-inspired aphorisms, construct links to their publications and publicize their connections to popular culture icons, resulting in the celebrification of prominent clergy (Cheong 2016).

In this way, the mediatization of religion proceeds from multilevel, multimedia communication, shaped by strategic church related practices that entail user engagement and interactivity across media. Accordingly, it becomes imperative to examine transmediation of religious texts and symbols in spiritual settings. In recent years, new transmedial practices have emerged in light of new church digital applications and social media campaigns, which reflect the creative work of an assemblage of religious actors in the shaping of action, interaction and consequently, change in Asian societies. Here, these practices are discussed and comprehended in the context of a highly mediatized locale of Southeast Asia, Singapore.

Mediatization of Religion in Singapore

To illustrate the communicative meso-micro interplay and the agency of religious actors in shaping digital media use to build religious authority and community, this chapter draws upon recent key developments in the case of the NCC in Singapore. The Republic of Singapore is a multicultural, dense, technologically advanced city-state in Southeast Asia, and is a renowned global transportation and financial hub. According to the latest figures reported by Internet World Stats (2018) at the time of publication, more than 80% of the Singaporean population has access to the Internet, and many gain digital access connect via smartphones and mobile devices. Hence, as one of most internet connected and savvy countries in Asia and worldwide, with nationwide high speed broadband and a plethora of religious organizations that have a digital presence and adopted digital media for their work, Singapore is a particularly well-suited context to examine the phenomenon of mediatized religion (Cheong et al. 2009, Kluver and Cheong 2007).

Founded in 1983, the NCC is one of the largest non-denominational Christian churches in Singapore, with more than 31,000 attendees, who meet in seven service venues every week. The organization is highly media savvy, with an extensive website and online digital presence across multiple social media platforms including Facebook, Twitter and Instagram, and international television broadcasts in America, Africa, Middle East, Europe and Asia. The size and wide-ranging medial practices of the NCC render it a rich case study for religion in a pluralistic society, as Christianity is the second most-practiced religion in Singapore, after Buddhism. Christianity is also a growing religion in Singapore. According to the latest census statistical release, Christians in Singapore grew from 14.6% in 2000 to 18.3% of the country's population in 2010, with the majority identifying as Protestants (Ministry of Trade & Industry, Republic of Singapore 2011).

For the purposes of this chapter, I will discuss two recent media innovations that entail organizational and grassroots mediated interactions. First, I will discuss the NCC application (app) which can be downloaded for free from the App Store or Google Play, and has real-time capabilities to sign up for events, get seats and carpark availability updates. Following that, I will proceed to discuss the #gracerevolution campaign.

Cultivating Religious Actors through Digital Applications and Premediation

First, the NCC app has multiple affordances to facilitate regular and repeated connections between members and the church leadership, particularly the cultivation of a loyal following to the Senior Pastor, Joseph Prince. Devotionals, excerpts of sermons, announcements and excerpts from books written by the Senior Pastor are available, to help consolidate the performance and *presentification* of his spiritual authority beyond the pulpit to online users' everyday situations (Brummans, Hwang and Cheong 2013, Cheong, Hwang and Brummans 2014).

According to the NCC's app landing page, "[s]taying ahead with the latest church information has never been easier. Access our daily devotions, latest announcements and calendar of events on the go" (New Creation Church App 2016). Through the app, members and seekers of the faith worldwide can access, share and post comments on various social media, which magnify Pastor Prince's teachings that are updated weekly, if not daily. These include the daily devotionals, monthly *e-solid rock* magazines, online videos of Pastor Prince's sermons, the tweets that embed his spiritual instruction or lessons, and the Instagram posts of his teaching events in Singapore and worldwide.

Furthermore, several novel digital functions, which are online and accessible through the church app, help members and visitors to connect to the church before their midweek and weekly main gatherings. For example, contrary to most church practices of congregants, the walking into church for regular services, entry to NCC's main 5,000-seater auditorium, the *Star theatre*, on the first two Sunday and midweek services is by online advanced seat reservation. This means that congregation members must access the app or log in to the Church's online system, named *NOAH*, to book their seat in church a week in advance to ensure that they can enter through the access gates to their reserved seats.

Interestingly, although NOAH is the acronym for the NCC's Online Access Hub, this nomenclature also refers to a prominent Old Testament Biblical figure. In order to reserve a seat for the service, members must first create an account on NOAH, which requires them to submit personal information including their name, their passport or national identification number, gender, date of birth, email, country of residence. Access to NOAH subsequently grants one access to the Star Theatre's seating plan, and detailed instructions on how to book seats for oneself and up to four immediate family members, friends or relatives, as well as instructions to book one's children into the church's classes. On Sunday, church attendees are required to bring their *access media* (which can be a registered public transportation cash card, credit card or the Church's commemorative card) in order to gain entry to the right access gates to their specifically numbered and reserved seats. Furthermore, according to the NCC website's page entitled, *Attending Services At The Star PAC*, members who have booked their seats are required to enter the service venue at least 15 minutes before the service starts or they "will be treated as 'no show'" and their "seats will be given up to walk-in congregation members" (New Creation Church Website 2016).

Besides the management of pedestrian traffic, entry into the local church is also facilitated by their carpark feature accessible through the church app. The NCC app offers news on traffic jams, congestion, road closures and roadworks; variations in traffic conditions common in densely populated and highly urbanized environments like Singapore.

For instance, news of a traffic advisory that was issued on the 2nd of October 2016 read:

> If you are attending our 1st service tomorrow at Marina Bay Sands (MBS) or The Star Performing Arts Centre, do note that the west-bound portion of East Coast Parkway and part of Marina Coastal Expressway will be closed in the morning for a cycling event. You can use Pan-Island Expressway, Kallang Road and Seletar Expressway to get to MBS. If you are heading to The Star for service, please take Pan-Island Expressway instead. Find out more at bit.ly/TA28Sep or look out for the announcement on our website. #nccsg.

Another transportation update issued about two months later read:

> Attending our 1st or 2nd service at Marina Bay Sands (MBS) this Sunday, 4 December 2016? Please note that some roads leading to MBS will be closed till 1.30pm due to a public run. To get to MBS, we encourage you to take the public train system. If you drive, do consider using either Pan-Island Expressway, East Coast Parkway or Central Expressway. For more information, please visit bit.ly/MBS4Dec2016 or look out for the announcement on our website. #nccsg.

Moreover, the app features "car park availability check in real time" on Sunday English services and selected weekday nights (New Creation Church App 2016). This application allows members and visitors to the church to obtain real-time updates on vacant parking spaces available at the service venue before or while on their way to church. To facilitate traffic flow in and out of the church building, this update highlights the number of open parking spaces at specific levels of the carpark structure. By providing crucial transportation information and regulating access to church premises, the use of this church app is woven into the mediatized itineraries and life worlds of congregational members.

Thus, in these ways, the use of these digital applications points to how mediatization is manifest through specific techno-spatial transformations in church life. As Jansson (2013, 281–282) stressed, mediatization enabled by transmedia technologies is defined by "sociospatial regimes of dependence" enhanced by interactivity, new media interfaces and technological convergence. Specifically, premediation, a concept introduced by Grusin (2010), refers to how the media help alter preconditions of material contact such that it "not only shape our expectations and anticipations of future events and experiences, but also generate particular forms of action and interaction that are performed, or staged, in order to become mediated within a certain representational register"

(Jansson 2013, 284). This premediation of experience can alter beliefs of space and place as:

> premediation works by mobilizing affect in the present, by deploying multiple modes of mediation and remediation in shaping the affectivity of the public, in preparing people for some field of possible future actions, in producing a mood of structure of feeling that makes possible certain kinds of actions....
>
> (Jansson 2013, 284)

Here, it is striking to observe how in the NCC case, the use of their app helps to premediate the experience of church gatherings, to produce a compelling experience in theatricalization of worship performance, both in the literal and metaphorical sense. Digital applications construct a sense of *conceived church space* by deploying various online scripts and interactions to prepare their members, both physically and emotionally, to produce a fitting mood and structure for weekly physical interactions. According to the church's website, NOAH was introduced to "enhance church life" with "more restful Sunday and midweek experiences" as members are assured that they have a designated seat when they book their seat in the church's sanctuary one week in advance (New Creation Church Website 2016). Thus, the meso-micro interplay of agency and action in mediatization is activated as the church designs and facilitates the use of digital applications by members and visitors. These online users are in turn, engaged with premediating church experience through the sharing and circulation of information within a digital infrastructure that nurture the habitual and punctual (and purportedly, more "restful") attendance of church in a cavernous auditorium (New Creation Church Website 2016). In other words, communicative practices facilitated by congregational digital interactions before weekly church services are seen to affect the quotidian operations of church life and its conditions of assembly, including the basic protocol governing the premeditated access into the house of God.

The above examples also pointedly illustrate how church leadership, members and online interactants appropriate the latest digital affordances to communicate to themselves, and by doing so, co-enact their organization through the creation of linguistic and material boundaries with its environment. "Auto-communication" or self-referentiality in organizing (Broms and Gahmberg 1983, 484) in spiritual sites include practices such as making clergy teachings readily present on an iterative basis and coherent languaging to notify members about the organization's news and developments frequently (Cheong, Hwang and Brummans 2014).

Here, we specially also observe how the mediatization of religion is achieved through app technologies facilitating various forms of auto-communication. These forms of organizational auto-communication include making the senior pastor's teachings present in multiple forms on diverse platforms accessible via the church app so that members are regularly informed and edified by these teachings and news. Auto-communication in this case also involves notifications and repetitive messaging about gaining vehicular and pedestrian entry into the church sanctuary (e.g., "Attending our 1st or 2nd service at Marina Bay Sands (MBS) this Sunday...?"), and customary transportation notifications "straight to your smart phone" to facilitate the commute to church (e.g., "use Pan-Island Expressway, Kallang Road and Seletar Expressway to get to MBS [church]," "we encourage you to take the public train system"). In this way, these types of mediated auto-communication practices via the integration of digital services in congregants' everyday lives serve to co-enact the church, produce the social conditions that facilitate weekly services, and establish institutionalized modes of interaction that support the contemporary growth of religious authority and community.

Cultivating Religious Actors through Branding and Social Media Campaigns

Second, church-led social media campaigns by the NCC in recent years has involved the use of hashtags to build momentum around online and grounded activities timed in concert with the promotion of the Senior Pastor's latest book release; typically released first in Singapore, and then worldwide. For example, the #gracerevolution was a two-month-long program beginning in October 2015 that coincided with the launch of Pastor Prince's book, titled *Grace Revolution: Experience the power to live above defeat* (2015). A grace revolution app was created which enabled users to access the first chapter of the book, a five-day devotional plan, *grace-inspired stickers* to be added to photos, and *grace-based wallpapers* for the their mobile devices. As users were encouraged to share the stickers with #gracerevolution, small groups in the church, called *care groups* took welfies (group selfie-like pictures) and added grace-inspired stickers with messages like *grace supplies* and *perfect love casts out fear* on their care group pictures.

Furthermore, congregants were encouraged to share their *story of grace* through various events that highlight the meso-micro communicative interplay via grassroots activities that involve congregants' production and consumption of mediatized events created by NCC. Activities fostered with #gracerevolution include collective jigsaw puzzling and asking believers to fill a card with personal testimonies, taking a snapshot of it and posting it on social media (using the #gracerevolution). Specifically, on 14 November 2015, the news on this activity on social media read:

> We're giving out Grace Revolution jigsaw cards at our English services today! Have fun joining your card with others to complete the

jigsaw puzzle. You can also write your story of grace on the back of the card, take a picture of it and share it on social media. #gracerevolution #becauseofgrace #nccsg.
(New Creation Church Singapore Facebook 2016)

Multiple reminders were also sent online to increase individual and community engagement. For example, on 22 November 2015, an update on the NCC Facebook to goad individual and collective participation said:

> Picked up the Grace Revolution jigsaw cards from our ambassadors or ushers at our English services today? Encourage others by filling in the back of the card with your story of grace and share a photo of it on social media using the hashtag#gracerevolution. You can also join your card with others and have fun forming the complete jigsaw puzzle. #nccsg #becauseofgrace.
> (New Creation Church Singapore Facebook 2016)

The #gracerevolution campaign also deployed photo booths, which were set up for several weeks in the church's service venues on Sundays, to help take pictures of members so as to facilitate the creation and sharing of personalized #gracerevolution photo cards. Full-length colored posters on floor stands were placed in the church foyers to provide instructions on the process. These instantly produced photo cards included the photograph of the members and writing space where participants penned their *stories of grace* and shared them online or with their friends.

Here, it is significant to note in more detail how this card writing practice represents processes of both customization and standardization; an interplay of individual input and institutional structure in storytelling. Specifically, while the cards were individualized with portraits, which were taken on church premises, the content and presentation were nonetheless structured to a certain degree. The cards were produced using a template that showcased the headshot on the top, and a space for a short narrative of several sentences below, which uniformly began with the words, "[b]ecause of Grace...." Examples of these photo card narratives which have been subsequently reposted on the Church's social media platforms such as Facebook and Instagram and print media include, "[b]ecause of Grace, I have been delivered from depression and found hope again in my life," and "[b]ecause of Grace, I was brought out of a lifestyle where I could have been killed in a gangfight and drug overdose. Because of grace, I am alive today to serve the next generation in the youth ministry" (New Creation Church Website 2015). The strategic integration of these photo cards in the #gracerevolution campaign illustrate how the mediatization of religion unfurls not merely as a one-way, institutionally orchestrated movement to transform the beliefs and behaviors of congregational members. Instead, the above discussion reflects how the campaign is contingent on actions and participation through meso-micro interplays, as top-down church-led promotional activities solicit the bottom-up and lay communication processes to help to literally and figuratively fuel the titular "grace revolution".

Hence, the above exemplars illustrate various forms of church-designed and collaborative activities, which are staged and scripted to a certain degree, in order to be socially shared, in embodied and virtual forms. These socially mediated activities highlight how individual as well as group acts of communicative production and consumption via hashtag activism can scale up to vivify the church-led #grace revolution campaign and legitimize the church. As congregational members use digital communication platforms like Instagram, Twitter and Facebook to engage in the posting of these stories of grace, as well as to share, *like* and celebrate their testimonies, they rally and galvanize others toward communal engagement, and in doing so, co-labor in building a consensual universe of meaning that constitute religious organizations (Cheong, Hwang and Brummans 2014). In this regard, the mediatization of religion is not causally determined in a technologically deterministic manner, but proceeds via the meso-micro interplay as dynamic social media appropriations sustain the development and outreach of religious institutions.

Concluding Thoughts: Mediatization of Religion

To contribute to the theoretical conceptualization and empirical basis of the mediatization of religion, this chapter has applied a communication-centered approach to spotlight the agency of organizational and individual religious actors as they enact distinct communication practices that constitute everyday spiritual organizing. By foregrounding communicative interactions afforded by the latest smart phone and social media applications, this article notes the vital role of digital media in contemporary religion, and how its criticality is both literal and figurative as networked flows of religious information and services build and sustain the church (Cheong 2016). In this sense, this work echoes the key thrust of work by other commentators arguing for more illumination on cultural conditions and the social constructivist paradigm to mediatization whereby communication is the linchpin of mediatization (Hepp 2013, Knoblauch 2013, Krotz 2009) and serves as the elemental artery by which society, including religious life is constructed and nourished.

Furthermore, by focusing on the communicative interplay between religious organizational and lay actors, this chapter has extended work on the concept of mediatization, which can be observed in communicative interlaces in the intermediate zone across traditional levels of analysis

(Hepp and Hasebrink 2014). By documenting micro practices of individual consumption, interaction and production of religiously related texts, as well as meso practices of how the church is involved in and transformed by mediatization, this article highlights how communication builds and lubricates religiously affiliated expectations and practices, and in turn, sustains and extends church outreach.

Yet contrary to some theorists in the field of mediatization, this chapter has also tried to highlight how the power of digital media has become inseparable from and dependent on the work of institutions, in this case, intricate and strategic church organizational processes and the products of church leadership. While mediatization has been coined to describe the broad, intensifying and extended implications of media, less research has focused on the role of religious organizations in constructing and cultivating mediated news, information, goods and services that circulate vigorously and form the lifeblood of many contemporary religious and social practices. This gap in the literature may reflect the course of events in certain Western societies where denominational Christian institutions are losing adherents and prominence. Thus, to a certain extent, the influence and presence of powerful religious institutions are enervated and diminished in recent literature.

Notably, Couldry and Hepp (2013) in their review of mediatization research observed that one key research stream has downplayed the role of institutions, and emphasized

> the emergence, and increasing dominance from the mid-1990s, of approaches to power that no longer located it inside powerful institutions, let alone powerful people, but saw it being reproduced everywhere in a huge network of linkages, apparatuses, and habits within everyday life.
>
> (2013, 194)

By highlighting multiple meso-micro interactions here, it is hoped that alongside the rise of individual networks and management of religious information online, data in this case also illustrate the principal influence and expansive reach of the Church, as still, a fairly influential organization in Singapore and in many other countries in the world. In the case of NCC, one cannot discount the role of religious leadership orders and executive plans in the creation, prompting and purposeful staging of various communication acts that involve and mandate certain congregational interactions. As this study shows how church members need to repeatedly access online services in order to stay attached to the church and even gain physical access to the sanctuary, we witness that power is still connected to religious leadership. Religious organizations can enact communicative norms to elicit reciprocal actions, support their physical rituals, extend the opportunistic and timely promotion of their campaigns, and consequently, fire the growth of their institution. In other words, the church clergy and its directors and workers remain a formidable aspect of mediatization, and are amongst the influential actors of contemporary socio-technical change, worthy of more in-depth and future research on this topic.

In this sense, this chapter further contributes to the internationalization of the mediatization of religion by locating its study in a specific cultural context that is intensely mediated, and where religious leaders of different faiths are highly supportive of the use of communication technologies for church innovation and growth (Kluver and Cheong 2007). Unlike the cultural circumstances and prominent secularization in the Nordic and North American contexts where the bulk of mediatization research has been conducted, Singapore is a locale whereby religion, media and the marketplace interact and function vibrantly in an information economy (Poon, Huang and Cheong 2012). There appears to be no inherent contradiction between modernization and religious life, and no prominent surge in secularization and the attendant demise of religious authority. Christian megachurches in Asia are experiencing growth as they construct intense experience-oriented religious activities fueled by state of the art technologies (Cruz 2009). Thus, to study the mediatization of religion in this context is to examine the intensely, personally mediated as well as institutionally led communication practices that help enact micro processes of everyday spiritual organizing as many churches influence what their members can concretely experience and apprehend.

It is also interesting that in light of the collectivistic Asian values, which are historically and culturally embraced by many Singaporeans, the mediated interactions that are facilitated by the church app are often taken up not just in individualistic ways or settings. Instead, it has been observed that mediated interactions also unfold in communal, place-based and group activities (e.g., the use of collaborative puzzling in church, and the spread of group photo-taking like the *Usie* or group *Wefie*, instead of egocentric selfies, framed with #gracerevolution stickers). Indeed, allocentric representations and familial displays of group cohesion, which align with the local value system, may be more significant in collectivistic cultures experienced in many parts of Asia. Therefore, this chapter also provides a case in point on the need for further research in the mediatization of religion in Asia and beyond, which investigates the motivations and practices of an array of religious actors not only within situated contexts that share some similarities to Western contexts but also where social and power arrangements differ in many marked ways. As mediatization research grows beyond non-American and non-European centric perspectives and sites of data, a wider and more colorful domain of inquiry can augment our understanding of the ramifications of digital and social media in everyday life.

References

Broms, H. and Gahmberg, H., 1983. Communication to Self in Organizations and Cultures. *Administrative Science Quarterly*, 28(3), 482–495.

Brummans, H. J. M., Hwang, J. M. and Cheong, P. H., 2013. Mindful Authoring through Invocation: Leaders' Constitution of a Spiritual Organization. *Management Communication Quarterly*, 27(3), 346–372.

Cheong, P. H., 2014. Tweet the Message? Religious Authority and Social Media Innovation. *Journal of Religion, Media and Digital Culture*, 3(3), 1–19. Available at www.jrmdc.com/journal/article/view/27, accessed 2 January 2015.

Cheong, P. H., 2016. Religious Authority and Social Media Branding in a Culture of Religious Celebrification. In: Hoover, S., ed. *The Media and Religious Authority*. University Park: Penn State University Press, 81–104.

Cheong, P. H., 2017. The Vitality of New Media and Religion: Communicative Perspectives, Practices and Authority in Spiritual Organization. *New Media & Society*, 19(1), 25–31. doi:10.1177/1461444816649913.

Cheong, P. H., Huang, S. H. and Poon, J. P. H., 2011a. Religious Communication and Epistemic Authority of Leaders in Wired Faith Organizations. *Journal of Communication*, 61(5), 938–958.

Cheong, P. H., Huang, S. and Poon, J. P., 2011b. Cultivating Online and Offline Pathways to Enlightenment: Religious Authority and Strategic Arbitration in Wired Buddhist Organization. *Information, Communication & Society*, 14(8), 1160–1180.

Cheong, P. H., Hwang, J. M. and Brummans, H. J. M., 2014. Transnational Immanence: The Autopoietic Co-Constitution of a Chinese Spiritual Organization through Mediated Communication. *Information, Communication & Society*, 1(1), 7–25.

Cheong, P. H., Poon, J. P., Huang, S. and Casas, I., 2009. The Internet Highway and Religious Communities: Mapping and Contesting Spaces in Religion-Online. *The Information Society*, 25(5), 291–302.

Clark, L. S., 2011. Considering Religion and Mediatisation through a Case Study of J+ K's Big Day (The JK Wedding Entrance Dance): A Response to Stig Hjarvard. *Culture and Religion*, 12(2), 167–184.

Couldry, N. and Hepp, A., 2013. Conceptualizing Mediatization: Contexts, Traditions, Arguments. *Communication Theory*, 23(3), 191–202.

Cruz, J. N., 2009. A Spectacle of Worship: Technology, Modernity and the Rise of the Christian Megachurch. In: Lim, F. K. G., ed. *Mediating Piety*. Leiden: Brill, 113–138.

Grusin, R., 2010. *Premediation: Affect and Mediality after 9/11*. Basingstoke: Palgrave Macmillan.

Hepp, A., 2013. *Cultures of Mediatization*. Cambridge: Polity Press.

Hepp, A. and Hasebrink, U., 2014. Human Interaction and Communicative Figurations: The Transformation of Mediatized Cultures and Societies. In: Lundby, K., ed. *Mediatization of Communication*. Berlin/Boston: De Gruyter Mouton, 249–272.

Hjarvard, S., 2008. The Mediatization of Religion: A Theory of the Media as Agents of Religious Change. *Northern Lights: Film & Media Studies Yearbook*, 6(1), 9–26.

Internet World Stats, 2018. *Usage and Population Statistics. Singapore Internet and Telecommunications.* Available at www.internetworldstats.com/asia/sg.htm, accessed 10 May 2018.

Jansson, A., 2013. Mediatization and Social Space: Reconstructing Mediatization for the Transmedia Age. *Communication Theory,* 23(3), 279–296.

Kluver, R. and Cheong, P. H., 2007. Technological Modernization, the Internet, and Religion in Singapore. *Journal of Computer-Mediated Communication,* 12(3), 1122–1142.

Knoblauch, H., 2013. Communicative Constructivism and Mediatization. *Communication Theory,* 23(3), 297–315.

Krotz, F., 2007. The Meta-Process of Mediatization as a Conceptual Frame. *Global Media and Communication,* 3(3), 256–260.

Krotz, F., 2009. Mediatization: A Concept with which to Grasp Media and Societal Change. In: Lundby, K., ed. *Mediatization: Concept, Changes, Consequences.* New York: Peter Lang, 21–40.

Lövheim, M., 2011. Mediatisation of Religion: A Critical Appraisal. *Culture and Religion,* 12(2), 153–166.

Lundby, K., 2014. Mediatization of Communication. In: Lundby, K., ed. *Mediatization of Communication.* Berlin/Boston: De Gruyter Mouton, 3–35.

Lynch, G., 2011. What Can We Learn from the Mediatisation of Religion Debate? *Culture and Religion,* 12(2), 203–210.

Ministry of Trade and Industry, Republic of Singapore, 2011. *Census of Population 2010. Statistical Release 1. Demographic Characteristics, Education, Language and Religion.* Available at https://web.archive.org/web/20110303155259/; www.singstat.gov.sg/pubn/popn/C2010sr1/cop2010sr1.pdf, accessed 5 August 2016.

New Creation Church App, 2016. Available at https://play.google.com/store/apps/details?id=sg.org.newcreation.ncc&hl=en, accessed 1 August 2016.

New Creation Church Singapore Facebook, 2016. @nccsg. Available at www.facebook.com/pg/nccsg/posts/, accessed 20 December 2016.

New Creation Church Website, 2015. *Share your Story of Grace.* Available at www.newcreation.org.sg/news/announcements/latest-news/2015/10/24/share-your-story-of-grace, accessed 15 November 2015.

New Creation Church Website, 2016. *Attending Services at the Star PAC.* Available at http://thestar.newcreation.org.sg/attending-services-at-the-star-pac.php, accessed 6 July 2016.

Pallas, J., Strannegård, L. and Jonsson, S., 2014. *Organizations and the Media: Organizing in a Mediatized World* (Vol. 30). London: Routledge.

Poon, J. P. H., Huang, S. H. and Cheong, P. H., 2012. Media, Religion and the Marketplace in the Information Economy: Evidence from Singapore. *Environment and Planning A,* 44(8), 1969–1985.

Prince, J., 2015. Grace Revolution: Experience the Power to Live above Defeat. New York: FaithWords.

Radde-Antweiler, K., 2017. Digital Religion? Media Studies from a Religious Studies Perspective. In: Nord, I. and Zipernovszky, H., eds. *Religious Education in a Mediatized World.* Stuttgart: W. Kohlhammer, 138–150.

Part 3
South Asia

8 Ravidassia

Neither Sikh nor Hindu? Mediatized Religion in Anti-caste Contexts

Dhanya Fee Kirchhof

Introduction

If a globally interconnected socioreligious movement of North Indian origin and related to anti-caste movements[1] proclaims a new religion, what methodical implications will it have for analyzing mediatized religion? Drawing upon a case study on a currently emerging mediascape in the context of the spatially highly mobile (religious) Ravidassia community, this is the initial question I seek to discuss in this chapter. Findings are based on a multimodal qualitative content analysis of YouTube music videos, a sample analysis of related online discussions in social media as well as on media ethnographic research on Ravidassias in Germany and their mediated interpersonal communication.

The argument is twofold: First, this mediascape of global dimensions and related new modes of articulating belonging are expressions of an upheaval, resulting from mediatization processes and their complex, contextual entanglements with socioreligious, political and economic changes and increased spatial mobility of various actors. Second, these entanglements and particularities of media communicative change in this context require an actor-centered, differentiated mediatization approach. This approach needs to consider the intertwining between various mediated communicative forms and multidirectional communication flows across borders and beyond the digital. Emphasizing this necessity, I will discuss the applicability of actor-centered, socio-constructivist mediatization approaches (especially by Krotz and Hepp 2011) before exemplifying benefits of the communicative figurations approach (e.g., Hasebrink and Hepp 2016, Hepp 2013) for analyzing transformation processes related to mediatized Ravidassia religion. As I will illustrate, this actor-centered approach combines different research perspectives on mediatized religion. According to Hasebrink and Hepp (2016, 6–7), a multilevel analysis is essential to relate the level of individual practices to larger social domains instead of analyzing transformation processes and their interconnections either from a micro perspective or from a meta perspective.

Changing Religious Affiliations, Anti-caste Movements and Mediatization in Punjab

On 30 January 2010, the religious organization *Dera Sachkhand Ballan*, based in the Indian state of Punjab, declared the split from Sikhism and the establishment of an autonomous Ravidassia religion. While a large number of members of the globally interconnected (religious) Ravidassia community are based all across the world, the followers, or their ancestors, are of South Asian origin – mainly from the Indian Punjab region. The affiliation to that religion seems to be strongly entangled with a specific caste background related to the traditional occupational field of leather working. People associated with this background have been facing caste-based discrimination, exclusion and violence – albeit to varying degrees – based on the stigma of *untouchability*.[2] The eponym of this religion is Guru Ravidass, a saint poet who had been a leather worker presumably during the 15th century and propagated equality and the vision of a casteless and classless society.

The striving for an autonomous Ravidassia religion is deeply intertwined with the struggle against caste-based discrimination and oppression aiming at social upward mobility and an overall social change. Within this struggle, religious change is seen as a prerequisite for social change, since a large number of involved people seem to perceive caste-based oppression as an integral part of Hindu religion, and spiritually and philosophically justified by its religious texts (Dirks 2001, 267–268, Juergensmeyer 1982, 269). Consequently, they had the firm belief "that shifts in religious alignment pose serious threats to the old bases of social power" (Juergensmeyer 1982, 269). In order to better their social status within society, conversion to Islam, Sikhism and Christianity was one strategy employed by anti-caste movements. Numerous ancestors of Ravidassias tried to reach equality in social status through the conversion to Sikhism, a religion that is based on the principle of universal equality. But as caste-based discrimination persisted after conversion – both within the everyday life as well as within the places of worship – the construction of a new autonomous religious identity seemed to be the prerequisite for social equality and dignity (cf. Ram 2016, 371–372, 2017, 55, Singh 2013, 186–187, 196). However, as Takhar's study (2014) related to Ravidassias in Britain revealed, there seems to be disagreement between followers of Guru Ravidass on whether the complete split from Sikhism is an appropriate decision.

Why is a mediatization perspective relevant in this context? Caste-based discrimination also causes exclusion from the Indian media sector and misrepresentations in its news coverage, since India's largely privatized news media sector is mainly controlled by dominant socioreligious groups as several publications in the field of *Dalit*[3] media studies have illustrated (e.g., Anand 2005, Jeffrey 2001, Loynd 2008, Nayar

2011, Thirumal and Tartakov 2011). Simultaneously, those authors stress that the access to means of communication can enhance opportunities to participate in public discourses and that it can improve the social position of those discriminated against on the basis of caste. The relevance of accessing and appropriating means of communication to bring about social change seems to become even more evident in times of deep mediatization in which various fields in society seem increasingly saturated and shaped by media-based communication. According to the socio-constructivist tradition of mediatization theory, this might even be true for all our constructions of sociocultural reality (cf. Hepp and Krotz 2014, 3). Following these arguments and Castells' framework of *network society*,[4] it seems likely that "power relations [...] as well as the processes challenging institutionalized power relations are increasingly shaped and decided in the communication field" (Castells 2007, 239).

As several authors and findings from my previous research have revealed,[5] those groups attempt to create their own media, but often face financial problems resulting from difficulties to acquire advertisers and a sufficient number of paying subscribers. Numerous authors express new hopes that the Internet can provide new alternatives (e.g., Nayar 2011, Thirumal and Tartakov 2011, Zaslavsky 2016).

Thus, the phenomenon of a currently emerging multidirectional Ravidassia mediascape of global dimensions seems to be an expression of a significant upheaval. In the course of renegotiating religious belonging, a large variety of media is evolving. This chapter focuses on the related music industry. It is characterized by a broad thematic and stylistic spectrum ranging from devotional *kīrtan* or *bhajan*[6] performances to popular music genres of Punjabi music. In addition, a large variety of online and print media, literature, television channels and radio stations becomes apparent.[7] In a broader sense of the term media, this equally includes iconography, flags, car stickers and textile prints with expressions of self-pride and shared (religious) symbols, statues and pilgrimage sites as well as mobile bodies. *Mobile bodies* shall be understood as either singers or religious leaders who are touring across India and the world, or masses gathering and moving on mediatized religious events. As I will demonstrate, mobile apps and forms of interpersonal mobile communication such as WhatsApp groups need to be equally recognized for understanding mediatization and meaning-making processes in this specific context. This also applies for the intertwining between various mediated communicative forms and multidirectional communication flows.

Using such means of communication, individual and collective actors all over the world, including the *Dera Sachkhand Ballan,* do not only negotiate religious belonging, but also articulate visions of their idols and create positive self-images as tools against caste-based oppression.

A quote by Ginni Mahi, a young singer who became a YouTube star in 2016, illustrates these issues vividly:

> We are no less than anyone, that's the message of my songs. I tell them, if being a girl, I can make it, so can you. Guru Ravidas dreamt of a casteless society where there's no sorrow, and that's what I am trying to project through my music.
>
> (Ginni Mahi cited in Kohli 2016, n.p.)

Her success on YouTube was followed by numerous performances in popular Indian talk shows, in music shows, at conferences on gender equality as well as interviews for newspapers and online news platforms. This quote was published in the *Hindustan Times*, a well-known Indian English language newspaper reading the headline: "Punjab's protest pop: How the Dalits are telling the world they've arrived" (Kohli 2016, n.p.). This example indicates that some actors are partially opening up access to so-called mainstream media and to public debates in various fields of society.

Although the emerging Ravidassia mediascape points to ongoing transformation processes, it has not yet been the focus of scholarly research.[8] Some scholars mention specific forms of media or technologies (e.g., Jodhka 2009, 2016, Juergensmeyer 1982, Lum 2014, Ram 2016, 2017) or illustrate topics discussed in related literature (Judge 2014) and virtual spaces (Judge 2015).

The Need for Contextualized, Actor-Centered Mediatization Approaches

Drawing on the example of the success and scope of actors related to the emerging music industry, the following sections seek to emphasize the necessity for a contextualized, actor-centered mediatization approach while relating micro-level analysis to larger domains and transformation processes. Therefore, I seek to answer the following question: Why is a technocentric mediatization perspective alone – with a specific focus on the Internet – insufficient for understanding ongoing transformation and meaning-making processes in the Ravidassia context? This question is threefold: First, why do particularities of mediatization processes require actor-centered mediatization approaches? Second, which particularities can we perceive if we look at media practices and articulations visible online and what are the limitations? Third, what can we perceive if we apply media ethnographic, actor-centered methods?

Particularities of Mediatization Processes in the Indian and Anti-caste Context

Looking at India and anti-caste movements, it becomes apparent that mediatization processes vary depending on the context. For example, the Indian print media sector has been experiencing a rapid growth and expansion in local markets during the last three to four decades, as Jeffrey (2000) and Schneider (2005) have illustrated. This is of specific relevance, since especially increasingly capitalized print media companies turned into media conglomerates expanding into television, radio and online sectors (Schneider 2011, 223, 228). Therefore, the Indian media system is characterized "by a growing inter- and crossmediality and media convergence" (2011, 227) including both digital and other communication media and practices. She further argues: "this wider context needs to be taken into consideration when conducting any media-related research, even when it deals with one particular medium" (2011, 228).

These arguments imply that it would be insufficient to focus only on particular individual media forms or technologies in order to analyze mediatization processes. They are substantiated by Krotz's (2007) understanding of mediatization as one among other long-term meta-processes of social and cultural change and other publications challenging the idea of a singular media logic and analysis (see especially Hasebrink and Hepp 2016, 5, Krotz and Hepp 2011, 141, Radde-Antweiler 2017, 147–148). Krotz argues that it is not the media that actively drives change of the everyday and culture, but rather humans through appropriating media in specific ways (Krotz 2007, 33). Following those elucidations, an actor-centered research, focusing on how people constitute change through their changing mediatized practices, seems highly relevant. Applying this argumentation to the study of mediatized religion, this chapter argues in line with approaches of mediatization of religion which understand media and religion as closely intertwined (see especially Lövheim 2011, Radde-Antweiler 2017), rather than as two separate entities. As Radde-Antweiler summarizes with regard to Meyer and Moors (2006): "religion should be primarily understood as a range of practices which will always have to be communicated in some form or other. Religion is inconceivable without media, because media is always a part of religious practice" (Radde-Antweiler 2017, 145).

Particularities regarding media appropriation in anti-caste contexts and new information and communication technologies (ICTs) further substantiate the need for a non-technocentric, actor-centered mediatization perspective. Due to the aforementioned bias in media coverage, mainstream media have been not very useful for enforcing political objectives in the anti-caste context. Additionally, a large proportion of target groups of anti-caste mobilization may also face difficulties in accessing certain forms of media due to the poor economic and educational background of many. Therefore, related parties, such as the *Bahujan Samaj Party*[9] (BSP) since the 1980s, have been utilizing a large variety of means of communication, with specific relevance to personal communication, based on grassroots structures. Initially, the BSP produced print products, post mailings and organized *cycle yātrās* (mobilizing bike tours through the villages) and theater performances (cf. Jeffrey and Doron 2013, 147–148, Loynd 2008, 80, Narayan 2006, 50–84). Especially in recent years, the relevance of mobile communication has increased significantly as means of mobilization, motivation and organization (Jeffrey and Doron 2013, 149). This also applies to broader Indian contexts, as Jeffrey and Doron (2013) illustrate throughout their book titled *Cell Phone Nation*.

The increasing significance of mobile communication characterizes media communicative change in India. While the computer, due to its high cost and insufficient infrastructure in various rural regions, has not yet become a mass technology in India, the number of mobile phone subscribers increased from 165 million in 2007 to 1.174 billion in 2017 (Telecom Regulatory Authority of India 2017, 1). According to the findings of the 2016 IAMAI and KANTAR IMRB Report (IAMAI and KANTAR IMRB 2017, 3, 7), India was expected to have 269 million Internet users in urban areas and 163 million in rural areas in December 2017 of which 92% of rural users and 77% of urban users use their mobile phone as a primary device for accessing the Internet. However, these findings also suggest that the majority of India's population still does not access the Internet through their own devices. This issue, the mobilization strategies of the BSP and the aforementioned entanglements between different forms of media indicate that it is insufficient to focus solely on particular forms of online media to explore mediatization processes under such conditions.

Articulating Change and Belonging Online and Its Analytical Limitations

Looking at media articulation available online, one might get the impression that musicians related to an emerging Ravidassia mediascape have unfolded their visibility especially on YouTube. Music videos are accompanied by comments and discussions between fans and opponents. Considering media contents of television shows from the online archive of *Kanshi TV* (Kanshi TV 2017), a Ravidassia satellite television channel based in England, it becomes visible that regular television programs also broadcast such music videos. Analyzing music videos and related comments online, one gets various insights. For example, it reveals changing articulations of self-identification, orienting topics and topical entanglements as well as the scope and relevance of specific actors and ideas – at least for those actively commenting on YouTube. Related findings are relevant to contextualize the case study. Therefore, this perspective provides at least some insights in meaning-making processes and entanglements between ongoing transformation processes in the Ravidassia context, which need to be considered while developing a framework for analyzing mediatized Ravidassia religion.

Entanglements between the religious and other domains are of specific relevance in this context. When articulating a shared collective identity, artists do not only refer to themselves as Ravidassias in terms of a religious identity, but in various songs also as descendants of Guru Ravidass or *Chamar*. For centuries, the term *Chamar* has been used as an offensive and denigrating term for people associated with the occupational field of leather working. Singers utilize the term to express a positive self-image and self-respect as responses to the lyrics of popular Punjabi *Bhangra* music in which Jats (a dominant caste group in Punjab) proudly articulate caste pride and masculinity (cf. Dogra 2011, n.p., Lum 2014, 101, Takhar 2014, 108–109). In numerous music videos, singers refer to visions of Guru Ravidass or depict his images or religious symbols, while simultaneously singing about self-pride and staging young, strong, muscular men along with expensive cars, motorcycles or houses. The characters – male and female – are portrayed as economically upwardly mobile and as being powerful enough to counter violence by dominant groups mostly in a non-violent manner (e.g., Amar Audio 2014 [video], Amar Audio Official 2016 [video], EKJOT Films 2016 [video]).

In addition, entanglements with political aspects, especially with the context of anti-caste movements, as well as entanglements between different religious traditions become visible. Thus, not all songs emphasize *caste-pride* and clear distinctions from other caste groups or religious traditions. A larger number of songs are not solely devoted to Guru Ravidass, but equally to Dr. B. R. Ambedkar (1891–1956, respectfully referred to as Babasaheb), one of the most popular leaders in the history of anti-caste movements and the first law minister of independent India. As main contributor to the Indian constitution, Ambedkar, who himself experienced caste-based oppression, imposed affirmative action policies to enhance the opportunities for certain defined minority groups regarding education, job opportunities within the public sector, as well as political participation. For example, in her song *Fan Baba Sahib Di* [Fan of Babasaheb] (Amar Audio 2017 [video]), Ginni Mahi communicates her deep gratitude toward Ambedkar and her own *arrival* resulting from Guru Ravidass' and Ambedkar's legacies. The translation of some of the Punjabi lines of her song reads as follows: "He was such a lion, who made arrows out of his pen. The one who fought for truth and justice, who changed our fate. He became our messiah" (cf. Dalit Camera 2017 [video]).

This example illustrates not only the intertwining between the religious, the social and the political, but also that different religious traditions in this context seemingly intersect. Ambedkar chose himself to convert from Hinduism to Buddhism in 1956, driven by his conviction that "the stigma of untouchability could not be erased simply by political means" (Dirks 2001, 271). Although related people in the state of Punjab did not follow his call for mass conversion in large numbers, his images are visualized and his ideas are uttered in various forms of media and public spaces in the context of the communicative construction of what is declared as Ravidassia religion (cf. Judge 2015, 57). The video of Rajni Thakkarwal's song *Bheem Da Mission* [Ambedkar's mission] is even shot in front of a Buddhist temple (EKJOT Films 2017 [video]).

Singers and characters in related videos seem to serve as role models in terms of upward economic mobility through illustrating personal (economic) success. Thus, those music videos illustrate the close relation between religious and social change and equally underline a related economic dimension. The economic dimension is closely entangled with the processes of migration, improved education and job opportunities in the Indian Punjab region. Especially resources from abroad have been crucial for the *Dera Sachkhand Ballan* to bring forward community building and welfare projects and the construction of religious places (Jodhka 2009, 84), and are highly relevant for the emerging mediascape as well. For example, Ravidassias abroad financially support music careers of singers through donations for producing songs and videos (cf. Dogra 2011, n.p.) or through inviting singers to perform in their places of worship.

Economic aspects as well as the relevance for people's lives become visible, when looking at numerous fan comments on YouTube and uploads of concert recordings and dance performances based on these songs. For example, one comment on Kant Kalers' song *Putt Ravidass Guru De* [The sons / descendants of Guru Ravidass] reads "hope we will learn something from u bhaji [brother] … thxx" (bhupinder singh, comment on Amar Audio 2014). Commenting on Ginni Mahi's song *Danger 2* (Amar Audio Official 2016), Harpreet Sandhu writes: "Really proud that I'm a chamar's girl. Thanks Ginny Mahi for this beautiful song. We all are really proud of you." Concurrently, young fans upload their own dance performances based on these songs presenting specific images, symbols and textile prints. Compared to official music videos, the comments on these fan videos suggest that those performers partly receive almost similar respect from their peers (see Bindas Dance and Fun 2017 [video], Kanhyalal Singh 2017 [video]). Thus, these examples point to an emerging youth culture as well, which seems to be closely entangled with digital media practices and communicative constructions of *Ravidassianess*. Furthermore, the multidirectional character of media flows turns visible.

Comments on aforementioned YouTube videos imply that related songs are relevant for a larger number of people besides members of Ravidassia religion originating from Punjab. The communication through those comments is carried out multilingually – mostly in Punjabi, Hindi and English. Several people are located in other Indian regions and countries abroad. Not all identify as Ravidassia in terms of religious affiliation, as exemplified by the following comment: "I am Hindu but guru ravidass maharaj ji is holy bless to all human being. [...]" (Saurav Kanda, comment on Amar Audio 2014 [video]). Additionally, some fans underline that they have a different caste background (e.g., comments on Amar Audio Official 2016 [video]).

It can be summarized that digital media practices seem highly relevant for the communicative construction and negotiation of what is understood as Ravidassia religion – especially due to its proclamation amidst the information age and its global dimensions. Online discourses can illustrate how an actively engaging group of people attribute meaning to mediatized articulations of belonging online at certain moments of their life. However, it leaves us unaware of how those people attribute meaning to other contexts and how flows of media, ideas and meaning are transmitted through a variety of means of communication. Meanwhile, this perspective bears the risk of limiting the identification to preassigned categories such as *Ravidassia*. This is of specific relevance in research fields characterized by changing (religious) affiliations and close entanglements between multiple modes of identification. If analyzing media practices only related to the term *Ravidassia*, it would lead to a very restricted perspective on affiliations. Furthermore, the majority of followers of Guru Ravidass is still based in different regions in India. Considering the particularities of anti-caste mobilization and Internet access in India, it might only be a small number of people who actively participate in online debates. The way in which other people attribute meaning to this phenomenon may differ from perceptions articulated in such communicative spaces.

Applying an Ethnography-Based, Actor-Centered Mediatization Perspective

As the former sections have revealed, the Ravidassia context is characterized by complex entanglements concerning media ensembles, (religious) affiliations as well as the religious and other domains. Because of this complexity, it seems necessary to focus on what this actually means for peoples' lives and how they attribute meaning to this phenomenon; instead of understanding Ravidassia religion as a fixed entity with clearly defined borders (see also Radde-Antweiler 2017, 142 related to the field of religious studies in general). Drawing on media ethnographic research on Ravidassias in Germany and their mediated interpersonal communication, conducted in 2017, I seek to exemplify how actor-centered ethnographic methods can prevent research biases resulting from technocentric mediatization perspectives, which focus especially on online discourses.

The *Gurughar Frankfurt* is so far the only place of worship in Germany dedicated to Guru Ravidass. Interviews, conducted with members of this *Gurughar,* illustrate that singers achieving large numbers of clicks on YouTube are not necessarily the most relevant artists for Ravidassias in Germany. For example, Ginni Mahi is rather unknown in Germany, although Indian news coverage attributes a larger relevance and scope to Ginni Mahi's aforementioned success, coinciding with the number of clicks on YouTube. A large variety of communicative flows, the spatial mobility of members and singers, direct communication at physical places as well as personal preferences and networks need to be considered. Many members store CDs and DVDs of singers at home. If members travel to the Punjab region or other places, or if relatives are coming to Germany, they carry those commodities in their suitcases and distribute them at the *Gurughar* or to their relatives and friends. At the same time, the *Gurughar* frequently invites singers or religious leaders from Punjab to perform in Frankfurt. Some of those singers are a part of private social networks – as one interviewee mentioned (male member 2017, personal communication 11 October, Frankfurt). Compared to other artists, those singers were mentioned more often in discussions and within a related WhatsApp group. This group is of specific relevance, since members from other German regions are not able to be physically present very often. It serves as a mean for multidirectorial information and discussions about current activities, events and occurrences at the *Gurughar* as well as at other places in Europe and in India, for recording and exchanging religious recitations, sharing songs or iconography or videos. Members also use the group to share and comment on videos and pictures of performing singers and religious leaders in the *Gurughar.* In contrast, the related website and Facebook page are not used very actively which, once again, emphasizes the relevance of basing actor-centered mediatization perspectives on ethnographic methods.[10]

This example illustrates as well that media practices and meaning attribution related to the newly proclaimed religion are not placeless, although Ravidassias and media producers in the related mediascape are spread across the world. The ongoing establishment of new places of worship around the world as well as pilgrimage sites emphasizes the persisting relevance of physical places for processes of meaning making. Simultaneously, those places are closely interwoven with other communicative spaces.

In this context, it might be useful to understand communicative constructions related to Ravidassia religion as a *mediatized world,* a concept introduced by Krotz and Hepp (2011). They summarize their understanding of this concept as follows:

> Mediatized worlds are in our understanding mediatized, small life-worlds. As such, they are structured fragments of life-worlds with a certain binding intersubjective knowledge inventory, with specific

social practices and cultural thickenings. Mediatized worlds are the everyday concretization of media societies and media cultures. They are the level where mediatization gets concrete and by this can be analyzed empirically.

(Krotz and Hepp 2011, 146)

This conceptualization could make comprehensible how media practices are related to physical places and people's lives and which shifts of meaning attribution take place in various spatial contexts. Furthermore, it is beneficial when analyzing which forms of media and communication are exactly involved in and entangled with processes of meaning attribution and various forms of change. When analyzing mediatization of religion, the understanding of *mediatized worlds* as "fragments of life-worlds" is useful to illustrate that people's "life-worlds" are not only characterized by religious affiliations and practices. This understanding enables us to grasp intersections with other fragments of broader "life-worlds" and to comprehend segmentations within specific mediatized worlds (Krotz and Hepp 2011, 147).

Grasping those intersections seems of special importance in view of the variety of entanglements between different domains, transformation processes and forms of communication related to communicative constructions in the Ravidassia context, as illustrated throughout this chapter. Simultaneously, the following question arises: How should we comprehend those complexities and how can we bring an ethnography-based, actor-centered perspective together with overarching transformation processes?

Conclusion: Benefits of the Communicative Figuration Approach

I suggest utilizing the communicative figuration approach (e.g., Hasebrink and Hepp 2016, Hepp 2013) as an extension of the concept of mediatized worlds in order to combine different research levels and perspectives on mediatized religion. In the concluding chapter of this book, Radde-Antweiler discusses the broader relevance of this concept for studying mediatized religion. According to Hasebrink and Hepp (2016, 6–7), a multilevel analysis is essential to relate the level of individual practices to larger social domains instead of analyzing transformation processes and their interconnections either from a micro perspective or from a meta perspective. This approach is based on Elias' (1978) *figuration* concept, describing the social intertwining of actors "which constitute a larger social entity through reciprocal interaction" (Hepp 2013, 623). In the context of the emerging Ravidassia mediascape, this is of specific relevance considering close entanglements between different transformation processes, everyday practices of individuals and the emergence of material infrastructures – such as the emerging music industry, emerging television channels or the *Dera Sachkhand Ballan* as a central religious institution and important media producer.

Hepp defines, "communicative figurations as patterns of processes of communicative interweaving that exist across various media and have a 'thematic framing' that orients communicative action" (Hepp 2013, 623). The approach is aiming at making sense to mediatization from a transmedial perspective through examining "changing communicative figurations of mediatized worlds" (Hepp 2013, 623). To do so, Hasebrink and Hepp (2016, 7), and in a similar manner Hepp (2013, 623), identify three levels of analysis:

- First, the analysis of the specific *constellation of actors* as an assemblage of individuals and organizations which are communicatively interrelated and serve as the structural basis of communicative figurations.
- Second, determining *relevance frames* understood as action guiding and orienting topics, which enable us to comprehend communicative figurations in its entirety.
- Third, examining *communicative practices* which are interlaced with other social practices and related with a characteristic media ensemble.

Looking back at the multiple entanglements in the Ravidassia context, as illustrated above, the benefits arising from using a communicative figurations approach are as follows: Analyzing the *constellation of actors* allows us to explore the multidirectional interactions between various professional and nonprofessional individual and collective actors as well as larger institutionalized actors on a global level. It can therefore illustrate what Cheong (in this book) calls the multidirectional "micro-meso interplay" between those actors. The aforementioned global dimensions of multidirectional flows of media, people and economic resources related to Ravidassia religion and the emerging Ravidassia mediascape substantiate the need to conduct research across national borders.

Exploring *relevance frames* and communicative *practices* enables us to comprehend Ravidassia religion and the related mediascape through their communicative constructions and interactions instead of understanding them as fixed entities. This is important for developing a differentiated and comprehensive understanding of the aforementioned entanglements between different religious traditions and changing affiliations, between the religious, media and other domains, as well as between various action-orienting topics. Since interlacements with other social practices become visible, the entanglements between mediatization processes and socioreligious, political and economic changes and increased spatial mobility in the Ravidassia context can be analyzed in a more differentiated way. Simultaneously, this allows us to observe moments or contexts where mediatization might not be the determining process of change.

Through exploring characteristic *media ensembles* from the perspective of communicative practices, the communicative figurations approach meets the aforementioned particularities of mediatization processes in the Indian context. This perspective allows us to incorporate a wide range of media and communicative forms beyond the digital. It can equally be used to consider the significance of *mobile bodies* such as traveling singers, religious leaders or members, or gathering masses as transmitters of meaning. Additionally, this focus, along with the analysis of *actor constellations*, facilitates the consideration of interactions between a wide range of media flows, taking into account blurring boundaries between media producers and consumers.

While the multiple interdependencies under these conditions seem to be specific at first glance, a communicative figurational approach might be equally useful for various contexts. Focusing on communicative practices, media ensembles, characteristic actors and frames of relevance in place of specific digital media and predetermined research subjects, it is context-sensitive, open toward manifold communicative forms and combines micro levels of research with broader meso and meta levels for a comprehensive analysis of transformation processes.

Notes

1 Since the 19th century, long-term administrative, political and social changes have facilitated the emergence of anti-caste movements in different parts of India, questioning the legitimacy of Hindu social stratifications and discrimination based on specific caste backgrounds. New education and employment opportunities, provided by the colonial administration and other actors, such as the Hindu reform organization *Arya Samaj*, partially reinforced the agency and economic independence of a few among those who experienced caste-based discrimination and exclusions (e.g., Zelliot 2001 [1992], 34–36, 96).

2 In the context of this chapter, *untouchability* is understood as the practice of discriminating or excluding certain hereditary groups on the basis of their assumed impurity related to specific traditional occupational fields, mainly by dominant social or socio-religious groups in society. Historically, this stigma caused, for example, dress and behavior regulations, exclusions from educational institutions, pilgrimage sites or temples (e.g., Zelliot 2001 [1992], 38–39). While caste-based discrimination is forbidden by law, certain forms of discrimination, exclusion and violence still persist. Associated castes or sub-castes neither constitute a homogenous group with clearly defined borders nor are caste structures based on a unified system (cf. Jodhka 2014, 584–585; Koschorreck [now Kirchhof] 2014, 202–205). Regional differences of caste structures and related power structures must be taken into consideration as well. This applies especially to the Indian Punjab region

where nowadays Sikhism is the predominant religion (for deeper insights, see Jodhka 2014). Since the ascription 'untouchable' is highly offensive, I avoid the term.

3 The term *Dalit* seems to have become the most widely used category to describe persons associated with the stigma of *untouchability* (cf. Guru 2004, 257). The literal meaning of the Hindi and Marathi word Dalit is *ground*, but it is often translated in the context of anti-caste movements as *oppressed* or *downtrodden*. Since the 1970s or 1980s, the term *Dalit* has been used as a *self-chosen* term to counter denigrating labels such as *untouchable*, and has become a commonly used term in academia, the news, and the NGO sector (Michael 2007, 16). However, the term is deeply entangled with identity politics and therefore seems to be a powerful, discursive construct (cf. Guru 2004, 256). Despite the widespread use of the term *Dalit* and its continuing relevance for specific contexts, I avoid the term as an overarching category for all persons associated with the stigma of *untouchability*, since not all of my interviewees identify with the term.

4 The framework or concept of *network society* is based on the hypothesis that media would increasingly become the space where power is negotiated and that it would enable new actors to challenge old, especially institutionalized, power structures. Castells' assumption that the development of interactive, horizontal communication networks, the emergence of the information age led to new ways of structuring societies is fundamental for the understanding of this hypothesis. According to him, the *network society* is characterized by a new form of communication which is characterized by multi-directional ways of communication from many to many. In contrast to one-way forms of mass communication, he employs the term mass self-communication. Crucial for this chapter is Castells' argument that this type of communication would enhance the opportunities of social movements to intervene in communicative spaces of society, since they would provide a decisive organizational structure and new platforms for public debate (Castells 2007, 238, 249–250).

5 In 2013, I conducted qualitative interviews with persons involved in the production of so-called *Dalit media*, especially in the production of small newspapers and journals in Delhi and in the Indian state of Rajasthan.

6 *Kīrtans* or *bhajans* are performances in which spiritual ideas, here especially sacred *śabads* (hymns), are recited through devotional singing. Singers are often accompanied by traditional instruments.

7 Examples are the England-based 24-hour satellite channel *Kanshi TV* (Kanshi TV 2014) and related *Kanshi Radio* (Kanshi Radio 2017), the Punjab-based channel *Kranti TV* (Kranti TV 2017), and the trilingual Punjabi-Hindi-English newspaper *Begumpura Shaher* (Begumpura Shaher 2017) as a mouthpiece of the aforementioned religious organization *Dera Sachkhand Ballan*. The *Facebook* site with the highest number of subscribers (more than 100,000) is *GuruRavidassGuruJi.com* (GuruRavidassGuruJi.com 2017). For deeper insights in some examples of recently published literature, see Judge (2014).

8 There exists at least one non-scholarly magazine article (Dogra 2011) illustrating some interrelationships between the related emerging music genre of so called *Chamar pop*, t-shirt prints and car-stickers in the context of identity assertion in Punjab. This article provides an important basis for the illustrations in this chapter. In an earlier publication, I already provided a brief overview of the emerging mediascape and its means of communication (Koschorreck [now Kirchhof] 2014), but the mediascape was not the focus of the research.

9 *Bahujan Samaj Party* means literally the party of the majority community, based on the perception that ruling dominant groups in society constitute only a minority in numbers.
10 These findings are based on conversations with members of the Gurughar Guru Ravidass Ji Frankfurt (Germany) as well as on participatory observation between September and October 2017 and further content analysis of related mobile communication between October 2017 and February 2018.

References

Amar Audio, 2014. *New Punjabi Song 2014 | Putt Ravidass Guru De | Kanth Kaler | Full HD Latest Punjabi Songs 2014.* [video] Available at www.youtube.com/watch?v=gCeztNEzGks, accessed 17 November 2017.

Amar Audio, 2017. *New Punjabi Shabad 2016 || FAN BABA SAHIB DI || GINNI MAHI || Guru Ravidas Ji Shabad 2016.* [video] Available at www.youtube.com/watch?v=H5XzHJBNyoI, accessed 17 November 2017.

Amar Audio Official, 2016. *New Punjabi Songs 2016 || DANGER 2 || GINNI MAHI || Punjabi Songs 2016.* [video] Available at www.youtube.com/watch?v=Gc4wh3YczJw, accessed 12 December 2017.

Anand, S., 2005. Covering Caste: Visible Dalit, Invisible Brahmin. In: Rajan, N., ed. *Practising Journalism: Values, Constraints, Implications.* New Delhi, Thousand Oaks, and London: SAGE Publications Inc., 172–197.

Begumpura Shaher, 2017. *Home.* Available at http://begumpurashaher.net/, accessed 12 December 2017.

Bindas Dance and Fun, 2017. *me chhora chamar ka by ajay|| mansoor pur||.* [video] Available at www.youtube.com/watch?v=om3G09PoQao, accessed 12 December 2017.

Castells, M., 2007. Communication, Power and Counter-power in the Network Society. *International Journal of Communication*, 1, 238–266.

Dalit Camera, 2017. *Ginni Mahi Interview.* [video] Available at www.youtube.com/watch?v=VSbbP72ZDK8, accessed 19 November 2017.

Dirks, N. B., 2001. *Castes of Mind: Colonialism and the Making of Modern India.* Princeton: Princeton University Press.

Dogra, C. S., 2011. The First Law: Sing My Name: Chamars Assert their Identity through Songs, T-shirt Slogans, Upward Mobility. *Outlook India*, 11 July. Available at www.outlookindia.com/magazine/story/the-first-law-sing-my-name/277445, accessed 12 December 2017.

EKJOT Films, 2017. *Dr. Bheem Da Mission | RAJNI THAKKARWAL | FULL HD SONG | Guru Ravidass Ji Shabad | Latest Song 2017.* [video] Available at www.youtube.com/watch?v=1IbTOXJrQQA, accessed 12 December 2017.

Elias, N., 1978. *What is Sociology?* London: Hutchinson.

Guru, G., 2004. The Language of Dalitbahujan Political Discourse. In: Mohanty, M., ed. *Class, Caste, Gender: Readings in Indian Politics: Readings in Indian Politics.* New Delhi: SAGE Publications India Pvt Ltd, 256–267.

GuruRavidassGuruJi.com, 2017. *Home* [Facebook group]. Available at facebook.com/GuruRavidassGuruJi/, accessed 12 December 2017.

Hasebrink, U. and Hepp, A., 2016. *How to Research Cross-media Practices? Investigating Media Repertoires and Media Ensembles.* Universität Bremen. Available at www.kommunikative-figurationen.de/fileadmin/redak_kofi/Arbeitspapiere/CoFi_EWP_No-15_Hasebrink_Hepp.pdf, accessed 12 December 2017.

Hepp, A., 2013. The Communicative Figurations of Mediatized Worlds: Mediatization Research in Times of the 'Mediation of Everything'. *European Journal of Communication*, 28(6), 615–629.

Hepp, A. and Krotz, F., eds., 2014. *Mediatized Worlds: Culture and Society in a Media Age.* Basingstoke: Palgrave Macmillan.

IAMAI and KANTAR IMRB, 2017. *Internet in India – 2016.* Available at http://bestmediainfo.com/wp-content/uploads/2017/03/Internet-in-India-2016.pdf, accessed 12 December 2017.

Jeffrey, R., 2000. *India's Newspaper Revolution: Capitalism, Politics and the Indian-language Press, 1977–99.* London: Hurst.

Jeffrey, R., 2001. [NOT] Being There: Dalits and India's Newspapers. *South Asia: Journal of South Asian Studies*, 24(2), 225–238.

Jeffrey, R. and Doron, A., 2013. *Cell Phone Nation: How Mobile Phones Have Revolutionized Business, Politics and Ordinary Life in India.* Gurgaon: Hachette Book Publishing India Pvt Ltd.

Jodhka, S. S., 2009. The Ravi Dasis of Panjab: Global Contours of Caste and Religious Strife. *Economic and Political Weekly*, 44(24), 79–85.

Jodhka, S. S., 2014. Changing Manifestations of Caste in the Sikh Panth. In: Singh, P. and Fenech, L. E., eds. *The Oxford Handbook of Sikh Studies.* Oxford: Oxford University Press, 583–593.

Jodhka, S. S., 2016. From Zaat to Qaum: Fluid Contours of the Ravi Dasi Identity in Punjab. In: Rawat, R. S. and Satyanarayana, K., eds. *Dalit Studies.* Durham und London: Duke University Press, 248–269.

Judge, P. S., 2014. Existence, Identity and Beyond: Tracing the Contours of Dalit Literature in Punjabi. *Economic and Political Weekly*, 49(29), 209–216.

Judge, P. S., 2015. Dalit Culture and Identity: Valorisation and Reconstruction of Tradition among the Chamars in Punjab. *Economic and Political Weekly*, 50(34), 53–60.

Juergensmeyer, M., 1982. *Religion As Social Vision: The Movement against Untouchability in 20th-Century Punjab.* Berkeley: University of California Press.

Kanhyalal Singh, 2017. *Danger chamar.* [video] Available at www.youtube.com/watch?v=yiP0AiuJIA0, accessed 12 December 2017.

Kanshi Radio, 2017. *Home.* Available at http://kanshiradio.com/, accessed 12 December 2017.

Kanshi TV, 2014. *Home.* Available at www.kanshitv.co.uk/, accessed 12 December 2017.

Kanshi TV, 2017. Videos. [YouTube channel] Available at www.youtube.com/user/rajbangar/videos, accessed 12 December 2017.

Kohli, N., 2016. Punjab's Protest Pop: How the Dalits are Telling the World They've Arrived. *Hindustan Times*, 3 November. Available at www.hindustantimes.com/india-news/punjab-s-protest-pop-how-the-state-s-dalits-are-telling-the-world-they-have-arrived/story-8UxGda8YwWcf0PDT6dc1RJ.html, accessed 12 December 2017.

Koschorreck [now Kirchhof], D. F., 2014. Ravidassia – Weder Sikh noch Hindu? Aushandlung und Festigung von Identität innerhalb einer global vernetzten (religiösen) Gemeinschaft. *Südasien-Chronik/South Asia Chronicle*, 4, 200–227.

Kranti TV, 2017. *Home*. Available at http://krantitv.com/, accessed 12 December 2017.

Krotz, F., 2007. *Mediatisierung: Fallstudien zum Wandel von Kommunikation*. Wiesbaden: VS Verl. für Sozialwiss.

Krotz, F. and Hepp, A., 2011. A Concretization of Mediatization: How 'Mediatization Works' and Why Mediatized Worlds are a Helpful Concept for Empirical Mediatization Research. *Empedocles: European Journal for the Philosophy of Communication*, 3(2), 137–152.

Lövheim, M., 2011. Mediatisation of Religion: A Critical Appraisal. *Culture and Religion*, 12(2), 153–166.

Loynd, M., 2008. Politics without Television: The BSP and the Dalit Counter-public Sphere. In: Mehta, N., ed. *Television in India: Satellites, Politics, and Cultural Change*. London: Routledge, 62–86.

Lum, K., 2014. Manufacturing Self-Respect: Stigma, Pride and Cultural Juggling among Dalit Youth in Spain. In: Toğuşlu, E., Leman, J. and Sezgin, İ. M., eds. *New Multicultural Identities in Europe: Religion and Ethnicity in Secular Societies*. Ithaca: Cornell University Press, 95–118.

Meyer, B. and Moors, A., eds., 2006. *Religion, Media, and the Public Sphere*. Bloomington: Indiana University Press.

Michael, S. M., 2007. Introduction. In: Michael, S. M. and Fitzgerald, T., eds. *Dalits in Modern India: Vision and Values*. 2nd ed. Los Angeles: SAGE Publications, 13–47.

Narayan, B., 2006. *Women Heroes and Dalit Assertion in North India: Culture, Identity, and Politics*. New Delhi: Sage.

Nayar, P. K., 2011. The Digital Dalit: Subalternity and Cyberspace. *Sri Lanka Journal of Humanities*, 37(1–2), 69–74.

Radde-Antweiler, K., 2017. Digital Religion? Media Studies from a Religious-Studies Perspective. In: Nord, I. and Zipernovszky, H., eds. *Religious Education in a Mediatized World*. Stuttgart: Kohlhammer Verlag, 138–150.

Ram, R., 2016. Religion, Identity and Empowerment: The Making of Ravidassia Dharm (Dalit Religion) in Contemporary Punjab. In: Jacobsen, K. A., ed. *Routledge Handbook of Contemporary India*. London: Routledge, 371–383.

Ram, R., 2017. The Genealogy of a Dalit Faith. *Contributions to Indian Sociology*, 51(1), 52–78. Available at http://journals.sagepub.com/doi/pdf/10.1177/0069966716677411, accessed 2 March 2017.

Schneider, N.-C., 2005. *Zur Darstellung von "Kultur" und "kultureller Differenz" im indischen Mediensystem: Die indische Presse und die Repräsentation des Islams im Rahmen der Zivilrechtsdebatte, 1985–87 und 2003*. Berlin: Logos-Verlag.

Schneider, N.-C., 2011. Media Research beyond Bollywood: Some Thoughts on a Systematic Media Perspective in India-related Research. *Internationales Asienforum / International Quarterly for Asian Studies*, 42(3–4), 223–238.

Singh, G., 2013. Religious Transnationalism, Development and the Construction of Religious Boundaries: The Case of the Dera Sachkhand Ballan and the Ravidass Dharm. *Global Network*, 13(2), 183–199.

Takhar, O. K., 2014. The Place of Scripture in the Trajectories of a Distinct Religious Identity among Ravidassias in Britain: Guru Granth Sahib or Amritbani Guru Ravidass. *Journal of Contemporary Religion*, 29(1), 105–120.

Telecom Regulatory Authority of India, 2017. *Highlights of Telecom Subscription Data as on 30th April, 2017*. [press release] 13 June. Available at www.trai.gov.in/sites/default/files/PR_No_43_Eng_13_06_2017.pdf, accessed 12 December 2017.

Thirumal, P. and Tartakov, G. M., 2011. India's Dalits Search for a Democratic Opening in the Digital Divide. In: Leigh, P. R., ed. *International Exploration of Technology Equity and the Digital Divide: Critical, Historical and Social Perspectives: Critical, Historical and Social Perspectives*. Hershey: IGI Global, 20–39.

Zaslavsky, F., 2016. Quels médias pour se ré-approprier une voix? L'investissement d'internet par le mouvement dalit. *Observatorio (OBS*)*, 10 (Special Issue 'Media, Internet and Social Movements in the Context of Asymmetries'), 97–115.

Zelliot, E., 2001 [1992]. *From Untouchable to Dalit: Essays on the Ambedkar Movement: Essays on the Ambedkar Movement*. 3rd ed. New Delhi: Manohar Publishers and Distributors.

9 Digitalizing Tibet

A Critical Buddhist Reconditioning of Hjarvard's Mediatization Theory

Gregory Price Grieve, Christopher Helland and Rohit Singh

Na svato nāpi parato na dvābhyāṃ nāpy ahetutaḥ
utpannā jātu vidyante bhāvāḥ kvacana kecana.[1]

On 7 July 2014, on day two of the Preliminary Teachings of the 33rd Kalachakra, we observed his Holiness the Dalai Lama read from the 2nd century Indian Buddhist philosopher, Nāgārjuna's *Precious Garland* (*Ratnāvalī*) and *Letter to a Friend* (*Suhṛllekha*). We were participating in the 33rd Kalachakra ceremony, which was an esoteric Tantric empowerment centered on the *Kālachakra Tantra,* held in Leh, Ladakh, India, between 3 and 14 July 2014, and led by the 14th Dalai Lama, Tenzin Gyatso. The immediacy of the Dalai Lama's charisma was palpable. Ironically, however, what drew us three to this remote Himalayan location was that the ceremony was being digitalized – tweeted, blogged, Facebooked and video-streamed over cyberspace and across the globe (Figure 9.1). Moreover, we found that the digitalization of the Kalachakra, and the Dalai Lama's charisma, were not an afterthought, but had been calculated in advance and had been incorporated into the ceremony's discussions, community building and symbolism. For example, as the teachings began that day, the Dalia Lama thanked "those who are here physically, and those who are not."[2]

Because of the assumption that Buddhism concentrates on a mindful awareness of the body, digitalization might seem antithetical to authentic practice (Grieve 2017). As the oldest proselytizing religion, however, Buddhism has always had a penchant for utilizing the latest developments (Grieve and Veidlinger 2016). One might assume, *mutatis mutandis,* that the 2014 ceremony was merely transmitting the same old analogue *dharma* in new digitized bottles. Does not all communication, even the spoken word, rely on physical vehicles that extend communication practices (cf. Grieve 2006, Krotz and Hepp 2011, 143, Sorokin 1947, 51–52)? History shows, however, that the Buddhist use of different media technologies is not a neutral transmission of content, but

Figure 9.1 Geshe Lobzang Samstan reviewing live broadcast at the HHDL media center in Leh, Ladak (photograph by Christopher Helland, July 2014).

conditions how the teachings (*dharma*) are communicated (Grieve 2017, Grieve and Veidlinger 2016, Veidlinger 2006). For example, *dharma* screened on a television would not be received the same as read in a book, which in turn would not be the same as played in a video game (Campbell and Grieve 2014, 1–21, Grieve 2017). This is not simply the assertion that active media determine and penetrate passive religious messages (Goody 1986, Havelock 1986, cf. Innis 1951, McLuhan 1964, Ong 1967, Postman 1985). We found that the Kalachakra and digital technologies mutually conditioned one another (Campbell 2010, Grieve 2006, Hoover 2006).

In this chapter, to analyze the mutual conditioning of the Kalachakra and digital media technologies, we theorize the distinction between *digitization* and *digitalization*. What does the small grammatical difference of the *al* add to our analysis (Derrida 1988)? As opposed to analogue media, such as films and newspapers, which use a physical or chemical property to communicate, *digital media* consist of electronic, programmable bits (Grieve 2017, 217). Digitization refers to creating a digital copy of a physical phenomenon or an analogue object. For example, one can click on *www.dalailama.com/teachings/kalachakra-initiations* and see a digital image of the Dalai Lama.[3] Digitalization, on the other hand, is not the mere translation of the analogue into the digital but is furthermore the conditioning of social structures and practices through the process of being digitized. Usually, digitalization is used to describe the disruption to economies by digital media (McChesney 2013, Weinelt 2016). We extend the term to also refer to other social fields, particularly religion. For example, in the 2014 ceremony, the placing of colored grains of sand by the Dalai Lama to begin the construction of the Kalachakra's *maṇḍala* was scripted to allow for its video-streaming to a global audience.[4]

This chapter chronicles our first steps toward creating a theory to describe, analyze and understand Tibet's digitalization. To begin the process we undertake a critical reconditioning of the work of the Danish scholar, Hjarvard (2011), who describes mediatization as a long-term process by which media transform society and culture. We maintain that Hjarvard's overemphasis on secularization occurs because of his reliance on a Protestant understanding of religion as a more or less reliable communication with the supernatural. Our chapter is not a rejection of Hjarvard's theory, per se, but rather a Buddhist reconditioning (cf. Dissanayake 2009b, 453).

A critical Buddhist reconditioning of Hjarvard's theory of the mediatization of religion is significant for two reasons. First, it affords the tools to understand the digitalization of the Dalai Lama's charisma, and thereby to understand the Tibetan diaspora's contemporary multimedia, multifaceted, and multi-situational virtual conditions. Despite *geographical* Tibet being subsumed under the Chinese State, these conditions have allowed the Tibetan government in exile, official religious organizations, and politically and religiously motivated individuals to imagine a nation. Second, a Buddhist reconditioning expands Hjarvard's theory beyond the Procrustean bed of its Protestant normative framework and affords a theory of mediatization for analyzing Asian religions.[5] Reconditioning Hjarvard's theory illustrates how scholars' own religious backgrounds shape research not only by affording particular content and symbolic forms, but also by privileging particular types of theorization (Grieve 2006, 11–13). Being aware of the second order categories through which we interpret religious phenomena allows researchers to be conscious not only of how society and culture shape religion but also of how religious media contribute to social change. Furthermore, it addresses how local theories of religion and media affect the understanding of the category of religion itself.

The Kalachakra's Digitized Mediascape

A Tibetan Buddhist (*Vajrayāna*) ceremony, the word Kalachakra means cycles of time, and involves practices of purification, teachings and Tantric empowerment. During the 33rd Kalachakra, the Dalai Lama spoke in person to an estimated 150,000 participants consisting of local Ladakhis, Tibetan refugees, Indian nationals and international spectators. The 2014 ceremony was also digitalized and disseminated across the globe. Since 1954, either in India or abroad, the Dalai Lama has conducted the Kalachakra teaching, usually every year or every other year, with the 2014 ceremony in Ladakh being his 33rd initiation.[6] The event in 2014 lasted 12 days, commencing on 3 July and concluding on 14 July, and consisted of three main components: ritual performances by monks, public teachings and the Dalai Lama initiating disciples into the Tantric traditions. Monks performed numerous rituals associated with Kalachakra including the earth-offering dance, the construction of a sand *maṇḍala*, apotropaic rites to ward off evil spirits, the production of talismans and offerings to deities associated with the Tantra.[7] The initiated disciples gained authorization from the Dalai Lama to practice and study the rituals and traditions of the *Kālachakra Tantra*, specifically under the guidance of gurus within the Kalachakra lineage. In 2014, between the Tantric ritual ceremonies, the Dalai Lama also gave a series of teachings on Buddhist philosophy, aimed at the global audience, that emphasized Buddhism as a universal *mind science* (a term used in English) (Singh 2016).

Time is a key aspect of the ceremony. The *Kālachakra* centers on a deity and *maṇḍala* that are replete with temporal significance and present a cosmology based on three connected temporal frameworks: inner cycles of time, outer cycles of time and the alternate cycles of time (Singh 2016). The inner cycle refers to internal states of the body including energy points (*chakras*) and channels. The outer cycles of time are associated with the movement of astrological entities like the sun, moon and stars. The alternate cycles of time are associated with Tantric meditations aimed at enabling practitioners to obtain enlightenment. These three cycles are unified within the cosmic body of the tutelary deity (*yidam*) of Kalachakra.[8] During the Kalachakra initiation, the consecrated grounds for the empowerment ceremony are ritually generated as the universe or *maṇḍala* of Kalachakra. The audience present become enveloped into the deity's sacred space. In the course of the rituals, the Dalai Lama, as Vajra Guru, assumes the identity of Kalachakra at the *maṇḍala*'s center. The ceremony concludes after he invites disciples to become symbolically reborn into the Kālachakra *maṇḍala* through a series of seven initiations, after which the Dalai Lama authorizes the initiates to practice traditions connected with the *Kālachakra Tantra*, such as the six-session Guru Yoga, and as well as the generation and completion stage rituals.

Besides offering a fascinating mythological drama, what drew us to the ceremony was that it took place not only in physical and mythical locations, but also in a digitalized mediascape, a term that describes the virtual environments created by digitized global media flows (Appadurai 1990, Helland 2016, cf. Baudrillard 1995).[9] Although Ladakh is a remote and isolated community in the Himalaya Mountains, network connectivity with the event was prioritized by the Indian

Government and an enormous effort was made to allow the live web streaming of the ritual. A dedicated team of people working for the *Office of His Holiness the Dalai Lama* ensured that the ritual practices were beautifully presented online for anyone to witness. This included the several rituals associated with preparing the site, the preliminary teachings, empowerments and a special camera above the Kalachakra sand *maṇḍala* so people could see its construction and development as the ritual progressed. By allowing for this form of intimate connection to occur through the Internet, new media allowed new observers to participate in fundamentally new ways.

Because Tibet's mediascape no longer merely augments actual geographic locations and physical events, and is not limited to synchronous time, but holds together and maintains (*dhṛ*) a global community (*sangha*) of practitioners, it can neither be understood through the categories of center and periphery, nor referent and represented (Appadurai 1990, de Saussure 1916). Yet, as we argue below, this is not merely the transmission of content, but the conditioning of distinct practices. For example, on that same day, a deeply devoted practitioner from the USA rested in a hotel room in Leh, located about eight kilometers from the teaching site. She had been lying in bed, exhausted, watching the Dalai Lama's teachings live on her computer. She held her prayer beads and a book of teachings on Nāgārjuna's texts that had been handed out during the first day of teachings. At the same time, she was online and supplementing the live teachings with additional materials, looking up terms and concepts and even posting information to her friends. That afternoon she told us that she was deeply grateful for the live webcasting of the teachings and that her exhaustion had not caused her to miss any of the day's important events. When we asked her if she felt part of the ceremony, she answered with no hesitation: "Oh yes, I was definitely there with you" (personal communication).

Hjarvard's Theory of the Mediatization of Religion

In order to analyze the Kalachakra's digitalization, our chapter aims to recondition Hjarvard's theory of the mediatization. Our first step is to describe it straightforwardly in this section, and critically recondition it in the following section. At its core, mediatization argues that media plays a part in the shaping of society and analyzes the long-term effects that media have on human life worlds (Hjarvard 2014, Krotz 2009, 2014, 137–139, Krotz and Hepp 2011, Lundby 2014, 7, Martín-Barbero 2003, 88, Schulz 2004). The driving purpose of Hjarvard's particular theory of mediatization, however, is to describe and analyze the role that religion and media play in what he calls high-modern societies – *the current globalized, highly mediated, and neoliberal consumeristic world* (passim. Hjarvard 2008a, 2011, 124).

Hjarvard's theory of the mediatization of religion can be analyzed through two propositions and three outcomes. He builds his theory of mediatization of religion upon an analytic and a synthetic proposition. The analytic proposition is the distinction he makes between the merely descriptive term *mediation* and the transformative *mediatization* (Couldry and Hepp 2013, 191, Livingston 2009, 6–7). As a theory, the descriptive term mediation analyzes how different types of media influence the content of their message. As Hjarvard writes, "mediation refers to the act of mediation via a medium, the intervention of which can affect both the message and the relationship between sender and receiver" (2011, 123). For example, in politics, mediation describes when a Tweet's 140-character limit changes the message that politicians deliver. For Hjarvard, mediatization is analytically different because it evaluates the transformative effect that media have on society and culture, and how media colonize other institutions. As Hjarvard writes:

> While the study of mediation pays attention to specific instances of communication situated in time and space (e.g., the communication of politics in blogs during a presidential campaign), mediatization studies are concerned with the *long-term* structural change in the role of the media in culture and society.
>
> (2013, 2–3 [italics in original])

These transformations allow media to dominate other social fields. As he writes: "mediatization denotes the social and cultural process through which a field or institution to some extent becomes dependent on the logic of the media" (2011, 119; cf. Hjarvard 2008b). In this case, Twitter and other social media become a "part of the very fabric" of life, not just on an individual political message, but on the field of politics more generally (Ess 1996, 9).

While analytic propositions point to a theory's internal logic, synthetic propositions refer to how the theory interprets the world. Hjarvard's synthetic proposition is that media and religion are similar because they play a part in constructing the reality of lived social worlds. This synthetic framework reflects early theories concerning the social construction of reality of the sociologist of religion Peter Berger (1967, 3–28; cf. Lövheim 2011, Schulz 2004). Citing Berger, Hjarvard maintains that "'religion has been the historically most widespread and effective instrumentality of legitimation' of socially defined reality'" (citing Berger 1967, 32, Hjarvard 2011, 130). Relying primarily on European survey data, Hjarvard posits that media, like a secular canopy, has taken over this role as a modern commercial version of the traditional religious world-constructing "sacred canopy" (cf. Berger 1967, Couldry and Hepp 2013, Lövheim 2011, 155–156).

From his analytic and synthetic propositions, Hjarvard delivers three outcomes, the first of which is disciplinary. He maintains that media theory about religion has been dominated by two major paradigms. On the one hand are those *effect-paradigm* frameworks concerned with how people are affected by exposure to various media, while on the other, the *audience centered* framework explores how people make use of media for their own purposes (passim. Hjarvard 2011, 121, 2013, 2, cf. Jenkins 1992, Preiss et al. 2007). Skeptical of these approaches, Hjarvard posits mediatization as a third approach, which stresses the interaction and transaction of actors and structures. "According to mediatization theory, media are not outside society, but part of its very social fabric" (2011, 121, cf. 2013, 3). As such, "mediatization studies move the focus of interest from the particular instances of mediated communication to the structural transformations of the media in contemporary society" (2013, 2).

Hjarvard's second outcome is that mediatization leads to secularization by colonizing many of the cultural and social functions that organized religious institutions traditionally held. Citing Berger, Hjarvard defines secularization as "the process by which sectors of society are removed from the domination of religious institutions and symbols" (citing Berger 1967, 107, Hjarvard 2011, 130). Hjarvard maintains that in high-modern societies media are an all-embracing force (Hjarvard 2008b, Lövheim 2011). Yet, the problem is not less religious content in the media (cf. Lash 2005). As Hjarvard writes, "with the help of the most sophisticated media technology, supernatural phenomena have acquired an unmatched presence in modern societies" (Hjarvard 2013, 78). Rather than less content, secularization occurs because "a series of structural transformations of religion in the modern world, including a decline in the authority of religious institutions in society, together with the development of more individualized forms of religious beliefs and practices" (2013, 79). Hjarvard knowingly sidesteps Berger's later work in which the American sociologist denounces his earlier secularization thesis (cf. Berger 1999, 2, Hjarvard 2011, 130). Hjarvard supports Berger's original secularization hypothesis by arguing that "increased public visibility is not to be equated with a growing support for religion, or involvement in religion" and that "secularization is still an important component of the modernization process of contemporary societies in Western Europe, USA and elsewhere" (2011, 131).

Hjarvard argues that secularization leads to an increase of what he terms *banal religion* – that process by which religious practices become loosed from the authority of organized religion, and become more and more individualized and subjective because they are guided by the logic of a commercialized media. "Banal religion is banal in the sense," Hjarvard maintains, that it is unnoticeable and does not constitute a highly structured proposition about the metaphysical order or the meaning of life, and it is religion in the sense that it evokes cognitions, emotions or actions that imply the existence of supernatural agency.

(2011, 128)

Hjarvard argues that banalization occurs because "media may not only provide information about religion but also create narratives and virtual worlds that invite people to have experiences of a religious-like character ... and community-building among people with similar religious orientation" (2011, 126). For Hjarvard, banalization occurs in a three-step process. First, he argues that data shows that banal religions serve media logics and not religious logics. As Hjarvard writes, popular culture's "religious representations serve the particular media genre in question and the religious meanings are not to be taken too literally" (2011, 129). Second, Hjarvard maintains that because they are not meant to be taken literally, banal religions are inauthentic. As he writes, "despite their pervasiveness and very explicit nature, the religious representations do not constitute a coherent religious narrative, nor are we, as an audience, to take them seriously as real religious symbols, practices or meanings" (2011, 129). Third, banal religious practices are anomic because, they "challenge the authority of existing religious institutions by disembedding specific religious meanings from their original context and rearticulating them in new ways" (2011, 129).

A Necessary Provincializing of Hjarvard's Mediatization Theory

Like a lens that focuses on a particular phenomenon, social scientific *theories* are second-order semiotic, analytic, synthetic frameworks that abstract, organize and interpret lived worlds in order to rationally explain, understand and predict types of human behavior (Morton 1980). At its core, Hjarvard's theory seems straightforward. "Our inquiry takes its point of departure in the classical question in the sociology of the media, namely, how the media come to influence the wider culture and society" (Hjarvard 2013, 1). This would seem to be the perfect tool to understand the digitalization of the Kalachakra. Theories, however, are not free-floating principles that exist untethered to the problems of human lifeworlds (Davidson Reynolds 1971). Theories of religion, no less than the religious phenomena they are theorizing, are bound by, entangled with and constituted by their historic-geographic location (Grieve 2006).

Hjarvard's theory is limited for understanding Asian religion because it was fabricated in, and built to analyze, as Hjarvard himself writes, the "historical developments in the north-western part of Europe" (2013, 27).

He understands the mediatization of religion, both as phenomenon and sociological theory, as stemming from and defining of modern Northern European society (2013, 5–7, cf. Thompson 1995). As Hjarvard writes, "the theoretical framework and analytic outline presented (...) may be more suitable to describe developments in north-western Europe than elsewhere in the world" (2013, 80).

Hjarvard maintains that "media are not a unitary phenomenon" and he argues that "the mediatization of religion may take different forms and generate different outcome in, for example, the USA, Brazil, or India, depending on religious, social and media context" (2013, 81, cf. Hoover 2006). Hjarvard is pushing in two directions. Mostly he wants to differentiate the Nordic experience from that which appears in North America (2013, 81). Hjarvard, however, also sees the Western experience as unique, and implies that if mediatization appears in the developing world, it is a product of European culture being exported through globalization (2013, 18).

Because of its unabashed eurocentrism, to be useful for analyzing Tibetan *Dharma*, and Asian religion more generally, Hjarvard's theory requires *provincialization*, a term which recognizes the limitations of using Western social sciences to explain and understand modern Asia (Chakrabarty 2000, cf. Eliade 1961). Provincialization, however, does not reject European thought out of hand, but rather reconditions it, as the anthropologist Chakrabarty, writes "from and for the margins" (2000, 16). Provincialization is not antithetical to Hjarvard's understanding of mediatization as a "meso-theory" (2013, 3–5). His "ambition is not to build a 'grand theory' in order to establish universal definition" (2013, 3, Hjarvard 2011, 124, cf. Krotz and Hepp 2011, 137–138). As he writes: "By considering mediatization theory as a middle-range theory, we have sought to avoid the pitfalls of both the grand claims typical of macro-level theorizing and the celebration of heterogeneity typical of certain micro-level analysis" (2013, 153). Hjarvard is skeptical about making broad meta-theories, because he is conscious that media's influence on religion will differ depending on historical and geographic location. "For instance," he writes, "mediatization may imply something rather different if we compare the use of media by Pentecostal movements in India" (2011, 120).

Hjarvard's theory, even for its stated awareness of its own limited nature, needs provincializing because it naturalizes a Protestant framework, which occurs because of the dominance of European survey data in his case studies, but also because of a *crypto-Protestantism* that informs and has shaped social thought since the late 19th century (Engelke 2012, Grieve 2006). Hjarvard defines religion as the "human ability to ascribe intentional agency to unexplainable occurrences, to make anthropological projections into a metaphysical world" (2011, 129). His substantive definition implies a *transmission theory of communication* that of content being transmitted more or less reliably through different media (Shannon 1948, Shannon and Weaver 1949). The substantive definition forces him to make a distinction between banal and institutional religion, between the small folk practices of a "common religion" and the greater institutionalized orders of "official religion" (Hjarvard 2011, 129–130). He defines banal religion as "the beliefs and practices held by ordinary people," and institutionalized religion as that which reflects "official religious texts and practices advanced by the priesthood" (2011, 130).

Because his theory necessitates a *church*, Hjarvard's institutional understanding of media needs to be provincialized as well. True, he poses his theory as pure social science. "Mediatization is, in our understanding, a *non-normative* concept" (2013, 18 [italics in original]). In the end, however, his use of mediatized religion is not a neutral sociological category. It is normative, because, as Hjarvard writes, "media are not in the business to preach" and "media's representation of religion does not originate from the institutionalized religion or have close resemblance with religious texts" (2011, 126, 132, cf. 120–121, cf. Grieve 2017, 79–87, Hjarvard 2013, 9–10). Hjarvard wants to understand media's effect on *institutions*, which he describes as social fields which organize "a number of very central aspects of life," and allocate both material resources and authority (2013: 21, 22, 43–44). This concentration on *church* reflects the strong role that organized institutions, such as the National (Peoples') Church of Denmark (Den Danske Folkekirke), have played in Nordic countries. One can also see the role Emile Durkheim has had in Hjarvard's sociological understanding of religion. As Durkheim writes, "the idea of religion is inseparable from the idea of a church, it conveys the notion that religion must be an eminently collective thing" (1995, 44).

A Buddhist Theory of Religious Mediatization

To recondition Hjarvard's theory of mediatization so that it is usable for understanding the Kalachakra's digitalization, we need to pry apart his core insight from his theory of religious communication. Hjarvard's core insight is that media influence society because their affordances "make certain actions possible, exclude others and structure the interactions between actor and object" (2013, 27). In fact, Hjarvard "recognize[s] the media as technologies, each of which has a set of affordances *that facilitate, limit, and structure communication and action*" (2013, 28 [italics in original]; cf. Grieve 2017, 48–50). While his overall theory focuses on the functions of religion, his model of religion is a normative one that requires a substantive or transmission theory of religious communication often assumed by many Protestants (Jennings 1969). In the postwar period, communication models have been dominated by the transmission theory of communication, pioneered in 1948 in an influential article by the American Claude E. Shannon. A transmission theory of communication describes the communication of a message as a unidirectional signal from an informational source, through a transmitter, and noise source, picked up by a receiver and finally decoded at its destination (A ⇒ B) (Table 9.1). A transmission theory of communication is unidirectional, has one outcome, is causal, has discrete variables, transmits information, is message centered, has a fixed sequence and communicates separate events. A transmission theory leads to the analysis of communication either as a more or less reliable transmission, or as an ideological distortion from the information source.

Table 9.1 A Mathematical Theory of Communication (after Shannon 1949)

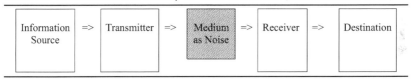

Information Source	=>	Transmitter	=>	Medium as Noise	=>	Receiver	=>	Destination

Painting with a broad brush, we describe what we call a *Buddhist theory of communication* as bidirectional, processional, reciprocal, continuous, meaning- and actor-centered, with flexible sequences and inseparable events (Table 9.2). Buddhist communication is distinct from a transmission theory, because it employs media practices to spread the *Dharma* through mutual conditioning. Rather than being a transmission theory of communication that models communication as the unidirectional transmission of data from source to destination, a Buddhist theory of communication models mediatization as the mutually dependent relationship between two different conditions (A ⇔ B) (*pratayaya*). In a transmission theory of communication media are neutral conveyers of information whose presence must be figured out as noise (A = m ⇒ B). In a Buddhist theory of media practice, media must be approached mindfully (*smṛti*) because they afford different types of interactions, which, depending on the mediascape, allow for the skillful teaching (*upāya*) of different types of *Dharmic* messages (A ⇐ m ⇒ B) (Table 9.3).

Table 9.2 A Buddhist Theory of Communication

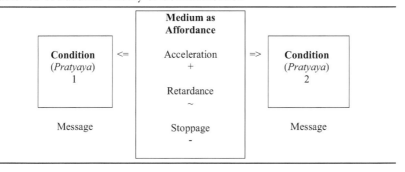

	Medium as Affordance	
Condition (*Pratyaya*) 1	Acceleration +	**Condition** (*Pratyaya*) 2
	Retardance ~	
Message	Stoppage -	Message

Table 9.3 A Mathematical Theory of Communication compared to a Buddhist
Theory of Communication (after Dissanayake 1983)

A Mathematical Theory of Communication	*A Buddhist Theory of Communication*
Unidirectional	Bidirectional
Outcome	Process
Causality	Reciprocity
Discrete variables	Continuous variables
Meaning transferred	Meaning created
Message-centered	Actor-centered
Fixed sequence	Flexible sequence
Events separable	Events inseparable

The difficulty with modeling the Kalachakra through a transmission theory is that rather than clarifying the ceremony, it further mystifies the highly digitalized mediascape that we encountered. During the Kalachakra, the Dalai Lama often referred to the religion (*dharma*) as a shield, and that its effectiveness depended on the context in which it was delivered. In Buddhism, *dharma* usually refers to the Buddha's teachings, which indicates not simply the transmitting of information, but also, with varying degrees of skill, the creation of efficient conditions that lessen suffering. *Dharmic* messages are not perceived by Buddhists as universal, but are dependent on the skill and means (*upāya-kauśalya*) of those that deliver them (Matsunaga and Matsunaga 1974). A transmission theory of religion leads to an interpretation of the Kalachakra's mediascape as a loss of fidelity to the essential teachings. Yet, while there was contention over the digital broadcast of the ceremony, the arguments given by the officials assembled were not about a loss of fidelity to the original sources, but about the dangers that the teaching might offer to those unprepared for the initiation (personal communication). The concern was not about the corruption of the message, but that the message might cause harm (*duhhka*) to the untrained (personal communication).

While the aim of Protestant communication is the transmission of symbols of belief about the supernatural, the aim of Buddhist communication is not merely to transmit content, but to create conditions which lessen suffering (Dissanayake 2009a). Because the Kalachakra did not just communicate information, but was aimed at lessening the suffering of its audiences, what we found was a complex relationship between event and digital communication. The communication was not the transmission of a passive referent (*svabhāva)* that was projected through the media, but rather a mutual conditioning (*pratyaya*) in which the ceremony and its mediascape were dependent on one and other (*pratītyasa-mutpāda*). With this in mind, to analyze the Kalachakra, we turned to a Buddhist model of communication that emerged from the ceremony.

Following the groundbreaking work of the media scholar Dissanay-ake, we assemble a Buddhist Theory of Communication by focusing on the work of the 2nd-century Buddhist philosopher, Nāgārjuna (Dis-sanayake 1983, 2009b). Nāgārjuna is the founder of the Mādhyamika (Middle-way) school of Mahayana Buddhism, and we are particularly interested in Chapter 1, *Examination of the Conditions*, from his mag-num opus, the *Fundamental Verses on the Middle Way (Mūlamadhya-makakārikā)*. In this treatise, Nāgārjuna makes a distinction between causes (*hetu*) and conditions (*pratyaya*). By *cause (hetu)* he means that something has as an essential quality of its nature to bring about an effect on something else. For example, one might argue that in high-modern societies media have caused (*hetu*) changes to religion. By condition (*pratyaya*), on the other hand, he indicates that phenomena are not es-sential, but that different phenomena bring about each other's state of existence. In this case, while distinct, religion and media would not be essential separate phenomena, but would mutually determine each other.

Key to understanding a theory of Buddhist communication is the con-cept of dependent co-origination (*pratītyasamutpāda*). *Pratitya* trans-lates as "having depended" and *samutpada* as "arising", and is the notion that everything that comes into existence is dependent on some-thing else (Lopez 2001, 29). Often argued to be the defining ontological heart of Buddhism, dependent co-origination states that all phenomena (*dharmas*) arise only in relationship to other phenomena, nothing ex-ists on its own (*Majjhima Nikaya* 1.90). Rather than causing *data*, in-formation that can be stored and transmitted, to be sent from a source to receiver, a Buddhist theory understands communication as mutual conditioning. While distinct, poles in a communicative act are not dif-ferent. Conditioning indicates how person, event or process plays a role in generating, and being generated by, another person, state or process. A Buddhist theory of communication, then, analyzes media practices not as the broadcasting of data between sender and receiver (A ⇒ B), but rather as the mutual conditioning of two or more communicators (A ⇔ B).

Digitalizing the Kalachakra

The Kalachakra's digitalization creates an oscillation between the desire for transparent immediacy, the experience of what it was like sitting at the Dalai Lama's feet, and the opaque hyper-mediation of multiple media that highlighted mediatization. Rather than being transmitted as information from source to destination, the ceremony made visible how media condition each other by commenting on, reproducing and replacing one another. Kalachakra practitioners wanted to both multi-ply media sources – printed books, the use of translation radios, large television screens and the Internet – but at the same time to erase all apparent mediation, and experience the Dalai Lama's teachings directly in all their charismatic immediacy. What holds the Kalachakra's knot of media together is the Dalai Lama, who stands at its center? Yet, rather than acting like a broadcast tower, which unidirectionally transmits a single message, the Dalai Lama conditions between distinct audiences using distinct media channels. This mediation is interactive, flexible and between two or more people, and is not merely the one-way exchange of information but rather conversely, is a bidirectional exchange in which the message conditions both the sender and receiver.

On 10 July, after days of teaching, the first day of the actual initiation began. Around noon, The Dalai Lama explained that these were an engagement between master and disciple, in which he becomes the deity at the center of the Kalachakra. The Kalachakra's immediacy arises (*samutpada*) from the Tantric empowerment that emerges between the ceremony's physically assembled audience and the Dalai Lama as a Buddhist protector deity. Immediacy refers to a feeling of being with the Dalai Lama. As Ong writes, immediacy "the existential relationship of person to person (I am in your presence; you are present to me), with the concept of present time (as against past and future)" (1967, 101). As the French moral philosopher Levinas (1985) theorizes, in such face-to-face encounters, people are responsible to one and other as people rather than because of roles, institutions or other social structures. In other words, the immediacy of Tantric empowerment functions because, as the Dalai Lama said, on 7 July, during the second day of teachings, he looked straight at the camera and pointing to his eyes and then to the assembled initiates, "You see me. I see you." (personal communication).

Transmission theories of communication are complicated by secrecy. The Kalachakra was described by the Dalai Lama as secret.[10] The use of secrecy in the ceremony indicates the difference between a Protestant influenced transmission theory of communication and a Buddhist influenced conditioning theory of communication (cf. Guhyasamājatantra). In a transmission religious model, secrecy would indicate when content was not delivered. This model does not work for the Kalachakra for two reasons. First, there were over 150,000 people assembled for the Kalachakra. In fact, because of the large numbers, the ceremony was televised on enormous monitors to the assembled crowd. Second, the ceremony was broadcast and simultaneously translated into a number of languages that could be listened to over small transistor radios. In other words, even the face-to-face immediacy was always already mediatized.

In a Buddhist conditioning model of communication, secrecy is not merely the stoppage of content, but the blockage of media affordances in order to influence and affect the mediatization. For example, on 3 July, from our position just outside the main stage, we could see movement and hear chanting from the inner sanctum. The chanting was being broadcast over the radios, and the large monitors displayed close up, televised images of the Dalai Lama and his senior monks. A transmission theory of communication could only describe this as a loss of signal. A conditioning model of communication could indicate how such secrecy was used to heighten immediacy. Many of the people in the crowd that we spoke to, felt as if they were having a direct and personal, even secret, conversation with the Dalai Lama. Many people said that they felt as if the Dalai Lama were speaking directly to them, and many claimed that the Dalai Lama had made eye contact just with them. For example, a German woman sitting next to us, thought at this point that the Dalai Lama had invited to her to the stage, and pushed through the crowd until stopped by security. The Dalai Lama was both very intimate and at the same time unreachable. For example, when the Dalai Lama spoke with the chief oracle, he leaned in close and pulled a curtain-like cloth over his head and around the two of them, but at the same time there was an extreme close up of the event that was broadcasted on the big screens.

Conditioning is key for the Kalachakra, because the ceremony was not merely the conveying of information but (ideally) a transformative, empowering and salvific Tantric ritual. Tantric rituals feature practices associated with specific classes of Tantric deities: tutelary deities (*yidam*), *ḍākinīs* (*khandroma*), and various types of *Dharma* protectors (*dharmapāla*). These invocations and use of these deities are ideally aimed toward soteriological ends, specifically, ultimately transforming the practitioner into the enlightened tutelary deity (*yidam*) residing at the center of its particular universe (*maṇḍala*). The Tantric specialist visualizes himself as the *yidam* residing in a *maṇḍala* surrounded by retinues of other deities including *ḍākinīs*, *Dharma* protectors, and lesser mundane gods and goddesses. In Buddhist Tantric theory, by using the Tantric *yidam* to harness the power of the mind, one obtains spiritual powers (*siddhi*) to aid others in mundane matters that include healing, rainmaking, averting disasters and helping others to achieve the state of enlightenment. All practices, however, first require initiation by a guru. The guru takes on the persona of the *yidam*. Acting as the *yidam*, through a series of ritual empowerments they bring disciples into the *maṇḍala* and authorize disciples to engage in the practices of the *yidam's* corresponding *sādhana*.

The current Dalai Lama's Kalachakra initiations, such as the one held in Ladakh, signals important shifts in this particular empowerment. The Dalai Lama positions himself not only as a Tibetan addressing a Buddhist community, but also as a member of a broader global *humanity* (usually a term used in English). This is apparent by the fact that in the context of preliminary teachings for the Kalachakra initiation, he addressed global concerns, such as the limitations of science and modernity, the need for inter-religious harmony and the significance of *secular ethics* (a term used in the English) (Singh 2016). As a practitioner of mind science, the Dalai Lama positioned himself as a post-secular teacher, and presented Buddhism as fundamentally ecumenical, secular and scientific. Everyone, regardless of their religious background, may benefit from the scientific and philosophical aspects of Buddhism, while foregoing what the Dalai Lama calls *Buddhist religion* (a term used in the English). Scientific and philosophical Buddhism offers interreligious and nonreligious audiences with secular means of transforming the mind. For the Dalai Lama, *Buddhist science* (a term used in the English) and Western science thus become mutually enhancing forces for improving modern humanity, the former capable of transforming the mind and the inner capacities of humans, and the latter a medium for material progress and development (Singh 2016).

While one could argue that mediatization is occurring, and one could argue for secularization, just the opposite of Hjarvard's prediction of anomie is occurring. Digitalization is increasing feelings of community and the authority of the central clergy. When the Dalai Lama commenced the Kalachakra ceremony, he began by claiming that all religions are ultimately united under the concept of *Dharma*. Here, he appropriates the concept of *Dharma* not as constituting religious values *per se*, but rather as a source of protection, specifically a defense against negative mental states and immoral actions. For the Dalai Lama, this sense of *Dharma* manifests in all religions and acts as a post-secular moral force for transforming human consciousness (Singh 2016). When all religions find this common post-secular *Dharma*, they can work together to foster shared human values such as compassion, love and tolerance. In this framework, the Kalachakra initiation in Ladakh – like most of the Dalai Lama's large public teachings – is not merely a Buddhist ritual ceremony; it is a period for all people, regardless of religion, to engage in dialogue and reflect upon their shared secular ethics. For the Dalai Lama, this secular ethics is both traditional, in that its precepts and ideals, including compassion, love and generosity, manifest in all religions, and modern to the extent that it provides what he calls an *ethics for a new millennium* (a term usually used in English).[11]

Conclusion

Later that evening, after we had left the ceremonial grounds, we analyzed what at first blush appeared the privileging of the digital representations of the ceremony over the ceremony itself. We puzzled over why Tibetans allowed the face-to-face ceremony to be overshadowed by its digitalization. Yet, as the night wore on, and we explored the data more closely, we started to reflect on how images of the Kalachakra are treated by Tibetan Buddhists themselves, and we realized that the fault might lie with our own biases, and not with the use or abuse of digital media technologies. Still, a central question remained. In the rich, dynamic, hyper-mediatized hubbub of the Kalachakra's digitalized mediascape, between the face-to-face interactions, enormous video monitors, amplified sound, websites, streamed videos and other social media, as well as radios used for simultaneous translation, printed books, even mass produced sacred images, it became unclear as to where the actual ceremony stopped and its representations began. What was the thin skin between sign and referent? Between the virtual and the actual? Between the object and its mediation, not to mention the effects of its mediatization?

To answer this cluster of questions, our chapter has turned to the notion of digitalization, which models not merely the translation of the analogue into the digital, but the conditioning of social structures and practices through the process of being digitized. Think, for example, of how Amazon.com has conditioned the economy of local bookstores.[12] To build our model, we have relied on Hjarvard and his theory of the mediatization of religion conditioned by Dissanayake's critical Buddhist theory of communication. For Hjarvard, the mediatization of high-modern society is a "'Trojan horse' that challenges the authority of institutionalized religion", and ultimately Nordic culture (2011, 132). We found just the reverse happening for Tibet. Digitalization increased the Dalia Lama's authority and charisma, ran against banalization's anomie, as well as created if not a virtual, at the least an augmented Tibet. Yet, our goal in this chapter has not been mere critique. Instead, we have taken the first steps to recondition Hjarvard's theory of mediatization so that is productive as a theory by which to analyze Buddhist mediascapes such as the Kalachakra.

Conditioning Hjarvard's theory of mediatization with critical Buddhist communication theory has illustrated how a scholar's definition of religion affects how they theorize its mediatization. We maintain that since Protestant models of communication remain deeply embedded in how many scholars of communication approach mediatization, if one wants to understand non-Western religions, one cannot simply add token Asian content. Instead, one needs to rethink the theories by which we model communication. Our observation and analysis of the Kalachakra ceremony necessitates a theory of mediation not as a one-way transmission of information about an essential referent (*svabhāva*) from source to destination (A ⇒ B), but as media practices that mutually condition (*pratyaya*) each other (A ⇔ B). As the chapter's epigraph hints, while built upon the research of Dissanayake, our model is ultimately indebted to the Indian philosopher Nāgārjuna's ontological viewpoint that maintains that phenomena lack any intrinsic and self-arising nature. Instead, everything conditions everything else, and relies upon numerous causes and conditions.

We have spilled much ink illustrating what Nordic theories of mediatization can learn from critical Buddhist theories of communication. In this denouement, we assert that Buddhist communication theory can learn two important lessons from mediatization. First, mediatization models how Buddhist social worlds, like all social worlds, are imagined by their inhabitants through technologies of communication, and that these social worlds are conditioned by these media practices. Accordingly, mediatization theory enables researchers to analyze the effect media have on determining Buddhist content, to map the social worlds held together ($\sqrt{dhr}$) by digital media, and also to illuminate the historic transformations caused by digitalization of Tibetan ceremonies such as the Kalachakra. For example, mediatization theory allows the understanding of the 2014 Kalachakra ceremony's mediascape and its religious practices, as well as trace a shift by the Dalai Lama from media as information, to an increasing use of cyberspace as a place of participatory and interactive media practices.

Second, generalizing from the case study of the 2014 Kalachakra, we can now extend our theory of digitalization to understand how Tibetan Buddhism, in diaspora, uses online religious practices for nation building. A reconditioned mediatization theory gives us the conceptual tools to explain (1) why far more than other religious traditions, Tibetan Buddhism flourishes in digital spaces and affords the use of the Internet not just for the transmission of information but for ceremonial practice, and also (2) how long-distance religious practices afford a diaspora community. Obviously, there are both historical and technological conditions in play. Historically, living in diaspora creates a situation in which long-distance forms of digitally mediated religious practice are not a choice but a necessity. Technologically, digital media allows for the types of interactive, real time communication that ceremonies such as the Kalachakra require. Beyond the historical and technological, however, a reconditioned mediatization theory reveals that a religion's ontology also plays a major role in its digitalization. Key to understanding a theory of Buddhist communication is the concept of dependent co-origination (*pratītyasamutpāda*), which maintains that everything that comes into existence is dependent on something else. As the Dalai Lama said on the second day of the Kalachakras teachings, "Nothing exists objectively, nothing exists on its own side."

Notes

1 Nāgārjuna, Mūlamadhyamakakārikā [I.1]; for our translation, we use Jay Garfield. 1995. *The Fundamental Wisdom of the Middle Way*. Oxford: Oxford University Press.
2 Cf. 33rd Kalachakra Empowerment Preliminary Teachings.
3 Cf. Office of His Holiness the Dalai Lama, n.d., *Introduction to the Kalachkra*.
4 Cf. Office of His Holiness the Dalai Lama 2014. *Kalachakra Initiation – Part 1* [online video].
5 A *Procrustean bed* describes a scheme that produces uniformity by arbitrary, often violent methods. It is named after Procrustes, the villain from

Greek Mythology who stretched or amputated the limbs of travelers to make them fit to the length of his bed.
6 For a full list of initiations, see www.dalailama.com/teachings/kalachakra-initiations, accessed 4 October 2017.
7 For more on the rituals of the Kalachakra, see: Dalai Lama XIV, 1999a. *Kalachakra Tantra: Rite of Initiation* 3rd Edition. Translated by J. Hopkins. Boston: Wisdom Publications. See also A. Berzin, 1997. *Taking the Kalachakra Initiation.* Ithaca: Snow Lion Publications.
8 For a nuanced treatment on the themes of selfhood, temporality, and embodiment in the *Kālacakra Tanta,* see V. A. Wallace, 2001. *The Inner Kālacakra: A Buddhist Tantric View of the Individual.* New York: Oxford University Press.
9 To examine the 2014 Kalachakra, we draw on three sources: Field notes we wrote while attending the ceremony; news reports of the event by local Ladakhi media outlets and news reports issued by the Office of the Fourteenth Dalai Lama; and English translations of the Dalai Lama's teachings found at the following websites: www.dalailama.com/webcasts/post/323-33rd-kalachakra-empowerment-preliminary-teachings, www.dalailama.com/webcasts/post/322-his-holiness-the-dalai-lamas-79th-birthday-celebration, and www.dalailama.com/webcasts/post/321-introductory-teaching—kalachakra-in-ladakh-2014.
10 Kalachakra: The Public and The Secret Initiations.
11 For more on the Dalai Lama's take on ethics, religion, secularism and modernism, see Dalai Lama XIV, 1999b. *Ethics for the New Millennium.* New York: Penguin and Dalai Lama XIV, 2011. *Beyond Religion: Ethics for a Whole World.* Boston: Houghton Mifflin Harcourt.
12 Cf. Amazon to Scuppernong Books.

References

Primary Sources

33rd Kalachakra Empowerment Preliminary Teachings, n.d. Available at www.dalailama.com/videos/33rd kalachakra-empowerment-preliminary-teachings, accessed 4 October 2017.
Guhyasamājatantra. Translated from Sanskrit by F. Fremantle, 1971. *A Critical Study of the Guhyasamājatantra.* London: University of London Library.
Kālacakra Tantra. Translated from Tibetan by J. Hopkins, 1999. *Kalachakra Tantra: Rite of Initiation.* New York: Wisdom Publications.
Kalachakra: The Public and the Secret Initiations. Available at www.trimondi.de/SDLE/Part-1-06.htm, accessed 4 October 2017.
Mūlamadhyamakakārikā. Translated from Sanskrit by J. Garfield, 1995. *Fundamental Wisdom on the Middle Way: Mūlamadhyamakakārikā.* Oxford: Oxford University Press.
Office of His Holiness the Dalia Lama, 2014a. *Kalachakra Initiation – Part 1.* [video] Available at www.youtube.com/watch?v=654CdfMEOoc, accessed 4 October 2017.
Office of His Holiness the Dalia Lama, 2014b. *33rd Kalachakra Empowerment Preliminary Teachings.* [video] Available at www.dalailama.com/videos/33rd-kalachakra-empowerment-preliminary-teachings, accessed 4 October 2017.

Ratnāvalī. Translated from Sanskrit by M. R. Kale, 2002. *The Ratnāvalī*. Delhi: Motilal Banarsidass Publishers.

Suhṛllekha. Translated from Sanskrit by B. Dharmamitra, 2008. *Letter From a Friend [The Suhṛllekha]*. Available at www.kalavinka.org/Jewels/book_ excerpts/Letter_excerpts/Letter_X-13_X-01.pdf, accessed 4 October 2017.

Secondary Sources

Amazon, 1994–. Available at www.amazon.com, accessed 5 October 2017.
Appadurai, A., 1990. Disjuncture and Difference in the Global Cultural Economy. *Theory Culture Society*, 7(2), 1–24.
Baudrillard, J., 1995. *The Gulf War Did Not Take Place*. Indianapolis: Indiana University Press.
Berger, P., 1967. *The Sacred Canopy: Elements of a Sociological Theory of Religion*. Garden City: Doubleday.
Berger, P., 1999. *The Desecularization of the World: Resurgent Religion and World Politics*. Grand Rapids: William B. Eerdmans Publishing Company.
Berzin, A., 1997. *Taking the Kalachakra Initiation*. Ithaca: Snow Lion Publications.
Campbell, H., 2010. *When Religion Meets New Media*. New York: Routledge.
Campbell, H. and Grieve, G., 2014. What Playing with Religion Offers Digital Game Studies. In: Campbell, H. and Grieve, G. P., eds. *Playing with Religion in Digital Games*. Indianapolis: Indiana University Press, 1–21.
Chakrabarty, D., 2000. *Provincializing Europe: Postcolonial Thought and Historical Difference*. Princeton: Princeton University Press.
Couldry, N. and Hepp, A., 2013. Conceptualizing Mediatization: Contexts, Traditions, Arguments. *Communication Theory*, 23(3), 191–202.
Dalai Lama, 1999a. *Kalachakra Tantra: Rite of Initiation*. 3rd ed. Trans. J. Hopkins. Boston: Wisdom Publications.
Dalai Lama, 1999b. *Ethics for the New Millennium*. New York: Penguin.
Dalai Lama, 2011. *Beyond Religion: Ethics for a Whole World*. Boston: Houghton Mifflin Harcourt.
Dalai Lama, n.d. *33rd kalachakra Empowerment. Preliminary Teachings*. Available at www.dalailama.com/webcasts/post/323-33rd-kalachakra-empowerment-preliminary-teachings, accessed 4 October 2017.
Dalai Lama, n.d. *His Holiness the Dalai Lamas 79th birthday celebration*. Available at www.dalailama.com/webcasts/post/322-his-holiness-the-dalai-lamas-79th-birthday-celebration, accessed 4 October 2017.
Dalai Lama, n.d. *Introductory Teaching. Kalachakra in Ladakh 2014*. Available at www.dalailama.com/webcasts/post/321-introductory-teaching—kalachakra-in-ladakh-2014, accessed 4 October 2017.
Davidson Reynolds, P., 1971. *A Primer in Theory Construction*. Boston: Allyn and Bacon.
Derrida, J., 1988. *Of Grammatology*. Baltimore: Johns Hopkins University Press (corrected edition).
Dissanayake, W., 1983. The Communication Significance of the Buddhist Concept of Dependent Co-Origination. *Communication*, 8(1), 29–45.
Dissanayake, W., 2009a. The Production of Asian Theories of Communication: Contexts and Challenges. *Asian Journal of Communication*, 19(4), 453–468.

Dissanayake, W., 2009b. Buddhist Communication Theory. In: Littlejohn, S. W. and Foss, K. A., eds. *Encyclopedia of Communication Theory.* Thousand Oaks: SAGE Publications, 84–85.

Durkheim, E., 1995. *The Elementary Forms of Religious Life.* New York: The Free Press (Simon & Schuster).

Eliade, M., 1961. History of Religions and a New Humanism. *History of Religions,* 1(1), 1–8.

Engelke, M., 2012. Angels in Swindon: Public Religion and Ambient Faith in England. *American Ethnologist,* 39(3), 155–170.

Ess, C., 1996. The Political Computer: Democracy, CMC, and Habermas. In: Ess, C., ed. *Philosophical Perspectives on Computer-Mediated Communication.* Albany: State University of New York Press.

Garfield, J., 1995. *The Fundamental Wisdom of the Middle Way.* Oxford: Oxford University Press.

Goody, J., 1986. *The Logic of Writing and the Organization of Society.* Cambridge: Cambridge University Press.

Grieve, G., 2006. *Retheorizing Religion in Nepal.* New York: Palgrave Macmillan.

Grieve, G., 2017. Mind the Gap: Screens, Ontologies, and the Far Shore. In: Grieve, G., *CyberZen: Imagining Authentic Buddhist Identity, Community, and Practices in the Virtual World of Second Life.* New York: Routledge, 194–214.

Grieve, G. and Veidlinger, D., 2016. Buddhist Media Technologies. In: Jarryson, M., ed. *Oxford Handbook of Contemporary Buddhism.* London: Oxford University Press, 469–486.

Havelock, E., 1986. *The Muse Learns to Write: Reflections on Orality and Literacy from Antiquity to the Present.* New Haven: Yale University Press.

Helland, C., 2016. Digital Religion. In: Yamane, D., ed. *Handbook of Religion and Social Institutions.* Switzerland: Springer, 177–196.

Hjarvard, S., 2008a. The Mediatization of Society. A Theory of the Media as Agents of Social and Cultural Change. *Nordicom Review,* 29(2), 105–134.

Hjarvard, S., 2008b. A Theory of Media As Agents of Religious Change. *Northern Lights,* 6(1), 9–26.

Hjarvard, S., 2011. The Mediatisation of Religion: Theorising Religion, Media and Social Change. *Culture and Religion,* 12(2), 119–135.

Hjarvard, S., 2013. *The Mediatization of Culture and Society.* London: Routledge.

Hjarvard, S., 2014. From Mediation to Mediatization: The Institutionalization of New Media. In: Hepp, A. and Krotz, F., eds. *Mediatized Worlds. Culture and Society in a Media Age.* Basingtoke: Palgrave Macmillan, 123–139.

Hoover, S., 2006. *Religion in the Media Age.* New York: Routledge.

Innis, H., 1951. *The Bias of Communication.* Toronto: University of Toronto Press.

Jenkins, H., 1992. *Textual Poachers: Television Fans & Participatory Culture.* New York: Routledge.

Jennings, R., 1969. Policies and Practices of Selected National Religious Bodies as Related to Broadcasting in the Public Interest. PhD Dissertation, New York University.

Krotz, F., 2009. Mediatization: A Concept with Which to Grasp Media and Societal Change. In: Lundby, K., ed. *Mediatization: Concept, Changes, Consequences*. New York: Peter Lang, 19–38.

Krotz, F., 2014. Mediatization As a Mover in Modernity: Social and Cultural Change in the Context of Media Change. In: Lundby, K., ed. *Handbook Mediatization*. Berlin: de Gruyter, 131–161.

Krotz, F. and Hepp, A., 2011. A Concretization Of Mediatization: How 'Mediatization Works' And Why Mediatized Worlds Are A Helpful Concept For Empirical Mediatization Research. *Empedocles: European Journal for the Philosophy of Communication*, 3(2), 137–152.

Lash, S., 2005. *Intensive media—Modernity and Algorithm*. Available at http://roundtable.kein.org, accessed 4 October 2017.

Levinas, E., 1985. *Ethics and Infinity*. New York: Duquesne University Press.

Livingstone, S., 2009. On the Mediation of Everything. *Journal of Communication*, 59(1), 1–18.

Lopez, D., 2001. *The Story of Buddhism*. New York: HarperCollins.

Lövheim, M., 2011. Mediatisation of Religion: A Critical Appraisal. *Culture and Religion*, 12(2), 153–166.

Lundby, K., 2014. *Mediatization of Communication*. Berlin: De Gruyter Mouton.

Martín-Barbero, J., 2003. *La Educación Desde la Comunicación*. Bogotá: Grupo Editorial Norma.

Matsunaga, Daigan and Alicia, 1974. The Concept of Upāya in Mahāyāna Buddhist Philosophy. *Japanese Journal of Buddhist Studies*, 1(1), 51–72. Available at https://web.archive.org/web/20140608152609/, http://nirc.nanzan-u.ac.jp/nfile/2297, accessed 4 October 2017.

McChesney, R., 2013. *Digital Disconnect: How Capitalism is Turning the Internet Against Democracy*. New York: New Press.

McLuhan, M., 1964. *Understanding Media: The Extensions of Man*. Cambridge: MIT Press.

Morton, A., 1980. *Frames of Mind*. Oxford: Oxford University Press.

Office of His Holiness the Dalai Lama, n.d. *Introduction to the Kalachkra*. Available at www.dalailama.com/teachings/kalachakra-initiations, accessed 4 October 2017.

Office of His Holiness the Dalia Lama, 2014. *Kalachakra: The Public and the Secret Initiations*. Available at www.trimondi.de/SDLE/Part-1-06.htm, accessed 4 October 2017.

Ong, W., 1967. *The Presence of the Word: Some Prolegomena for Cultural and Religious History*. New Haven: Yale University Press.

Postman, N., 1985. *Amusing Ourselves to Death: Public Discourse in the Age of Show Business*. New York: Penguin Books.

Preiss, R. W., et al., 2007. *Mass Media Effects Research: Advances through Meta-Analysis*. Mahwah: Lawrence Erlbaum.

de Saussure, F., 1916. *Course in General Linguistics*. Chicago: Open Court.

Schulz, W., 2004. Reconstructing Mediatization as an Analytical Concept. *European Journal of Communication*, 19(1), 87–101.

Scuppernong Books, 2014–. Available at www.scuppernongbooks.com/, accessed 5 October 2017.

Shannon, C., 1948. A Mathematical Theory of Communication. *Bell System Technical Journal*, 27(3), 379–423.

Shannon, C. and Weaver, W., 1949. *The Mathematical Theory of Communication*. Chicago: University of Illinois Press.

Singh, R., 2016. Buddhists and Muslims in Ladakh: Negotiating Tradition and Modernity. PhD Dissertation, University of California, Santa Barbara.

Sorokin, P., 1947. *Society, Culture, and Personality*. New York: Harper & Brothers.

Thompson, J. B., 1995. *The Media and Modernity. A Social Theory of the Media*. Cambridge: Cambridge University Press.

Veidlinger, D., 2006. *Spreading the Dhamma: Writing, Orality and Textual Transmission in Buddhist Northern Thailand*. Honolulu: University of Hawaii Press.

Wallace, V. A., 2001. *The Inner Kālacakra: A Buddhist Tantric View of the Individual*. New York: Oxford University Press.

Weinelt, B., 2016. *Digital Transformation of Industries (White Paper)*. Cologny: World Economic Forum.

Part 4

West Asia

10 Being Religious through Social Networks

Representation of Religious Identity of Shia Iranians on Instagram

Narges Valibeigi

Introduction

This study focuses on the relationship between new communication technology and religion in Iranian contexts. This chapter focuses on how the Internet, as a new digital communication tool and forum, influences the process of religious identity construction for Shia Iranians. To answer this question, I will explore the relationship between religion and media as two societal institutions that were once separated. The framework of *mediatization* suggested by Hjarvard (2008, 2013) is applied to analyze how religious identity may undergo transformation through the use of online social media, which currently permeates religion.

Religious experience, in the smartphone era, is not limited to a specific time or place, the two necessary characteristics of traditional institutions, defined by Hjarvard (2008). The Internet extends interaction in time and space, which means new social networking tools, such as Facebook, Instagram and Twitter, allow for instant communication where individuals can more easily perform their identity, and in several stages and spaces simultaneously. These changes are important for religious communities since the logic of the media not only influences the form communication takes, but it also influences the nature and function of social relations as well as the sender, the content and the receivers of the communication (Hjarvard 2008).

The fact that religion and religious acts have become more publicly visible because of the Internet may result in more engagement in religious content, for both believers and others, since religious subjects constantly appear on all their electronic devices through their various social networks:

> The presence of religion in the media is not just a mirror of a religious reality 'outside' the media. It is also an outcome of a complex set of processes in which the importance of religion and particular religious beliefs and actions are contested as well as reasserted,

both in and by the media, at the same time as religion undergoes transformation through the very process of being mediated through various media.

(Hjarvard 2016, 9)

For Shia believers, among other religious communities, compression of time and space makes religious products available everywhere, anytime. This chapter will examine if being religious – or, more specifically, performing religion in a new, fast, live and connected online sphere – has become a different experience compared to the pre-Internet era. Reading or listening to religious texts or asking questions about religious issues on clerics' websites are not the only and ultimate ways Shia Iranians use the Internet. Shia Iranians have become the agents of producing new religious structures, style, content and symbols through their activities on social media. This means that the traditional structure of Iranian Shia community is under a perceptible transformation in the process of mediatization.

One of the distinctive rituals that distinguishes Shia, specifically Iranians, from other denominations of Islam is the *Muharram Mourning and Processions*. The anniversary commemorates the tragedy of Karbala, in which Prophet Muhammad's grandson, Imam Hossein, along with a group of his family members and associates, was massacred in Iraq, Karbala, by the troops of the Caliph in a historically unfair battle on the tenth day of the first month (Muharram) of the Islamic calendar in the year of 61 AH (10 October 680 AD). A few examples of the religious and cultural behaviors that have a significant visual expression of the Shia identity online include wearing black attire to express sorrow for the Ashura incident; attending *Rowze* (gathering and mourning); marching in procession in *Dasteh* (marching in large groups on the streets while reciting religious poems and playing traditional musical instruments); performing and attending *Ta'ziah* (theatrical performance of the Karbala story); and decorating homes, mosques and streets with black flags and calligraphic signs during the month of Muharram each year.

Instagram, an online social media used specifically for photo and video sharing, has become one of the most popular applications on smartphone devices among the Iranian youth who are actively communicating with each other and people around the world. There are no concrete statistics regarding Instagram users in Iran. However, according to the Iranian Student Polling Agency (ISPA), as of August 2016, 30–35 million Iranians have Instagram accounts. This application is the second most used social media in Iran, after Telegram, an instant messaging app (ISPA 2016). The most observable themes of the images constantly uploaded to Instagram by religious Iranians, specifically during the holy month of Muharram, relate to the subject of *Rowze, Mourning, Ziar'a*, and the Procession for Imam Hossein as one of the most highlighted elements of Shia identity.

This chapter posits that a cultural transformation in religious identity is occurring in the process of taking snap shots, using different filters on pictures, uploading and sharing them on social media and getting likes and comments on them. This process has significant meaning within the religious experience of Shia Iranians and makes identity formation an individual but reciprocal experience, not a traditional and organizational one. In order to demonstrate this, this chapter focuses specifically on pictures shared by Shia Iranians on Instagram that contain symbols or performances of a ritual surrounding Muharram events. I chose the cases based on my own observation of daily activities of Shia Iranians on Instagram between 2015 and 2016. This research uses longitudinal online observation as the main method for gathering photos selected for analysis. I have been observing twenty Shia Iranian Instagram profiles from September 2014 to December 2016 on a daily basis to discover the trends surrounding how often and how much religious content is shared. The pictures are from public profiles that provide religious icons, such as religious biography, and posts containing religious symbols or connotations, such as profile pictures of Hijabi women. This research undertakes a visual qualitative methodology (Glaw et al. 2017). Visual methodologies are used to understand and interpret images including photography, film, painting, sculpture, artwork and other pictorial forms. Different layers of meaning can be discovered by using this method. To apply this method first we need to categorize the gathered photographs into different themes, in this case, the related metaphors, and then through thematic analysis, each photograph will be studied for repeated patterns and meanings they illustrate. Based on this observation, I bring five examples to discuss mediatization process with regard to three metaphors of media suggested by Meyrowitz (1993): media as environments, media as conduits and media as languages.

Representation of Religious Identity in the Process of Mediatization

According to Turkle (1995), identity refers to a process by which individuals develop the capacity to grasp the meaning of situations in everyday life and their own position in relation to them. Based on this definition, identity has two dimensions. The first is the individual's experience of himself or herself as a separate, unique person, capable of acting in a situation. The second refers to the location of the individual in relation to meanings, practices and positions that organize social life (Lövheim 2013). In the digital era of networked society, computers have become a tool for organizing personal life and social interactions. The Internet has conceptualized and prioritized our commitments and self-expression through various types of texts, images and sounds. Widespread use of online social networks, as Miller and Shepherd (2004) point out, provides new genres in which individual self-performance is combined with interactivity through likes and comments. Therefore, the reactions of audiences can be considered as an effective element for collaborative formation of identity in networked society.

The role of social groups in identity formation should also be noted here: "membership of social groups is internalized as part of the self-concept and as such forms an integral part of the identity of an individual" (in Bornman 2003, 26, Tajfel 1981). For religious individuals who have been active in online platforms, membership within social media is a part of their identity formation. Moreover, since religious identity can be considered a part of cultural identity, based on Hall's (1996) explanation of the twofold interpretation of religious identity, there is on the one hand cultural identity that "reflects common historical experiences and shared cultural codes that serve to unify and to provide stable, continuous and unchanging frames of reference of meaning amidst social and political changes" (Bornman 2003, 26). In this conceptualization, identity is shaped based on the struggles to represent the true essence of a particular identity. For example, when Shia Iranians try to search for the origins of being Shia, their attempt is associated with the investigation of history in order to reveal unseen aspects and roots of their belief. Even in online platforms, sharing and disseminating traditional so-called original texts, audio files and well-known religious symbols still get attention and are considered attractive and in some cases *authentic*.

On the other hand, there is a difference between *what we are* and *what we have become* (Hall 1996). The second one "provides a framework for the different ways in which people are positioned by, and position themselves in relation to, present realities and narratives of the past" (Bornman 2003, 26). This framework is used to show how Shia Iranians try to present their identity in a new way by using digital media and how the media become a necessary part of their religiosity through the process of mediatization. Based on the longitudinal online observation for this research, Shia Iranians use social media to connect to each other based on a shared origin, and they use these platforms to narrate their own version of religiosity, in an individualized format, that connects them with their historical roots as well. By uploading pictures containing both traditional religious symbols and new forms of religious expression, they display that their religious identity is more of a process of becoming than being.

The main frame that has been used for this research is mediatization theory presented by Hjarvard (2008, 2013, 2016). He presents an institutional approach in the study of media as agents of social and cultural change. Mediatization is a double-sided process of high modernity in which the media on the one hand emerge as an independent institution with a logic of its own that other social institutions have to accommodate to. On the other hand, media simultaneously become an integrated part of other institutions like religion, politics, family as more and more of these institutional activities are performed through both interactive and mass media. The logic of the media refers to "the institutional and technological modus operandi of the media, including the ways in which media distribute material and symbolic resources and make use of formal and informal rules" (Hjarvard 2008, 105). The public face of religion is changing through the process of mediatization (Hjarvard 2012). Hjarvard's focus is on Christianity and Western culture; however, the framework can be applied to examine other religious communities such as Muslim Shia Iranians and the interplay between media and culture in their society.

There are evidences and studies that show the media, specifically online social networks, became essentially constitutive in presenting religious issues, e.g., Campbell (2007, 2012), Campbell and Garner (2016), Dawson and Cowan (2004), Hoover (2006) and Helland (2007, 2008). They have also discussed that media obtained a significant role both in the transmission of religious imagery and in the very production and framing of religious matters and subjects. Regarding the interplay between media and religion in Nordic society, Hjarvard claimed that

> Religious organizations and advocates may still produce their own public representations of religion, but the extent to which these get circulated is heavily influenced by the media system, and religious organizations are more often forced to react to the media's representations of religious issues than the other way around. The majority of public representations of religion are not disseminated by religious organizations but are produced and circulated by the media and serve social functions other than those pursued by religious organizations.
>
> (Hjarvard 2012, 21)

The process of mediatization in Muslim communities has taken the same path. Bunt (2009, 2002) for example documented the influence of the Internet on Muslim communities, rituals, practices, and authority. He focused on what happens when Islam meets the new media, namely the Internet, with a specific focus on how the Internet shapes what Muslims recognize as Islam and its authority. In addition, Eickelman and Anderson (2003) talked about how a new sense of public is emerging throughout Muslim-majority states and how new and increasingly accessible modes of communication have played a significant role in fragmenting and contesting political, organizational authority. They refer to the ways in which formal state control is disrupted by the individualized interpretation of religious texts, meanings and beliefs through online networks.

This chapter is focusing on the process of mediatization among Shia Muslim Iranians based on the key developments in relation to

Meyrowitz's (1993) three metaphors of media. Hjarvard applied these metaphors to analyze media functions with regard to religion: media as conduits, media as languages and media as environments. In media as conduits, the media have become an important source of information and experiences concerning religious issues. The media, as Hjarvard (2012) mentions, use fragments of institutionalized religion and/or elements of folk religion and other cultural forms combined in new ways. Through this process, the media provide a constant framework of *banal religion* in society. Media as languages refers to the statement that says:

> ... the media not only produce and circulate religion but also format religion in different ways, in particular through the genres of popular culture, like adventure, consumer guidance, reality television. The spread of interactive media allows people to express religious ideas and feelings in a variety of genres that usually have not been available to institutionalized religion.
>
> (Hjarvard 2012, 27)

Regarding media as environments, Hjarvard explains that media contribute to the production and altering of social relationships and cultural communities and how they have become crucial for the public celebration of major national and cultural events. "The media ritualize social transitions at micro and macro levels; provide moral orientation, emotional therapy, and consolation in times of crises... the media promote various forms of worship through fan culture, celebrity culture, etc." (Hjarvard 2012, 27).

For this chapter, I will use the same framework to analyze the process of mediatization in the Shia community of Iranians. My focus will be on Instagram as an image-based online platform. Images, pictures, and photos have always played a significant role in religious experience and rituals. For example, paintings and pictures of holy places and Imams, or calligraphic flags, murals, stamps, and posters are inseparable objects in religious scenes and gatherings in Shia Muslim communities. As Morgan (2005) discusses, "images and how people look at them are evidence for understanding belief" (2005, 21). Instagram has an immense capability for representing and negotiating religious identity in a pictorial format. What is fascinating about images, as Morgan (2005) contends, is that images are part of the way of seeing. Seeing can be considered a social act that is a fundamental aspect of believing. Using images for practicing and presenting religion is not a new concept; however, global and instantaneous dissemination of religious pictures by believers is a new social phenomenon, which also magnifies how media enable a continuous dynamic of dis-embedding social interactions from local and traditional contexts and re-embedding them into larger and more modern settings (Hjarvard 2013). Based on this assumption, the social and cultural developments in modern society, which include the increasing mediation of self-representation and social interactions, challenge the traditional role of religion in the formation of identity. Religion, as a social institution, has undergone transformation through the use of online social media, which currently permeates religion.

The Iranian Shia Community and the Internet

As Dawson (2004) mentions, the possibilities introduced by digital media challenge the way religious identities have traditionally been formed. In pre-Internet society, as discussed by Campbell (2012), in most religious communities, religious identity had been dictated from specific authorized institutions and official organizations.

In Iran, after the Islamic revolution of 1979, the state has tried to invite and encourage people to perform their religious deeds in public. In addition, national television and radio, which are under government control, have become the main source of dictating values, norms, and even the form and structure of performing rituals based on the specific interpretation of Shiism. However, the religious structure that the state defines and operates has not necessarily been accepted and performed by all groups of believers. With the ever-expanding use of the Internet and smartphone applications, we need to discuss how and if localized and individualized versions of religiosity and new aspects of Shia identity have emerged. Hjarvard (2013) argues that the increased presence of religious themes in the media may appear to be a challenge for secularization (in Western society) as a necessary feature of high modernity. That means the development of media has increased tendency toward the desecularization or resacralization of modern society. Consequently, we may conclude that online social media as well have at least two major consequences for religious life in Iranian society: First, social media have made religion even more visible and different types of religiosity have developed and are observable. A new process of sacralization is mounting among online groups of Shiite Iranians. They utilize Instagram as a new tool for creating a sacred space and defining their lives as religious. Second, social media have become a resource for knowledge and experiences about religion, which also compels traditional religious organizations to play a different role in society. First, social media have changed the traditional sources of religious authority by providing all kinds of information and a new arena of criticism; and second, social media have changed the manner of religious elites and organizations. As Mazaheri (2007) notes, historically, in performing rituals, especially Muharram mournings and gatherings, some Shia Ulama (elites) have followed the desires and structures created and performed by local communities (non-elites). This has always been criticized by other groups of Ulama and clerics, who believe in a solid foundation of *original* and *authentic* Shia rituals that may or may not be preferred by the popular culture (Mazaheri 2007). It seems that social media have amplified the reflection of pubic desire on elites' behavior. In fact, the mutual impact of the public and the elites with regard to the desires, pace and format of religious rituals is considerably visible on Instagram pictures. Thus, the quality and quantity of changes in the status of authority, which is defined as an element of religious identity formation in the Shia Iranian community, needs to be discussed under the mediatization framework as well.

Hjarvard (2008) mentions three functions of mediatization on the macro level that impact how institutions relate to one another due to the intervention of media. First, they constitute an interface in the relations within and between institutions; in our case, social media bring religious rituals of Muharram into every moment of the individual's life, work, and leisure. Second, the media constitute a realm of shared experience; that is, it offers a continuous presentation and interpretation of *the way things are* and by doing so, contributes to the development of a sense of identity and community. For example, in the case of Shia Iranians using social media platforms, especially Instagram, celebrities have emerged from the elites and individuals whose religious performances – the *Majalis* (gatherings) they attend, the socio-religious campaigns they initiate, the *Rowze* (lyrics and music) they promote – not only get spotlighted, but they also become a specific type of identification for representing identity. Third, media help to create a public sphere within which institutions, such as religion, can pursue and defend their own interests and establish their legitimacy. For the Iranian Shia community, social media provide a public sphere in which all members of the community have an equal opportunity to defend their own interpretation and interest, which extends the meaning of being religious into the wider context of society.

The significant difference between practicing a religion in the pre-Internet world and the global networked society is not the re-combination of public and private spheres; rather it is in the individual's capability to explore their own version of religion and re-constructing religious identity in a reciprocal and cooperative context (Campbell and Garner 2016). The Shia Iranian community is now exploring religious identities through sources other than official organizations and scholars. The version of religiosity that they are now practicing is slightly different from other forms that they have experienced before, since both the tools of getting the information and the fields of representation involve new technologies and integration of different cultures. As Krüger points out, "as the Internet offers religious seekers a degree of autonomy, and as more religious information becomes available online, convergent practice facilitates a potential freedom in the acquisition of ritual knowledge that is individualized rather than absorbed from traditional gatekeepers" (Krüger 2004, 683). In the Internet era, believers can search for alternative points of view and criticisms about their religious thoughts. They can challenge or strengthen the traditional forms by redefining their identity online. They can choose between different versions of interpretation and/or interpret religious content based on their own thoughts and publish it publicly online to a worldwide audience.

To investigate various dimensions of change in the process of mediatization of Shia rituals and identity, I will use the metaphorical distinctions between media as environments, conduits, and languages suggested by Meyrowitz (1993) to investigate how the duality of online-offline religiosity has faded, how experiencing real-time religious practice will affect the presentation of religious identity, and how this new public platform has utilized the creation of the innovative frames for religiosity and new symbols around a traditional ritual. I will illustrate each metaphor through the examples from Instagram pictures.

#The_Flag_of_Imam_Hossein: Media as Environments

Collective Shia identity has always been reflected in special religious events like *Rowze* (Muharram gatherings) and *Dasteh* (processions). Symbols like black attire and flags, calligraphic signs and chains, *Nazri* (food donation), and the whole process of mourning and commemoration have been some of the most important (if not the most important) elements of Shia identity throughout its history (Aghaie 2004, Mazaheri 2007).

Since Muharram rituals play a significant role in Shia identity, it is not surprising that visual, vocal, and textual formats of it have been frequently and vastly presented by Shia Iranians on social media, namely on Instagram. For example, there is a hashtag *the flag of Imam Hossein* (in the Arabic font) on Instagram that was first offered by @moradishahb, Shahab Moradi, a young popular *rohani* (cleric), who invited Shia Iranians to hang one of the flags on a wall of their home or workplace and take a picture of it and share it on Instagram with the same hashtag or re-share other pictures of the flag with the same hashtag. In 2015 and 2016, more than 2,000 pictures were published following his request.

Figure 10.1 is a picture that illuminates a common scene in Muharram in Iran. It shows the living room of a house, clean and organized, before the gathering begins. The armchair is for a lecturer, and the three flags with pictures and calligraphy of Imam Hossein's name decorate the room. The caption contains the hashtag and a poem that says the account holder, nimrokh6, is in search for submission to Allah, purity, and peace in these Muharram gatherings. It seems that nimrokh6 runs a traditional gathering that takes place very early in the morning for a number of days in their home and they are proud of it. Although the setting and decoration in this picture is not unusual, the presentation of this picture on Instagram indicates a new process of mediatization of Shia rituals. This is one example of a reiterated subject in Shia Iranians' profiles during the month of Muharram. Through the lens of the metaphor suggested by Meyrowitz (1993), media can be analyzed as an *environment* in this context.

94 likes

nimrokh6 .

یا اباعبدالله...

مزه ی نوکریت را که چشیدم گفتم

سر این سفره نمک قدر عسل شیرین است

+ فردا بعد از نماز صبح، آخرین روضه خونگی. خدایا

حاجت همه ی دوستام رو بده..

#پیرق_حسینی

Figure 10.1 A house decorated by flags containing the name of Imam Hossein, symbolic pictures of burning candles, and poems. Shared on 29 October 2015, by @nimrokh6.

O'Leary (1996) mentions, religious adopters of the Internet consider it as a sacred space in which they can practice traditional rituals and create new forms of religiosity. In her review of the early studies about religion and the Internet, Campbell (2012) highlighted various forms of adaptation of offline religious rituals, such as prayer, in online environments (Schroeder, Heather and Lee 1998), the creation of cyber-altars or shrines (Brasher 2001, Cowan 2005), and the performance of religious ceremonies and worship services (Prebish 2004, Young 2004). She also referred to Helland (2008), who argues that

… the very structure of the Internet supports and even encourages importing diverse religious activities, especially those that facilitate members' connections to religious sites, festivals, or fellow believers with which they might normally be disconnected due to time–space limitations within contemporary life. Importing religious rituals and artifacts online means religious practitioners can reinterpret context and use.

(Helland 2012, 683)

Referring to the picture above, Instagram becomes a sacralized medium and an environment that has the capacity to reflect religiosity and connect Shia believers to each other. Shia Iranians reinterpret their religion through what they are sharing on social media. A photo of a black flag with Imam Hossein's name printed on it is not simply a picture casually shared on social media; rather, most of the time, it is a religious statement and a declaration of identity. It shows how the person who uploaded the picture wants to explain their religious belongings by projecting a new level of religiosity based on the photos they share on Instagram. For that person, social media have become a new platform for practicing Shia Islam.

Uploading pictures on Instagram and using the specific hashtags indicates three main points: First, people who participate in this movement wish to spread a sense of support and togetherness. They want to explain their choice of belief through sharing a picture of a flag that embodies religious values and meanings. As Berger (1999) describes, religious identity has shifted from being a *given* to a *choice* in the age of digital media. This new tool gives an individual the choice of being religious or not, and allows the individual to decide on the extent of their religiousness based on a collective identity that lifestyle provides. Their attendance in the movement, and the support via comments and likes on flag pictures posted by others, emphasizes the collectiveness of this identity.

Second, uploading a picture of a flag on their social media profile and commenting and liking may be considered as a religious duty since social responsibilities to support and practice religious deeds are now finding a new arena. In Helland's (2007) and Campbell's (2012) accounts, the Internet can be seen as an extension of religious life, not a substitute for it. In other words, social networks have added a new avenue to experience Shia identity that may be more malleable and individualized and less structured and attached to institutions and the state. This new identity can be experienced by sharing pictures, participating in an online campaign by using hashtags, or commenting on related posts.

Third, following a well-known traditional cleric's request online may suggest the empowerment of the offline authority structures in online platforms, as well. These pictures denote more meanings specifically about the position of religious authority in it. There are studies that have tried to explain how the Internet challenges traditional authority online following similar concerns by religious communities. However, these scholars often fail to clarify what aspects of authority are being challenged by the Internet and how (Campbell 2012). Recent works have sought to explore authority online in more tangible ways by distinguishing between authority roles, structures, ideological systems, and sources of legitimation as mentioned by Busch (2011) and Campbell (2007). The result has been that the Internet is framed as a threat to certain roles and hierarchies and as a tool of empowerment for others. This resembles the findings of Meyer and Moors (2005), who argue that the media's format, styles, and infrastructure

> … shape the specific modes by which religions go public, modes that are difficult to control by religious establishment. New media may both have a destabilizing and an enabling potential for established practices for religious mediation. In this sense, new media may resemble a Trojan horse.
>
> (Meyer and Moors 2005, 11)

If we refer to Weber's (1947) three forms of authority – charismatic, rational-legal, and traditional – we may conclude that these forms continue to play a role in the legitimation of religion in contemporary mediatized societies, and media may both reinforce and challenge them in various ways when engaging with religious affairs. The activities of Shia clerics in online social media such as Instagram, for example, are an example of the reassertion of charismatic religious authority in a modern media setting. In the Shia Iranian context, the traditional authority of clerics still plays a role in the media's ritualization of public events, specifically the religious ones. Weber's typology of authority also has descriptive power outside the realm of explicit and organized forms of religion. What can be seen with regard to the celebrity culture on Instagram indicates the ability of media industries to construct charismatic and traditional forms of authority. For example, in the case of Shahab Moradi or other clerics who can be considered Shia celebrities, charismatic and traditional versions of authority play a clear role. However, this is a mediatized version of charismatic and traditional authority that was unavoidably transformed by the media's logic.

"Real-Time" Religious Experience: Media as Conduits

In the Internet era, time and space have been compressed in the use of smartphone technology, even for practicing religion. The conduit metaphor suggested by Meyrowitz (1993) will explain how different mediums have different effects on the content because of their affordances and protocols. This means that experiencing religion in real time would reframe the presentation of religious identity as well.

All religious events can be broadcast *live* on both individual and organizational levels. At the same time, the information that is transmitted is fragmented and disintegrated. One can watch the video and pictures of the Muharram *Rowzeh* while waiting in line at Starbucks. This highlights two main concerns: (1) Not only is the religious information in a *mix and match* and disintegrated format, but it is also experienced out of its context in a nonrelated situation. What does that mean for religion and for the person's religious identity? (2) Religious concepts seem to lose their sacredness if they are accessible anywhere and at any time. That which is sacred is meaningful when it is located in a specific moment and in a holy place. Durkheim (1995) mentions that religious and profane life cannot coexist in the same space and time. Sacredness requires that special locations and times be set aside for religious rituals. How can the meaning of sacred be justified for Shia Iranians in a ceaseless stream of religious concepts on social media? Does religion become less sacred? Can we understand religion differently in the process of mediatization?

There are an increasing number of Shia Iranians who publish their religious experiences on their social media profiles in visual, vocal, or written formats. Official and non-official religious organizations also have created their own websites and profiles on social networks, where they broadcast their events and information and gain followers. This is usually how an individual can attend events and rituals from a distance. For Internet users, limitations of time and place have almost vanished from religious experiences in their everyday lives.

Figure 10.2 is a scene captured in Karbala, Iraq, by Farid Modarresi, an Iranian liberal journalist and a moderate Shia activist who traveled to Iraq for *Ziarat* (to visit the shrine) of Imam Hossein on the exact day of Ashura. He uploaded thirty photos from 22 to 26 October 2015, on his profile during the days he visited Iraq for Muharram commemoration. The frequently of uploading pictures explains the importance of the event for the person and how this medium has become one of the main source of presenting and communicating Shia rituals. Figure 10.2 shows the main door of the shrine of Imam Hossein and the crowd, all in black attire, trying to enter through the door. The red lights, shining gold wall, and black flags all symbolize the martyrdom of Imam Hossein and the rituals performed each year in this place. Uploading this picture on Instagram on the day of Ashura not only creates a unique experiential frame of reference, it also introduces and initiates a new way of being religious or of understanding religious ritual and identity in a new context. Using Instagram and taking a picture while he is at the live event of commemoration means converging different spaces, times, and contexts. The media's creation of a new, shared realm of experience may be conceived as a *re-embedding* of social interaction on a more general and abstract level than once characterized erstwhile place-bound cultures (Hjarvard 2008).

Figure 10.2 The crowd mourning the martyrdom of Imam Hossein on the day of
Ashur in Karbala. Shared on 23 October 2015, by @faridmodarresi.

With regard to the subject of mediatization of religion, part of
Instagram's success with creating an emotional and factual arena for Shia
Iranians to present their modes of religiosity is that sharing the moments
of religious events on Instagram has become as important as participating

in the event itself. Figure 10.2 exemplifies this point. The photographer, standing among all the crowds in the middle of the event and the holy place (in front of the shrine) took a picture. Not only that, but he connected to the Internet, uploaded the picture on his Instagram account, made a caption, and set the location for it, the supporting protocols that each medium comes with (Gitelman 2006). Although being online and the constant notification alerts are the sources of distraction from the event (which is known as a sacred and holy moment for the believers), at the same time the use of these media have become unavoidable for communicating about religious emotions and concepts. Being in different spaces (online and offline) simultaneously and disseminating/receiving various types of information (religious or non-religious) while participating in religious rituals are other new aspects that have been added to religious experience in the mediatization process.

It is important to mention that in the process of mediatization of religion in the Shia Iranian community, online social media such as Instagram provide a spontaneous version of religiosity that is a mélange of formal/institutionalized religion and an imaginative and personalized version of it. As can be seen in the pictures uploaded by Shia Iranians on Instagram, each adaptor narrates a new aspect of religiosity, which may not even be considered as the original element of Shiism, but it is being explicitly published as a part of Shia identity representation. Being an active member on social media for them means that it has become religiously important to participate in online expression of their beliefs, which shows the expansion of mediatization even more.

The feeling of connectivity in a real-time context makes religious performances fluid and condensed, since it happens in an instant and continues with other moments on social media, namely Instagram. Religious identity, as well, has become a situational and a real-time subject. Therefore, it seems that the Internet gives its audiences a broader sense of religiosity since it provides them with access to different traditions and rituals practiced by Shias in other places, inside or outside of Iran. Among the selected pictures for this study, some pictures have been taken from different cities in Iran that have various types of rituals regarding the same event, and other pictures are from Europe and North America, which show Shia Iranian communities in the West running and participating in the commemoration despite the limited resources (such as the lack of lecturers for the event, or lack of specific place to gather for the *Rowze*) typically faced in their new communities.

As the main indicators of religious identity, religious beliefs, religious structures and authority, religious practice, and religious community have all emerged and been performed by Shia Iranians on online social networks, but they have been practiced differently. Some traits of their religiosity are mixed with other contexts (using modern arts), some other parts are challenged (i.e., aspects of traditional leadership), and some traits are empowered and increased (i.e., visual and symbolic aspects of rituals). In other words, Shia Iranians' religious experience goes beyond orders and boundaries by utilizing new communication technologies. Therefore, the type of identity that has been formed online is more flexible and fluid.

Storied Identity: Media as Languages

Discussing the fluidity and malleability in identity formation, the meaning of *storied identity* by Campbell (2012) can denote the transformation of Shia identity through mediatization. Historically, the process of identity formation and the structure and ways of performing rituals were mostly controlled by official religious organizations and local authorities. There were rules and features assigned for religious rituals, particularly for performing them in the community of believers. Even in modern and secular societies, institutions usually define what is originally religious and what language is proper. In the Internet era, however, digital communication has been changing this tradition toward a more individualized version of identity and experience, and new forms and categories of religiosity have emerged. In Campbell and Garner's (2016, 68) account, "identity online often becomes an act of conscious performance, in which individuals select, assemble, and present their sense of self through a variety of resources available to them".

In the Shia Iranians' context, looking at the images shared on Instagram, there were many pictures taken of *a cup of tea in Rowze* (by searching the hashtag *Roze_tea* in Persian font, more than 1,000 pictures showed up) accompanied by poetic captions that symbolize a cup of tea as a sign for the love of Imam Hossein and the Muharram commemoration. *The Rowze tea*, which is served as a traditional drink during the mourning ceremonies, has become an icon of believing in the specific spirituality that this drink presents in that specific moment and context. In many cases, the poems and the captions associate this specific tea with physical health and spiritual peace. As Hjarvard (2012, 27) points out regarding the metaphor of media as languages: "since media do not have the intention to preach, but rather to get attention, they have a higher sensibility to the immediate cultural demands of various segments of the population". The metaphor of *cup of Rowze tea* in the picture symbolizes the love for Imam Hossein has become a fashion among the believers. They utilize Instagram as an interactive media which allows them to express religious ideas and feelings in a variety of genres that usually have not been available to institutionalized religion. No one had captured a picture of a cup of tea as a Shia identity indicator in the pre-Internet era (Figure 10.3).

Figure 10.3 Women's Muharram commemoration session in Tehran, Iran. Shared on 23 October 2015, by @fetemeseif.

The focus of the photographer is on the cup of tea placed in front of an old woman, who is among a row of women wearing a traditional hijab (Chador) seated on an Iranian carpet in Imam Hossein's mourning session. This is a very familiar scene in Muharram gatherings, which appears in a new context through a new medium. The poem in the caption can be translated as the following: *I am not a tea-drinker, but I drink this tea wishing for spiritual and physical healing and peace.*

We must acknowledge that in the mediatization process, information about religion is shaped based on the demands of various popular media genres such as news, drama, blogging, and in this case, attractive traditionally mournful pictures (Hjarvard 2016). The metaphor of media as languages provided by Meyrowitz (1993) discusses that not only is the content important, but the different tools (like grammar in language) will influence the communication and how it appears in a religious context. The pictures shared by Shia Iranians on Instagram contain familiar and eye-catching indications that can tell nostalgic stories with religious connotations, but the way they put these pictures together, how they narrate their sorrow, how they use the filters, what angles they choose to capture the picture, and what captions they write is also considered part of the mediatization of religious identity formation. On Instagram, each Shia Iranian becomes a religious agent who provides a source of religious knowledge and the narrator of their part of the story through pictures.

Creation (and re-creation) of local symbols, and sometimes personal symbols for Shia Iranians, is not an unexpected incident; however, it has happened only in very restricted ways and the symbols were rarely disseminated and published worldwide as is possible with social media. Also, most of the time, creating symbols was limited to religious leaders or artists who had the authority or the technology to do so. Currently, through social media and using different smartphone applications, religious individuals are making religious symbols that are welcomed and widely used.

There are other types of examples among the selected pictures that contain conceptual art designs mixed with the symbols signifying the meanings of martyrdom or justice and freedom to honor Imam Hossein. Figure 10.4 is one of the pictures of an art exhibition with the theme *Muharram* that took place in a *Hey'at* (a place and the community for Muharram gathering) and held by a group of artists from the Department of Art at the University of Tehran. The meaning implied in this picture is directly related to how these people, both the artists and the audiences who share the picture on Instagram, wish to perform their religious identity online. Using their professional skills to make a unique religious artwork and demonstrating it on social media is just an observable aspect of their religious goals. The more significant point is that the Internet has become a tool by which personalized versions of religious identity can be narrated. As Campbell and Garner note,

> … the Internet provides the sources and space that help religious individuals explore and present the beliefs and values they identify with. In this way the Internet becomes a tool to perform the religious persona they seek to portray to the Online public.
>
> (Campbell and Garner 2016, 68)

daszarrin ...

60 likes

daszarrin .

صحنه آرایی هنرمندانه هیئتی های دانشگاه هنر

#هیئت_هنر

View 1 comment

OCTOBER 21, 2015

Figure 10.4 An artwork symbolizing Imam Hossein and his associates as lights and other companions as the pigeons who follow them. It was part of an art exhibition with the theme *Muharram* along with the commemoration session at Tehran University, Iran. Shared on 21 October 2015, by @daszarrin.

These kinds of pictures can be contextualized through Hjarvard's (2013) concept of *banal religion*, as well; the term that Hjarvard borrowed from Michael Billig's (1995) idea of *banal nationalism* and used in the context of mediatized religion:

> … nationalism and national identity are not only created and maintained through the use of official and explicit symbols of the nation, but are also to a very great extent based on a series of everyday phenomena that constantly remind the individual of his or her belonging to the nation and the national culture.
>
> (In Hjarvard 2013, 90)

Billig also refers to official and unofficial, waved and unwaved flags to discuss manifested and less visible aspects of nationalism. This frame can be adopted for analyzing religion as well. The less noticed part of religion, which is usually not performed in the institutionalized version of religion and is not a formal way of presenting religious identity, is what we can call *banal religion*. It is a less coherent version of religion that is fragmented and appears in unfamiliar formats.

The artist captured in Figure 10.5, just as an example among all similar pictures, is performing religiosity in a completely new format. As a type of language, Instagram frames religion within discourses of debate,

Figure 10.5 An artist wearing black attire working on a sculpture in an exhibition with the theme *Muharram* along with the commemoration session at the University of Tehran, Iran. Shared on 21 October 2015, by @sfmotahari.

presentation and even disapproval of other forms of religiosity, rather than within the language of the institutionalized Shia tradition. These experiences which mostly relate to instances of individual history or profession are now becoming a part of representing religious identity for the Instagram adaptor. This is one of the most noticeable aspects of banal religion that have been occurred through the process of mediatization. The scene in Figure 10.5 showcases modern artists who now can narrate their own story of being Shia in online platforms, and the Shia community welcomes these personal narratives not only by attending their exhibition, but also by making comments and likes and following them on social media. In this way, media may destabilize existing forms of religious communication practices and identity performances and enable other practices to emerge, both inside and outside of established religious organizations and movements (Hjarvard 2016).

Using Instagram, as a tool and as a forum, these artists perform their unique version of Shia identity through the representation of artifacts. The pictures of this exhibition contain another connotation as well: These artists separate their professional identity from other artists who do not have religious belonging. Campbell and Garner (2016, 67) state that "religious identity represents the core characteristics or values with which a religious group or individual identifies as a way to distinguish themselves from others". For these people, making religious art scenery and sharing pictures of it online is not just fulfilling their leisure time or finding friends online. For them, acting religiously online is part of their Shia identity construction. However, they highlight the same concept, *Muharram rituals*, that have been the climax of the history of Shia identity as Aghaie (2004) and Mazaheri (2007) also discuss. The main point that should not be ignored in this regard is that these banal representations of religion are becoming as important, significant, expressive and representative part of Shiism as the formal and institutionalized versions of it. This describes how the mediatization process is affecting the function and form of religiosity and religious identity in the Iranian Shia community.

Conclusion

Shia Iranians' presentations on social media, particularly the process of photo sharing on Instagram with friends and the world, have changed their experience of being religious. Now we may ask a further question: Has the media arrogated religious experience from the religious institutions in the way they have become increasingly dependent on the media and have had to adapt to the logic of the media in the process of mediatization?

This study indicates that mediatization of religion offers new possibilities for studying and understanding religious identities. For example, when Shia Iranians share pictures related to the Muharram rituals, they want to emphasize their religiosity. However, the variety of the pictures and the selected options are deeply connected to the way they understand a specific event or how they want to define it. It seems that because of the compression of time and space, and using smartphones that connect individuals to religious content constantly, Shia Iranians overcome the limitations of reaching religious resources and become increasingly more engaged in religious contexts.

Using Instagram photos as examples, this research leads us to conclude that new media technology has individualized identity formation for Shia Iranians. As Campbell (2012) mentions, "such experiences can inhibit an individual's ability to develop a cohesive religious identity, or restrict one's reaffirmation of the accepted boundaries between traditional and personal religious identity" (2012, 687). For example, the objects and artifacts presented in these photos may not necessarily be considered religious in a traditional way; however, the photographer has used the artifact as an iconic object to present their religious identity. The term *banal religion* (Hjarvard 2016) which introduces how media affects religion, helps to clarify the contexts explored in this chapter.

In this chapter, three metaphors of media, media as environments, conduits and languages, have been discussed and the examples revealed that the Internet does not necessarily have a uniform influence on every aspect of religion. For example, in the Shia Iranian community, traditional origins of rituals get more attention and new symbols have even been created based on them, but the function of religious authority itself has been transformed in its appearance and form. Applying a three-metaphor framework explains that the mediatization of religion through social media entails that religious practices and rituals become increasingly dependent upon media and, more specifically, the Internet.

Pictures show that traditional Shia Islam is still the main discourse for religious Iranians. As Baym (1998) states, "over time researchers found that Internet users tended to create online identities that closely resembled their offline identities" (in Campbell 2012, 688). However, using the new communication technology to disseminate this ideology can be considered an innovation. New communication technology provides a free public sphere for Shia Iranians to discuss and form their religious identity. This is a new experience in their religious life since they can narrate and interpret religious concepts in their own way. Although the authoritative official perspective still spreads through the online sphere, the level of individuality cannot be ignored in how religious lifestyle is represented online.

Based on Shia Iranians' activities online, it seems that they have defined a new type of practice for themselves: being online and gathering all the information they can in real time to participate in a broader context of Shiism. This way, whether they are at work or school, inside Iran or outside, they can constantly experience religion online. If they attend any religious events or visit any holy city, they can disseminate their experience by sharing photos, recording audio and videos or writing about it on social media. Sometimes they use all of these formats to share their experience on their various social media accounts. This is how the media contribute to mold the religious imagination and performances in accordance with the genres of popular culture and individual lifestyle, specifically shown in the creation of religious symbols on social media.

The formation of religious identity has become a real-time and reciprocal process in which individuals and their choices perform a significant role. The body of information disseminated online and used by religious adaptors makes them active believers who have the chance to publish their experience worldwide. They also receive feedback and supportive comments from other active individuals. As a cultural environment, the Internet has become a sacred space for Shia Iranians to practice rituals. That means the media has partly taken over some of the social functions of the institutionalized and dominant version of religion that provides moral and spiritual structure and a sense of community among Shia Iranians.

References

Aghaie, K., 2004. *The Martyrs of Karbala: Shi'i Symbols and Ritual in Modern Iran*. Seattle: University of Washington Press.

Baym, N., 1998. The Emergence of On-line Community. In: Jones, S., ed. *Cybersociety 2.0: Revisiting Computer-Mediated Community and Communication*. Thousand Oaks: SAGE, 35–68.

Berger, P., 1999. *The Desecularization of the World: Resurgent Religion and World Politics*. Washington, DC: Ethics and Public Policy Centre.

Billig, M., 1995. *Banal Nationalism*. London: SAGE.

Bornman, E., 2003. Struggles of Identity in the Age of Globalisation. *Communicatio*, 29(1–2), 24–47.

Brasher, B., 2001. *Give Me That Online Religion*. San Francisco: Jossey-Bass.

Bunt, G., 2002. *Virtually Islamic: Computer-Mediated Communication and Cyber Islamic Environments*. Lampeter: University of Wales Press.

Bunt, G., 2009. *iMuslims: Rewiring the House of Islam (Islamic Civilization and Muslim Networks)*. Chapel Hill: The University of North Carolina Press.

Busch, L., 2011. To Come to a Correct Understanding of Buddhism: A Case Study on Spiritualizing Technology, Religious Authority, and the Boundaries of Orthodoxy and Identity in a Buddhist Web Forum. *New Media & Society*, 13(1), 58–74.

Campbell, H., 2007. Who's Got the Power? Religious Authority and the Internet. *Journal of Computer-Mediated Communication*, 12, 1043–1062.

Campbell, H., 2012. Religion and the Internet: A Microcosm for Studying Internet Trends and Implications. *New Media and Society*, 15(5), 680–694.

Campbell, H. and Garner, S., 2016. *Networked Theology: Negotiating Faith in Digital Culture*. Grand Rapids: Baker Academic.

Cowan, D., 2005. *Cyberhenge: Modern Pagans on the Internet*. New York: Routledge.

Dawson, L., 2004. Religion and the Quest for Virtual Community. In: Dawson, L. and Cowan, D., eds. *Religion Online: Finding Faith on the Internet*. New York: Routledge.

Durkheim, E., 1995. *The Elementary Forms of Religious Life*. New York: Free Press.

Eickelman, D. and Anderson, J., eds., 2003. *New Media in the Muslim World: The Emerging Public Sphere*. Bloomington: Indiana University Press.

Gitelman, L., 2006. *Always Already New: Media, History and the Data of Culture*. Cambridge: MIT Press.

Glaw, X., Inder, K., Kable, A. and Hazelton, M., 2017. Visual Methodologies in Qualitative Research: Autophotography and Photo Elicitation Applied to Mental Health Research. *International Journal of Qualitative Methods*, 16, 1–8.

Hall, S., 1996. Cultural Identity and Diaspora. In: J. Rutherford, ed. *Identity: Community, Culture, Difference*. London: Lawrence & Wishart, 222–237.

Helland, C., 2007. Diaspora on the Electronic Frontier: Developing Virtual Connections with Sacred Homelands. *Journal of Computer-Mediated Communication*, 12(3), 956–976.

Helland, C., 2008. Canadian Religious Diversity Online: A Network of Possibilities. In: Beyer, P. and Beaman, L., eds. *Religion and Diversity in Canada*. Boston: Brill Academic Publishers, 127–148.

Hjarvard, S., 2008. The Mediatization of Society: A Theory of the Media As Agents of Social and Cultural Change. *Nordic Review*, 29(2), 105–134.

Hjarvard, S., 2012. Three Forms of Mediatized Religion. Changing the Public Face of Religion. In: Hjarvard, S. and Lövheim, M., eds. *Mediatization and Religion Nordic Perspectives*. Göteborg: Nordicom University of Gothenburg.

Hjarvard, S., 2013. *The Mediatization of Culture and Society*. New York: Routledge.

Hjarvard, S., 2016. Mediatization and the Changing Authority of Religion. *Media, Culture and Society*, 38(1), 8–17.

Hoover, S., 2006. *Religion in the Media Age*. London: Routledge.

Iranian Student Polling Agency (ISPA), 2016. Available at http://ispa.ir/Default/Details/fa/1215/--یرانیا-از-نیمی-عضویت%E2%80%8Cدر-ها-شبکه%E2%80%8Cتلگرام-نفر-میلیون-20-از-بیش-اجتماعی-های, accessed 13 December 2016.

Krüger, O., 2004. The Internet As a Mirror and Distributor of Religious and Ritual Knowledge. *Asian Journal of Social Sciences*, 32(2), 183–197.

Lövheim, M., 2013. Identity. In: Campbell, H., ed. *Digital Media: Understanding Religious Practice in New Media Worlds*. London: Routledge, 41–57.

Mazaheri, M., 2007. *Shia Media*. Tehran: Sherkat-e Chap-o Nashr-e Bein-ol Melal.

Meyer, B. and Moors, A., 2005. Introduction. In: Meyer, B. and Moors, A., eds. *Religion, Media, and the Public Sphere*. Bloomington: Indiana University Press, 1–25.

Meyrowitz, J., 1993. Images of the Media: Hidden Ferment – and Harmony – In the Field. *Journal of Communication*, 43(3), 55–66.

Miller, C. and Shepherd, D., 2004. Blogging As Social Action: A Genre Analysis of the Weblog. *Into the Blogosphere: Rhetoric, Community, and Culture of*

Weblogs, 18. Available at http://blogs.ubc.ca/ewayne/files/2010/03/A-Genre-Analysis-of-the-Weblog.pdf, accessed 2 October 2015.

Morgan, D., 2005. The Sacred Gaze: Religious Visual Culture in Theory and Practice. Berkeley: University of California Press.

O'Leary, S., 1996. Cyberspace As Sacred Space: Communicating Religion on Computer Networks. *Journal of the American Academy of Religion*, 64(4), 781–808.

Prebish, C., 2004. The Cybersangha: Buddhism on the Internet. In: Dawson, L. and Cowan, D., eds. *Religion Online: Finding Faith on the Internet*. New York: Routledge, 135–150.

Schroeder, R., Heather, N. and Lee, R., 1998. The Sacred and the Virtual: Religion in Multi-User Virtual Reality. *Journal of Computer-Mediated Communication*, 4(2). Available at doi:10.1111/j.1083-6101.1998.tb00092.x/full, accessed 4 August 2015.

Tajfel, H., 1981. *Human Groups and Social Categories*. Cambridge: Cambridge University Press.

Turkle, S., 1995. *Life on the Screen: Identity in the Age of the Internet*. New York: Touchstone.

Weber, M., 1947. *Theory of Social and Economic Organization*. New York: Oxford University Press.

Young, G., 2004. Reading and Praying Online: The Continuity in Religion Online and Online Religion in Internet Christianity. In: Dawson, L. and Cowan, D., eds. *Religion Online: Finding Faith on the Internet*. New York: Routledge, 93–106.

11 Understanding Jewish Digital Media in Israel

Between Technological Affordances and Religious-Cultural Uses

Ruth Tsuria and Heidi A. Campbell

Introduction

Studying the religious Jewish community's engagement with the Internet within Israel has been an area of interest for many scholars, especially those seeking to understand how religious communities navigate between the resources offered by modernity and their traditional social-moral boundaries. This chapter offers a review and discussion of current studies on Israeli Judaism and digital media in light of the theoretical considerations of mediatization. It will begin by presenting how Israeli Judaism has historically been highly mediatized. Then it will provide an overview of past scholarly work on Israeli Judaism and digital media. Two specific case studies will be highlighted: religious community and identity construction through humor in social media, and religious communal boundary negotiation online. The chapter will conclude by discussing the benefits and disadvantages of using mediatization theories and suggest combining it with the theoretical approach of *Religious Social Shaping of Technology* (RSST).

Mediatization is an approach to media theory that is understood in a variety of ways. Two of the most prominent mediatization theories are articulated by European thinkers, such as Hjarvard (2013) and Hepp and Krotz (2014). Hepp and Krotz explain their version of mediatization in depth (2013). They describe mediatization as a long-term meta-process "of changing forms of communicative action" (2013, 138). They define media as "modifiers of communication" (2013, 142) and mediatization as a "non-linear concept and consists of a colorful bouquet of mechanisms and possible influences" (2013, 142). Those mechanisms and influences include the rules and regulations placed on media (media institutions), the technologies related to media (media technologies), media as molders of social reality (media as apparatus of staging) and media as form of communication (media as space of experience) (2013, 143–145). In other words, mediatization is understood as a process in which media plays an important role in cultural and social meaning-making. To explore this role, Hepp and Krotz look to social phenomenology, and utilized the concept of *life-worlds* (Luckmann 1970) to empirically analyze everyday *mediatized worlds*. According to Hepp and Krotz, we can begin to examine mediatization by looking at small-scale or context-specific mediatized worlds and exploring "in which way their communicative construction is shaped by various media, as well as how this communicative construction changes..." (2014, 149).

A different approach to mediatization is explicitly articulated in Hjarvard's work as a nuanced version of technological determinism. Unlike technological determinism, which sees every technology as a determining force, Hjarvard's mediatization theory focuses on the influence of media in the 20th and 21st centuries, in societies that live in highly-technological, highly-modern surroundings. Hjarvard claims that in those societies, media industries operate as social institutions. That is, media industries are organizations that inform or establish norms of social behavior. Furthermore, media as social institutions are increasingly gaining power. His theory about the *mediatization of religion*, therefore, claimed that these media institutions are replacing religious institutions, or that established religious institutions begin to function using media logics. According to Hjarvard,

> The overall outcome of the mediatization of religion is not a new kind of religion as such, but rather a new social condition in which the power to define and practice religion has changed.
>
> (Hjarvard 2013, 10)

That is, media as an institution and media logics are the forces shaping contemporary culture and religion.

Are these European approaches to media and society helpful when examining other contexts? This chapter offers Judaism in Israel as an interesting case study for exploring these notions of mediatization and for considering religion, culture, media and modernity at large. It is important to note that Judaism is not the only religion practiced in Israel – Christianity, Islam, Druze and Judaism are all officially recognized religions, meaning the Israeli government protects the rights of people to practice these religions. However, Israel is the only country in the world in which Judaism is the majority religion, and 75% of population are registered as Jews (Israeli Central Bureau of Statistics 2010). This means that Israeli Judaism is a different lived experience than diasporic Judaism. While most people in Israel are not actively practicing Jewish religion, Judaism as a culture or lived experience is present in many aspects of life in Israel.

Campbell argued that when studying digital media and religion, it is important to consider how the cultural and religious norms inform the adoption, rejection and negotiation of the new media (Campbell 2010). Judaism in general has an appreciation of text and media that makes it easy for new media to be adopted and used for religious purposes, which is the case with print, newspapers, radio and audio cassettes (Campbell 2011, Fader 2013). However, visual media such as television, cinema and visual art are less accepted in Jewish religious circles. Furthermore, digital media allow private communication without the regulation by the community, and therefore can be a threat to this community-based religion. In Israel, two major religious reactions to visual and digital media can be noted – rejection and negotiation (Campbell 2011, 365). While some religious communities almost completely reject television and digital media, most religious Jews in Israel consume these media. The negotiation practices include either consuming only religious content, consuming regulated content (e.g., using internet filters) or consuming mainstream Israeli media with self-regulation and in moderation. One should note that Israeli media is relatively secular. As a result, religious communities in Israel have created their own sectorial media (Cohen 2001, 96). This sectorial approach to media is still present in digital media, where religious Jews create "digital enclaves" (Campbell and Golan 2011, 709).

This chapter will focus on these religious individuals and communities who consume and use digital media, and will consider in what ways they use media, and how their use of media informs their religious practice. Mediatization asks us to pay careful attention to how the media work as a social institution and/or as a meta-process, which is, to some degree, replacing and contributing to existing social institutions and communication behaviors. In the case of Israeli Judaism, the religious social institution is comprised of the community, the religious schools (*Yeshiva* and *Midrasha*) and the synagogue. While digital media have not replaced the synagogue for religious Jews in Israel, they do, as this chapter will argue, serve as a complimentary and increasingly important site for identity construction and communal norms development. Two case studies will be used to support this claim: Aya Yadlin-Segal's work (2015) on community and identity construction via memes and social media, and Golan and Campbell's work (2015) on the strategic management of Orthodox websites in Israel.

This chapter will suggest combining *Religious Social Shaping of Technology and Mediatization of Religion*. This is important because we argue the ways media are used for the construction of religious norms in Israel are informed both by the religious cultural background and by media affordances. Although these two approaches stand in opposition regarding, for example, the way they understand the shaping of technology process – where RSST argues that religious communities shape technology and mediatization claims that technology as a social institution shapes society – this chapter argues that combining these approaches creates a productive dialectic tension. Through this combination we are able to consider both processes: the religious context and how it informs religious uses of technology, as well as the logics and affordances of the media and how these logics and affordances impact religious uses of technology. The rest of the chapter will contextualize religious media in Israel, review two specific case studies and examine the use of mediatization theories in this context.

Understanding Religious Digital Media in Israel

In order to understand religious digital media in Israel, we first provide some context on both the media sphere and the religious sphere in Israel. The religious context in Israel is unique in several ways. First, it is the only nation in the world in which Judaism is the majority religion and the official state religion. The Israeli government in its early days created what is known as the status quo of religious adherence regulated by the state, which includes restrictions on work during Jewish holidays and Sabbaths (Saturdays), restrictions on selling non-kosher food, religiously ordained marriages and burials, and the duty of the state to support and supply religious needs, such as a local rabbi, accessible *Mikvhe* (ritual bath) and synagogues (Barak-Erez 2009). While the official religion is Judaism, some Muslim, Bahai, Druze and Christian needs are also supported by the government, although these religions are not so dominant in the public spaces (for example, Christmas is not an official holiday). Most Israeli Jews are either secular (43% of the Jewish population) or traditional (23%). Twenty-five percent self-identify as religious, and 9% label themselves as ultra-Orthodox (Israeli Central Bureau of Statistics 2010). Since most Jews in Israel are secular or moderately traditional, these early status-quo regulations are being challenged by the secular majority. As of 2016, it has become legal to operate a business during Sabbath, although this pertains primarily to shopping centers and restaurants; to sell pork and seafood (although it is still illegal to raise pigs in Israel), and there is currently a public struggle to make public transportation operational during Sabbath and to make marriage a state issue instead of a religious one.

Within Judaism, two religious denominations are practiced by Jews in Israel: Orthodox National-Religious (also known as Zionist-Religious) and ultra-Orthodox. While the Conservative and Reform movements are gaining visibility in Israel, especially following the wave of American Jews immigrating to Israel in the last two decades, these religious movements are in the minority and are considered suspicious (Maltz and Ravid 2016). Therefore, Judaism in Israel is inherently different from that in the USA or Europe. Both the acceptable denominations are Orthodox, but a variety of what it means to be Orthodox has arisen in Israel, including hybrids such as Datlight (lightly religious), Hardal (between National-Religious and ultra-Orthodox) and more. Within Orthodoxy, a spectrum of reactions to modernity exist. On one end of the spectrum, ultra-Orthodox groups typically reject modern values and live in more closed-off communities. However, even within ultra-Orthodox society there are different degrees of exclusion, where some ultra-Orthodox communities work and interact with the secular world while fencing themselves off from possible challenges to their belief systems. Other communities try to live in complete isolation, with community-based education, commerce and media (Dosick 1995, 20). On the other end of the spectrum, modern-Orthodox communities strive to combine modern living and values with their religious tradition. Modern-Orthodox individuals may be consuming popular media, consider themselves feminist, and work and live in mixed neighborhoods. The National Religious group in Israel is a prominent example of combining modern and traditional values. This community believes in many modern values, most prominent of which is nationalism, namely, protecting and benefiting the state of Israel. They also view integration with general Israeli secular society as a positive value (Rosenthal and Ribak 2015, 148), and use and contribute to the advancement of science and technology. This community also has a more egalitarian approach toward rabbinical authority. Although rabbis still represent the religious institutions and knowledge, each (male) person is encouraged to study *Halacha* (Jewish law and interpretation) and be the master of his own life/home. Some of the ultra-Orthodox communities take a similar approach to epistemic authority, especially the *Mitnagdim* (Friedman 1991). In contrast, the Hasidic communities are groups in which the rabbi is the absolute leader of the community. In these communities, the rabbi is conceived of as a *Zadik*, a holy man, and his words and actions must be followed. Some of the distinctions within the spectrum of religiosity have to do with where you live – Is it a religious neighborhood? Mixed? Secular? – others with what you wear – Black suit? Long sleeves? Skirt? Skirt and thick socks? Head cover? Wig? Yet other ways to distinguish one's religious standing are through the type of media they consume. For more strict ultra-Orthodox communities, for example, secular media is unacceptable and community members mostly consume sect-specifically produced material, such as the *Hamodia* newspaper. The least religiously constrained people use digital media and secular media seamlessly. Generally, religious people in Israel consume a negotiated mixture of religious and secular, mass and digital media.

The media sphere in Israel is also important to consider as part of the context in which religious media negotiation takes place. Although a relatively young nation (est. 1948), Israel has an advanced modern media infrastructure. Already in the early days of Zionism, Hebrew communication through books, pamphlets and newspapers was prevalent. After the creation of the state of Israel, most media broadcast systems – especially radio and television – were government produced and controlled, secular in nature, with little to no diversity in content.

Newspapers were not government owned, and had much more freedom of expression (although some military censorship prevails to this day). For the religious groups in Israel, the main source of media produced for the community consisted of synagogue pamphlets, and religious radio and newspapers. From the 1980s onward communication technologies and media broadcasters have been privatized, resulting in a variety of Israeli-produced content, as well as the increased import of American, Australian and European television shows and films. More diversity and sector-specific content was also available, including religious television shows/channels, such as *Eruzt Meir* and *Eruzt Orot* (http://orot.tv/).

Digital media in Israel emerged in the 1990, through academic and military institutions. The Israeli market adopted the Internet relatively quickly, developed infrastructure and ISPs, and by 2014 Israel was rated as having the fifth fastest internet connection in the world. Mobile phones are also very popular in Israel, with Israel having the second fastest adoption rate in the world (Tsuria and Yadlin-Segal 2017, 146). Most Israelis are constantly connected, many have more than one device, and quite a few Israelis are involved in the creation, development and production of successful mobile apps and cybersecurity software (such as ICQ, Waze and Checkpoint). While the majority of Israelis quickly embraced digital technology, religious Jews in Israel were much more suspicious of the emerging technology. Most Orthodox Jewish communities in Israel initially viewed digital technology as a threat for a few reasons. First, internet access allowed little to no communal regulation, and for a society that centers on communal life, this was unwelcome social behavior. Second, right from its early days, the Internet was synonymous with access to pornographic material, which is forbidden for religious Jews. Third, it made moving between the community and the outside world seamless and invisible, and access to the vast amount of information online can lead to doubts or a rejection of religious and communal principles. As beautifully put in the short documentary *Bacon and God's Wrath*:

> ...two years ago I started using the Internet... my journey on the Internet began by accident... I was looking for a recipe but I quickly became fascinated... I would start typing a sentence and it would guess the ending [...] some of my most intimate thoughts and questions were shared... were so common... that feeling of connectedness – it was more than I ever got from going to synagogue! Well, as you can imagine it was a first step on a slippery sloop, and I went very quickly from Julia Child to Christopher Hitchens!
>
> (2015, Minutes 5:11–6:13)

Because of these concerns, the religious-Jewish reaction to mobile and digital media was either rejection or negotiation. While some religious communities completely reject digital media, most religious Jews in

Israel use these media. The negotiation practices include either consuming only religious content or regulated content (e.g., using internet filters), forming *digital enclaves* or consuming mainstream Israeli media with self-regulation. The following section discusses how to theorize the adoption and negotiation of digital media by religious Jews in Israel.

Understanding Digital Religion in Israel: Between *Religious Social Shaping of Technology* and Mediatization of Religion

The study of Judaism and digital media can be thought of as a continuation of the more general study of Judaism and media. This includes studies of mass media such as television, radio and newspapers (Katz 2012), as well as community produced media, such as books and audio cassettes (Barzilai-Nahon and Barzilai 2005, Fader 2013), and religious Jews' representation in Israeli media (Cohen 2005, 2012). Both research on *old* media and new media tended to consider the role media play in communal and religious norms construction and how these religious communities negotiate their relation with media (Blondheim and Caplan 1993, 59). This has been especially noted in the reaction to digital media, which are less easily restricted.

Jewish Religious communities in Israel have reacted to digital media in various ways, mostly through negotiation or rejection. It can be argued that the reactions reflect the religious spectrum in Israel – from *light* religiosity, or modern Orthodox, which by and large adopted digital media, to *strict* religiosity, or fundamental ultra-Orthodox, which mostly rejected and by-and-large do not use digital media. Of course, many religious users fall somewhere in between, creating their own version of a religiously motivated negotiation of digital media use. For some ultra-Orthodox communities, the threat posed by the Internet is such that rejection is the only option. To insure this rejection, rabbis and community leaders called on their disciples to ban the Internet. However, as Campbell and other scholars showed early on, this is not a complete rejection, but rather a complicated negotiation. Those religious Jews who embrace digital media do so, according to Yaron Katz, by utilizing the digital religiously. Katz found that the religious communities in Israel use the Internet for what he calls "religious purposes" (Katz 2012, 16). These uses include: (1) finding essential information about religious festivals, culture and education; (2) questions and answers; (3) *Torah* lessons; (4) websites for specific rabbis; (5) online communities; and (6) a space to share and consume creative work. Campbell (2010) also showcased how many Jewish religious communities negotiate new media in various ways. For example, the Chabad sect, which has a missionary vocation within Judaism, embraced the Internet fairly early on for missionary purposes. Furthermore, since the Internet supplies business opportunities, especially for women who could utilize the Internet for work while staying at home, ultra-Orthodox communities had to shape tools to allow access to the Internet whilst maintaining community boundaries and the authority of the religious leaders. In 2008, the ultra-Orthodox leaders allowed community members to use the Internet for work. As Barzilai-Nahon and Barzilai (2005) argued, this process is best understood as cultured technology, where specific communities localize the Internet for their needs, instead of simply rejecting or accepting it. One way in which the technology of the Internet is being cultured is by restricting certain online content. This can be done, for example, via the use of a specific internet program – *Internet Rimon* (www.neto. net.il/). This program filters internet content and provides access only to *kosher* content. Another way in which Jewish communities negotiate their relationship with new media is by creating local spaces: blogs, web pages or web portals specifically designed for their communities. These digital enclaves like the *Kipa.co.il* site (for the Israeli National-Religious community) or *Behederi Haredim* forum portal (for the Israeli ultra-Orthodox community), are where religious communities create safe havens online for their religious denominations. De facto, regardless of the ban, most Orthodox Jews in Israel use the Internet to some degree (Cejka 2009, 99).

These negotiation patterns suggest a relationship between media and culture that is informed by the religious and cultural worldview of the users. While mediatization theories are helpful to consider the ways media shapes social structures, they tend to belittle the role tradition plays in the adoption and negotiation of media and technologies. Therefore, we suggest a softer approach to mediatization, an approach that combines it with the important theoretical approach of *Religious Social Shaping of Technology*. The following case studies serve as empirical data to exemplify the complexity of religion and digital media in Israeli Judaism.

Filters, Memes and LOLs – Tension between Technology and Religion

In this section, two case studies are discussed: Aya Yadlin-Segal's (2015) study of National Religious internet memes and Golan and Campbell's (2015) work on the strategic management of Orthodox websites in Israel. These two studies provide empirical information for the examination of religious daily uses of digital media, and will be used as key case studies when trying to understand religious negotiation of media in Israel.

Golan and Campbell's (2015) work examines Israeli religious (Orthodox) websites and their negotiation between tradition and modernity. They looked at three sites – *Koogle.co.il, bhol.co.il* and *kipa.co.il* –

and conducted interviews with twenty-six people: webmasters, web-site designers and content providers, internet filter operators, and avid Orthodox website users of these three websites. Their study focused especially on webmasters' choices and voices, thus giving scholars a unique view into Jewish religious media negotiation from the designers' perspective. Here we can already note a different approach in researching media and culture – not examining the *mediatized worlds* of users, or users' adoption, but rather shedding light on the production and content creation that shapes and is shaped by religious worldviews. The findings from their interviews suggested three strategies of managing religious websites in Israel: control, layering and guiding.

These strategies include the tactics the webmasters' used when considering content, user vetting and user discourse. The first website, *Koogle.co.il*, uses a control strategy, meaning they intensely regulate both content and users. Koogle works as a combination between a web browser (Google) and Craigslist, allowing users to search among websites and shopping options. Each website and shopping product entered into Koogle's servers goes through strict examination – either by algorithm or human – to insure it is *kosher* (i.e., does not include sexually explicit material). Users are also vetted, and only people above the age of 18 can use the website. Thus, this website controls the type of information accessible and who has access to it. By utilizing the Internet in a controlled way, these webmasters actively resist media logic, rejecting interactivity (as possible gossip) and user-generated content (as possible heresy).

The second website, *Bhol.co.il*, uses what Golan and Campbell described as a layering strategy. The website consists of a series of forums specifically designated for the ultra-Orthodox community in Israel. In order to keep the boundaries of the community safe, even online, and because the ultra-Orthodox community in Israel has varying sects and splits, Bhol uses layers in their web portal design. The first layer is open to all and includes news specific to the ultra-Orthodox community. The second layer consists of forums, for which users need to sign up and are vetted. The third layer is comprised of topic- or sect-specific forums (*rooms*), for which further rules and vetting are required. This layering strategy allows not only control of the material, but also some agency on the part of the forum users – within the second and third layers, there is a lot of self- and communal surveillance. This is done in order to create a space where community members can actually feel safe, rather than be trolled or treated like a minority. According to one of the webmasters, "Some people trick us, but the forum managers eventually identify them and ban them. We have tens, perhaps even hundreds of forum managers" (Campbell and Golan 2015, 476).

The forum managers and webmasters work hard to maintain a balance between the different groups, as well as to keep these forums not only open on the one hand, but within the religious boundaries on the other hand. Bhol's content manager explains it so:

> There are two targets for the [vetting] questionnaire: The first is the assumption that people will provide truthful answers. Another is that there won't be an over representation of a single group over other groups, in comparison to the others, [...] If I see a new contributor to the forum – I check this person out. If I see that things don't seem right, I let the other [forum administrators] know to keep an eye on him.
>
> (Campbell and Golan 2015, 476)

Thus, the layering strategy uses technological affordances (such as forum vetting) as well as social norms and peer regulation to maintain online activities.

The last strategy, guiding, is mostly utilized by *Kipa.co.il*, a website for the Religious-National group in Israel. As previously noted, this group is the most open in its adoption of both technology and modern values, and the strategy adopted by the website creators reflects this attitude. Kipa webmasters are rather moderate in their regulation – of content they supply, user discourse and user access. According to Golan and Campbell,

> Rather than silencing discussions of potentially controversial issues, he [Kipa's CEO] encourages their proliferation because they yield increased web traffic. But this openness concomitantly intensifies the risk of losing legitimacy [...] for a community that stands between traditionalism and modernity; this delicate balance must be preserved.
>
> (Campbell and Golan 2015, 479)

This strategy suggests that the webmasters and content managers see their positions as guides, directing and stimulating conversations, bringing up challenging views or dismantling them when the boundaries are pushed too far.

In summary, Golan and Campbell's works showed how religious web users and entrepreneurs do not completely adhere to the logic of the media, nor do they reject new technologies. Instead, they use media tools while adhering to their own tradition, religion and worldviews. That is, to some degree, while these religious individuals use digital media for religious purposes, it is unclear how much that use of digital media has altered the religious experience or institution. Put differently, their *mediatized worlds* seem to be, primarily, culturally/religiously informed. Paying attention only to the *structural character* – the rules and technologies accessible to the religious individuals – does not lead us to question the choices these webmasters make. Rather, focusing, as Golan and Campbell do, on the creation and use of the technologies reveals an even more complicated relationship between media and society. It shows how these religious individuals use these technological affordances according to how they understand their religious needs. As Golan and Campbell argued:

> To create a community-based website, webmasters must navigate between building a new, unique platform to capture community attention and simultaneously reflect the group's established interests and boundaries. [...] Under these social circumstances, webmasters must carefully address the emergence of new technologies and new types of knowledge that can be disseminated through the Internet.
> (Campbell and Golan 2015, 481)

Golan and Campbell show how Jewish religious webmasters and content managers take their work seriously and negotiate both technological affordances and social-religious needs and knowledge. The webmasters they interviewed seem to understand digital media as a tool that will help reflect and spread established social and communal interests and boundaries, not a medium for shaping new religious norms. Here, the relationship between offline and online is an extension of the same space: The *mediatized world* is one in which the religious world is reflected, not shaped.

In her work, Yadlin-Segal (2015) examined a Religious Nationalist's Facebook group, titled *Tweeting Orthodoxies*, in which group members share internet memes, jokes and other light-hearted information related to Jewish religious life in Israel. The group is managed by five administrators, and at the time of Yadlin-Segal's writing, had around 75,000 Facebook users (as of July 2017, the group had 90,409 Facebook users). Yadlin-Segal conducted textual analysis of twelve internet memes created by this group's members and eight interviews with the group's administrators and avid users. Through memes and Facebook discussion, members of this group share, negotiate, make sense of their experiences in religious educational institutions, youth movements and synagogues, and discuss issues of fashion, rituals and customs. Yadlin-Segal suggested that we understand these online phenomena of religious memes as a type of religious participatory culture.

While Golan and Campbell's work touches on what could be considered Hepp and Krotz's structural characters, Yadlin-Segal's work examines the meaning-making, situational characters of media and mediatization. In this case study, the users utilize the Internet's interactive affordances (meme-making and Facebook sharing and commenting) to engage in the production of their own cultural and religious interpretations.

In other words, Yadlin-Segal suggests we understand these religious users as "prosumers" – an active audience that takes part in "creating and circulating digital cultural artifacts" (Yadlin-Segal 2015, 111–112). Furthermore, she understands the sharing and making of religious internet memes as a manifestation of lived religion, "a process in which ordinary men and women draw on religious sources to make sense of their world and experience of the sacred in everyday practices" (ibid, 112). Thus, religious internet memes are an interesting example of digital and religious *everydayness*.

Through her interviews and analysis, Yadlin-Segal highlights the need addressed by this digital media usage – the National Religious movement's need to have *entertainment* media that address their own subculture in the Israeli mediascape. As one of the interviewees pointed out:

> It [the Facebook group and content creation] was necessary since many members of the National Religious community could not find themselves and their values in mainstream media. Most of the content on Israeli mainstream television, radio and even newspapers are not focused on this community.
>
> (Yadlin-Segal 2015, 113)

Thus, the Internet is used in a surprising way for this religious community: not as a space for communal norms negotiations (as in *Bhol* and *Kipa*) or communal informational and material needs (as in *Koogle*), but as a space for creating entertainment and humorous media for this underrepresented subculture.

The interviews and analyses conducted by Yadlin-Segal also shows a relationship with general and even global mainstream media, specifically, popular culture. While the religious public in Israel is thought of as shying away from film and television – especially American popular culture – because of its exposure to sexual content, Yadlin-Segal reveals a religious public that constantly utilizes pop culture and internet culture – for example, the movie *The Matrix* or the Willy Wonka internet meme. According to Yadlin-Segal, "The memes in this study show two layers of meaning: One layer relies on the ability to recognize and decode nonreligious content derived from international popular culture. The second layer draws on religious Jewish content..." (ibid, 118). In the memes Yadlin-Segal analyzed, religion and popular culture go hand in hand, and one is used to make fun of the other. Put differently, here, media logics (Hjarvard) and media as an apparatus of staging (Hepp and Krotz) seem to play an important role in the creation of meaning: The joke and meaning of memes are dependent on certain media logic (or meme logic). Furthermore, according to Yadlin-Segal, "...the way religion is carried in mundane acts as sharing and posting in social media [is] opening the Jewish religion to new, individual meaning making" (ibid, 118) – that is, utilizing the media logics of the Internet allow religious users to engage in innovative worldview construction.

However, this mediatized content operates to maintain and strengthen the existing religious culture. While the media technologies allow religious users to engage in a participatory way, Yadlin-Segal's analysis pointed out that this engagement is, by and large, used to reinforce religious norms and identity. Many of the memes in her study "essentially function as an affirmation of the religious tradition…" (ibid, 118). That is, while the structure of the *jokes* and communication actions were digital and *mediatized*, the content, the staging and meaning-making of this media use were traditional and only made sense through a religious worldview.

This reinforcement of religious identity in a less rigid and more humorous way online also trickled back into the off-line communal space – the social institution of the synagogue – as memes were downloaded and printed in *Sabbath* synagogue pamphlets (ibid, 119). As internet use is forbidden during the *Sabbath* (because the use of electricity is forbidden), distributing memes in a printed form that is allowed for *Sabbath* consumption combines the digital and off-line religious life in an innovative way, reshaping the technological affordances to fit religious needs. As one of the interviewees points out,

> Technology can actually help spread religion. As I see it, the National Religious people do not see technology as conflicting with religion, rather as complementing each other. […] We always ask – how can I integrate it [a technological invention] into religion […].
> (Yadlin-Segal 2015, 119–120)

Thus, not only is technology not considered a threat in these cases, it is sought as a tool to complement religious needs: to help spread religion. Here again, we see a negotiation of media by religious users who view media not as an external force that will change their communication, but as a complementing tool that will help transfer their existing ideas.

Mediatization in Israel – Speaking Religious Language in Digital Media Affordances

Both the studies described above show the ways in which digital technology is used for *speaking* in religious terms and for allowing, maintaining and reinforcing religious identity and communal structures. The utilization of digital media for religious purposes works both on the level of community construction and maintenance, and identity construction and maintenance. Thus, these studies supply empirical data useful in examining the theorizing of media and (religious) society in Israel.

When considering mediatization as a set of theories that seek to explain the relationship between media and society, it is important to ask the following: what media and which society? We agree with the goal of this book, arguing that it is important to contextualize mediatization in various global settings. For example, Facebook and WhatsApp are very popular in Israel.[1] Twitter is less popular (statista.com, 2016).[2] One possible explanation has to do with the social institutions and the culture of sociability in Israel. Israel is a small nation with a small town sense, in which 'everybody knows everybody'. Therefore, one's actions – even digital actions – matter. Unlike Twitter, Facebook and WhatsApp reduce the notion of anonymity. Both these applications demand a certain amount of identifiability. Thus, in Israel, Facebook and WhatsApp are far more popular and are used to maintain familial bonds, social relations and work and life circles (for example, a popular use of WhatsApp is for school and kindergarten groups, see Bouhnik and Deshen 2014).

Furthermore, it is not only the global/local context that needs to be considered, but also the religious and traditional context. If mediatization is to be understood as a meta-process that interacts with other meta-processes, we need to carefully consider those other processes, settings and the worldviews that inform them; for example, the process of secularization or of individualization and the creation and maintenance of subcultures, as in Yadlin-Segal's work. Alternatively, the history and traditions, which inform the rulemaking and negotiation of technology, as showcased in Golan and Campbell's work. At the heart of mediatization theory – in most of its different versions – is the notion that media creates (dramatic) changes in social, political and religious worlds. As the socio-constructivist approach to mediatization theory reminds us, researchers have to be careful when attributing the changes in the religious scape in Israel merely to changes in *the media*. As can be seen from both the studies we reviewed above, religious Jews in Israel use new media gingerly, in controlled ways, which are informed by their religious and social worldviews, history and their relationship to community, authority and text.

Conclusion

We suggest that it might be helpful when considering mediatization in Asia to combine it to some extent with the histories and traditions of the religions/cultures. Here, Campbell's *Religious Social Shaping of Technology* (RSST) is useful for the study of digital religion. RSST claims that we should pay attention to the way society shapes technology, rather than the other way around (Campbell 2010). Coming from the tradition of ICT studies, *Social Shaping of Technology* is a theory adapted by Campbell to address religious users and uses. Within the theory of *The Social Shaping of Technology*, "Technology is seen as a social process, and the possibility is recognized that social groups may shape technologies towards their own ends, rather than the character of the technology determining use and outcomes" (ibid, 50). Social shaping of technology (SST) considers how technologies are created, shaped, used and negotiated in the societies that make and employ them. SST further stresses "the negotiability of technology ... and highlighting the scope for particular groups and forces to shape technologies to their ends..." (Williams and Edge 1996, 867). Campbell combined SST with religious studies to highlight the specificity of how religious groups negotiate technology, a process she called *Religious Social Shaping of Technology*. According to Campbell, this theory

> takes into account the factors informing a religious community's responses to new media – their relationship to community, authority, and text – and combines it with a social shaping approach that highlights the practices surrounding technology evaluation.
>
> (Campbell 2010, 41–42)

This theoretical approach offers an in-depth exploration of both religion and technology and views their interactions as processes of combined social factors instead of combating ones. It argues the necessity of, and urges researchers to ask, questions "about how technologies are conceived of, as well as used, in light of a religious community's beliefs, moral codes, and historical tradition of engagement with other forms of media technology" (ibid, 59).

The pervasiveness of digital media in everyday life, explained through the process of mediatization, is evident in the religious communities in Israel. However, as these religious communities embrace digital media, they do so consciously, not replacing one social institution with another, but finding ways in which digital media can complement their religious needs and reinforce religious norms and identities. As one of the interviewees said, "... we always ask – how can I integrate it [a technological invention] into religion" (Yadlin-Segal 2015, 120). We suggest combining RSST with Mediatization of Religion to allow for a theoretical framework that considers both religious worldviews and technological/media *logics*/the characters of media. This combination, we argue, helps one conduct a nuanced research and is especially useful in the case of researching the religion and media. This is because religions act as preservers of history, tradition and community. As such, theories that examine the communal or institutional are better able to explain digital religion. We would like to suggest that the ways media are used for the construction of religious norms in Israel are informed by both the religious cultural background and media affordances. Even more, we suggest that technological affordances are not used according to *media logics* at the social level (Krotz and Hepp 2011), but are used according to centuries-old communal boundaries and norms, as can been seen from the work of Golan and Campbell. Similarly, digital media in these communities do not replace the synagogue, but instead, serve as a complement to synagogue and communal life, as can be seen in Yadlin-Segal's work. Namely, in this combination, we need to consider both processes: The religious cultural context and how it informs religious uses of technology, as well as the logics, affordances, structural and situational characters of the media and how they impact and shape religious uses of technology. We suggest thinking about this as an ecosystem in which media/technology and religion/culture are two forces, which, in different ways, shape our lives, our worldviews, the ways we use technology and the ways we understand our religions. Further research into the ways in which combining mediatization with other approaches to media both in Israel and other loci can contribute to understanding the delicate and complex ways in which religious groups and individuals use digital media.

Notes

1 As of 2014, WhatsApp was used by 70% of Israeli population, see Elis, N., 2014. Survey—Israelis Addicted to WhatsApp Don't Pay for Streaming Movies. *Jerusalem Post*, 28 December. Available at www.jpost.com/Israel-News/Survey-Israelis-addicted-to-Whatsapp-dont-pay-for-streaming-movies-385980, accessed 7 May 2018.
2 As of 2014, less than 10%, see statista.com.

References

Bacon and God's Wrath, 2015 [documentary] Sol Friedman. Tornato, Ontario, Canada: Artbeast Production, Minutes 5:11–6:13.Barak-Erez, D., 2009. Law and Religion under the Status Quo Model: Between Past Compromises and Constant Change. *Cardozo Law Review*, 30(6), 2495–2507.

Barzilai-Nahon, K. and Barzilai, G., 2005. Cultured Technology: Internet and Religious Fundamentalism. *The Information Society*, 21(1), 25–40.

Behederi Haredim, 2018. Available at www.bhol.co.il/forums, accessed 7 May 2018.

Blondheim, M. and Caplan, K., 1993. Rish'ut ha-shiddur: tikshoret ve-kalatot ba-hevra ha-haredit (On Communication and Audio Cassettes in Haredi Society). *Kesher*, 14, 51–63.

Bouhnik, D. and Deshen, M., 2014. WhatsApp Goes to School: Mobile Instant Messaging between Teachers and Students. *Journal of Information Technology Education: Research*, 13(1), 217–231.

Campbell, H., 2010. *When Religion Meets New Media*. New York: Routledge.

Campbell, H., 2011. Religion and the Internet in the Israeli Orthodox Context. *Israel Affairs*, 17(3), 364–383.

Campbell, H. A. and Golan, O., 2011. Creating Digital Enclaves: Negotiation of the Internet among Bounded Religious Communities. *Media, Culture & Society*, 33(5), 709–724.

Cejka, M., 2009. Making the Internet Kosher: Orthodox (Haredi) Jews and Their Approach to the World Wide Web. *Masaryk University Journal of Law and Technology*, 3(1), 99–110.

Cohen, Y., 2005. Religion News in Israel. *Journal of Media and Religion*, 4(3), 179–198.

Cohen, Y., 2012. *God, Jews and the Media: Religion and Israel's Media*. New York: Routledge.

Dosick, W. D., 1995. *Living Judaism: The Complete Guide to Jewish Belief, Tradition, and Practice*. San Francisco: Harper

Elis, N., 2014. Survey—Israelis Addicted to WhatsApp Don't Pay for Streaming Movies. *Jerusalem Post*, 28 December. Available at www.jpost.com/Israel-News/Survey-Israelis-addicted-to-Whatsapp-dont-pay-for-streaming-movies-385980, accessed 7 May 2018.

Fader, A., 2013. Nonliberal Jewish Women's Audiocassette Lectures in Brooklyn: A Crisis of Faith and the Morality of Media. *American Anthropologist*, 115(1), 72–84.

Friedman, M., 1991. *HaChevra HaCharedit—mekorot, megamot vetahalichim. [Charedi Society—Sources, Trends and Processes.]* Jerusalem: Machon Yerushalayim Liheker Yisrael.

Golan, O. and Campbell, H. A., 2015. Strategic Management of Religious Websites: The Case of Israel's Orthodox Communities. *Journal of Computer-Mediated Communication*, 20(4), 467–486.

Hepp, A. and Krotz, F., eds., 2014. *Mediatized Worlds: Culture and Society in a Media Age*. London: Springer.

Hjarvard, S. P., 2013. *The Mediatization of Culture and Society*. New York: Routledge

Israeli Central Bureau of Statistics, 2010. *Israeli Population 1990–2009*. Available at www.cbs.gov.il/www/statistical/isr_pop_heb.pdf, accessed 26 September 2015.

Katz, Y., 2012. Technology Use in the Religious Communities in Israel: Combining Traditional Society and Advanced Communications. *The Journal of Religion, Media and Digital Culture*, 1(2). Available at www.jrmdc.com/journal/article/view/7/4, accessed 7 May 2018.

Kipa, 2018. Available at *Kipa.co.il*, accessed 7 May 2018.

Koogle, 2018. Available at *Koogle.co.il*, accessed 7 May 2018.

Krotz, F. and Hepp, A., 2011. A Concretization of Mediatization: How 'Mediatization Works' and Why Mediatized Worlds are a Helpful Concept for Empirical Mediatization Research. *Empedocles: European Journal for the Philosophy of Communication*, 3(2), 137–152.

Luckmann, B., 1970. The Small Life-Worlds of Modern Man. *Social Research*, 37(4), 580–596.

Maltz, J. and Ravid, B., 2016. Unprecedented Clashes As non-Orthodox Rabbis Bring Torah Scrolls into Western Wall. *Haaretz*, 2 November. Available at www.haaretz.com/israel-news/1.750459, accessed 7 May 2018.

Rosenthal, M. and Ribak, R., 2015. On Pomegranates and Etrogs: Internet Filters as Practices of Media Ambivalence among National Religious Jews in Israel. In: Campbell, H., ed. *Digital Judaism: Jewish Negotiations with Digital Media and Culture*. New York: Routledge, 145–160.

Statista, 2016. *Number of Twitter Users in Israel*. Available at www.statista.com/statistics/558324/number-of-twitter-users-in-israel/, accessed 7 May 2018.

Tsuria, R. and Yadlin-Segal, A., 2017. Israel. In: Steckman, L. M. and Andrews, M. J., eds. *Online around the World: A Geographic Encyclopedia of the Internet, Social Media, and Mobile Apps.* Santa Barbara: ABC-CLIO, 144–148.

Williams, R. and Edge, D., 1996. The Social Shaping of Technology. *Research Policy,* 25(6), 865–899.

Yadlin-Segal, A., 2015. Communicating Identity through Religious Internet Memes on the 'Tweeting Orthodoxies' Facebook Page. In: Campbell, H. A., ed. *Digital Judaism: Jewish Negotiations with Digital Media and Culture.* New York: Routledge, 110–123.

Part 5
Critical Reflection

12 Religion as Communicative Figurations – Analyzing Religion in Times of Deep Mediatization

Kerstin Radde-Antweiler

Religious groups and individual actors increasingly use digital media and become part of religious discussions on religious authority, dogmatic doctrine and belief systems themselves. An example of such processes is the discussion of a popular ritual carried out on Good Friday in the Philippines; namely, self-crucifixion that goes hand in hand with self-flagellation (for a detailed description, see Bautista 2011). The Philippines, with a population that is over 80% Roman Catholic, is one of the few Christian Asian countries. There, religion is still a part of public life: "media-sensationalized events such as human crucifixion during Lent and the overwhelming procession of the Black Nazarene at the start of every year, (...) suggest both the high level of piety and the theological conservatism of Filipino Catholics" (Cornelio 2016). This ritual itself was invented in 1962 and originates in the concept of self-flagellation:

> The colonial ambitions and missionary fervor of the Spaniards brought Passion plays and the practice of self-flagellation to Mexico and the Philippines. In both countries, the so-called Iberian "Calvary Catholicism" was introduced with great success. Flagellation in public became popular either as a theatrical element of Passion plays or as separate performances by confraternities or by individuals. The adoption of such rites of self-mortification was accompanied by local reinterpretation. In the Philippines, for instance, self-flagellation is associated with a private vow, the well-being of the family, corporeal purification, and healing, far less with guilt and atonement" as in the European history.
>
> (Bräunlein 2010b, 1122)

Public self-crucifixion became very popular and is performed in parts of the Northern Philippines, e.g., in the village of Papanga in Northern Luzon (Bräunlein 2010a).

Nowadays, this ritual is highly mediatized. This means the Internet is full of pictures, videos and descriptions of it; namely, on social media platforms such as YouTube, Facebook, Travel blogs and Instagram. These representations often provoke heated discussions. Furthermore, self-crucifixion seems to become one of the most important elements in Philippines religion. For example, if you run a Google search for the words 'Philippines' and 'religion', websites relating to self-crucifixion and self-flagellation are among the top ten search results. In addition (especially in Europe and the US), every Easter TV station reports the Filipino ritual; showing and presenting it in broadcasts. News magazines also write about it as a prominent event and being part of the cultural heritage. It is often labeled as one of the weirdest rituals worldwide. It is therefore not surprising that certain villages have become famous tourist spots. This fact is perfectly reflected in various travel guides such as *Lonely Planet*, which ranks the ritual as one of the *top things to see in the Philippines*:

> The country's most bizarre and controversial celebrations are the crucifixion re-enactments that occur in several towns, most famously in San Fernando (in the Pampanga Province), north of Manila, where devotees are literally nailed to wooden crosses.
>
> (Lonely Planet n.d.)

Furthermore, ritual actors who are engaged in the self-crucifixions have become famous as well. A popular example is Ruben Enaje, who has crucified himself for more than 18 years by now. He is interviewed every year by journalists as well as filmed by television stations during the rituals. In addition, tourists who travel to this village just to watch this Good Friday ritual usually take selfies with him and treat him like a local celebrity. It is therefore not surprising that the procession route with the self-flagellants and the people wearing the crosses as well as the field where the self-crucifixion takes place are spotted with outside broadcast vans and film crews. Thus, we can speak of a highly mediatized ritual.

Now, the interesting question is as follows: Can we observe a modified ritual due to media representation? What is the relationship between the self-crucifixion and the changing media environment?

Religion in Times of Deep Mediatization

This leads us to a more general question: How does religion change in times of deep mediatization? Moreover, what do we mean when talking about religion and mediatization? In contrast to an essentialist approach (e.g., Waardenburg 1986) which assumes that religion exists as such (i.e. as something preexisting that can be investigated), my approach is based on a discursive understanding; namely, that religion or religious symbol systems (Gladigow 1988) are constantly being redefined and negotiated by different actors according to time and context: "Religions are no longer seen as a clearly delimitable, consistent and homogeneous symbol system" (Radde-Antweiler 2017a, 142). Such interpretations and negotiation processes take place through the so-called communicative practices. Communicative constructivism (Keller, Knoblauch and Reichertz 2012) presupposes that "social reality is constructed in communicative action" (Luckmann 2006, 28). In this way, religious social realities are always processes within a communicative construction of religion (Knoblauch 2017) by religious actors. These religious actors can be individual persons (laypeople or religious experts alike), groups or organizations. Research on the communicative construction of religion – and along these lines, rituals, religious authority, identity, etc. – focuses on the way in which religious actors define something or someone through their communicative action as religion; how they assign meaning to it; and furthermore, how this changes with an evolving media environment. In the context of the Philippines case study, this means specifically that we are interested in how different actors (the involved ritual actors as well as the off-line and online audiences) ascribe meaning to the self-crucifixion and how this changes in relation to an evolving media environment.

Communication has changed (and continues to do so) through the development of new media technologies over time; this occurs worldwide. If we look at the evolution of the media environment from book printing up to today, we can see major changes that also play a role in the religious field. The pure amount of media has increased as well as their entanglement with everyday life practices. For example, in daily life, a religious person could use various media such as an app for religious prayers, songs or videos; watch televised bible clips; ask for the next service via WhatsApp; discuss ethical issues in a forum; or read various print media. In addition, actors can use these media in different aspects of their lives, such as in the workplace, during leisure time and more. Due to this enormous media entanglement, the actors' media usage is sometimes subconscious (Radde-Antweiler and Grünenthal forthcoming.).

Research positions tend to diverge concerning the transformation of religion in relation to mediatization (for a detailed overview, see Zeiler in this book). The majority of (mainly critical) discussions refer to Stig Hjarvard's mediatization approach (Hjarvard 2008). According to this concept, various fields of culture and society, such as religion, are determined by an inherent logic of the media that arises from economic interests (Altheide and Snow 1979). Media is thus defined primarily as journalistic media, which as a specific field has its own logic and rules. Due to the enormous and growing influence and relevance of media nowadays, other fields – and among them religion as well – "nonmedia actors have to conform to this *media logic* if they want to be represented in the (mass) media or if they want to act successfully in a media culture and media society" (Couldry and Hepp 2013, 196). One consequence of society's increasing mediatization is a decline in religion and, in line with that, increased secularization. Hjarvard's approach was mainly criticized because of his narrow definition of religion; namely, religion as organized religion, e.g., the Church in so-called Western (especially Nordic) societies. Lövheim (2011), Lundby (2009) and Radde-Antweiler (2017a), for example, made clear that especially individual actors or groups outside of religious organizations increasingly use digital and social media and are gaining influence on the construction of religious identity or authority.

Alternative definitions of mediatization have been offered and have since gained influence. Friedrich Krotz established the so-called social-constructivist tradition and stressed the fact that media can only be understood as inseparable from the construction of reality. In contrast to the concept of media logic, he understood mediatization as a meta-process of change, comparable to globalization or economization in its societal impact. It is meant to be a comprehensive framework for and approach to describing cultural and social transformation in a theoretically informed way. In contrast to Hjarvard (2013), who defined the invention of digital media as the starting point of mediatization, Krotz presupposed a historical understanding of mediatization. According to him, history as such can only be understood as a media history "during which communication media became increasingly developed and used in various ways" (Krotz 2001, 33). Couldry and Hepp (2013, 197) stressed that mediatization has two characteristics: A quantitative perspective history of mankind showed that the number of media has increased and in line with that, the possibility for an increasing number of people to gain access to it. Furthermore, older media such as television or radio have not disappeared but rather exist side by side. Additionally, in a qualitative perspective, mediatization refers to the fact that the communicative constructions of (religious) reality are increasingly entangled with digital media. Nowadays, our everyday life is more and more interwoven with media: a condition we call deep mediatization. All parts of life – even religion – are influenced by media. One prominent example is family life, which nowadays is organized by media, e.g., by using a shared online calendar to manage family activities as well as business appointments; communicating with each other by smartphone; or by using a cooking app that automatically generates a shopping list. According to Krotz, mediatization describes a process in which modernity and, as a consequence of this process, also institutions and whole societies are shaped. This includes

> changing media environments…, an increase of different media …, the changing functions of old media …, and changing communication forms and relations between the people on the micro level, a changing organization of social life and changing nets of sense and meaning making on the macro level.
>
> (Krotz 2008, 24)

It is therefore crucial not to take the media as an isolated phenomenon, but rather to reflect on the change in communicative forms that go hand in hand with media evolution. Therefore, methodologically, a specific medium such as television or the Internet should no longer constitute the research object, but rather it should be the individual actors in their mediatized worlds. In short, mediatization means a shift from media-centered to actor-centered research.

Furthermore, media alone is no longer assumed to be the only motor for transformation processes. Rather, it is part of a combination of various sociocultural processes, in which mediatization is one process among many. Thus, classifications such as *online* in contrast to *offline* (Helland 2000) or *virtual* versus *real* are quite problematic: "(t)he question arises how a dichotomy such as this can hold up, if presently everything is highly mediatized" (Radde-Antweiler 2012, 97) and off-line and online realms are interwoven. In contrast to Hjarvard's mediatization approach, Krotz stressed that mediatization (as shown above) did not start with digitalization or with the invention of the mass media bundle called the Internet (World Wide Web).

> Researchers studying the interconnection of religions and digital media are well-advised not to isolate monocausal relations, but to locate them in their interplay with other metaprocesses, e.g. individualization. This is not intended to relativize the significance of media or to neglect the specifics of various media genres, yet verdicts such as a propagated radicalization via the Internet should be called into question.
>
> (Radde-Antweiler 2017a, 147)

The different interpretation of the impact of media on religion can be easily illustrated by the Philippines case study. The two different mediatization approaches produce different results regarding the change of the ritual of self-crucifixion in relation to media. By applying the institutionalist mediatization approach, research would focus on the role of mass media. In this case, it would assess the impact of the press articles as well as the television broadcast and ask how the mediatization of such a ritual leads to a further deconstruction of the established religious organization; namely, the Roman Catholic Church in the Philippines. Such research would presuppose a declining importance of the Roman Catholic Church as well as its banalization by the mediatization thereof.

The socio-constructivist mediatization approach, however, would take the actors engaged in this ritual – be it the spectators, the actors who crucify themselves or the flagellants – in their mediatized world as a research object. It would then ask if, and when, media in all its forms play a role. In contrast to Hjarvard's hypothesis of a banalization of religion through its mediatization, it would analyze religion's transformation into popular religion. Like Hubert Knoblauch rightly pointed out, "changing communicative action, mediatization changes religious rituals and what used to be called 'religious membership'" (2014, 216). Mediatization could have consequences for organized religions. Still, it can increase individual religiousness at the same time. Furthermore, such research would relate its findings to research in this area with a focus on individualization, economization, globalization, etc. Whereas research with an institutionalist perspective presupposes a monocausal relationship between a changing ritual and media, the socio-constructivist perspective would try to investigate which role communication and, based thereon, media play in the processes of a changing ritual in relation to other meta-processes.

Both mediatization approaches are still used today, but they focus on different areas. Whereas the institutionalist approach still focuses on mass media, the socio-constructivist approach is mainly interested in everyday life communications in relation to media. It is therefore important to notice that

> 'mediatization' does not refer to a single theory but to a more general approach within media and communications research. Generally speaking, mediatization is a concept used to analyze critically the interrelation between changes in media and communications on the one hand, and changes in culture and society on the other. At this general level, mediatization has quantitative as well as qualitative dimensions.
>
> (Couldry and Hepp 2013, 197)

However, it is significant that we have been confronted with major changes during the last 20 years. We have to ask what is characteristic about the changing media environment in times of deep mediatization. The "Communicative Figurations" research network stressed that besides the multifaceted and self-reflexive media

> (t)he cross-media character of deep mediatization means that not the emergence of any one single medium has brought about the media environment's change, but the overall digitalisation and connectivity of various 'old' media and the emergence of 'new' digital ones.
>
> (Hepp and "Communicative Figurations"
> research network 2017, 14)

Furthermore, in times of deep mediatization, actors and society as such are confronted with specific trends such as differentiation, increasing connectivity, media's growing omnipresence, rapid pace of innovation and datafication. Differentiation points out that we can observe nowadays various media technologies that exist next to each other and allow a differentiated bundle of media forms. These media are increasingly connected to each other; likewise, people can connect to each other using them independently of space and time. This is still encouraged through the elevated ubiquity of media. With this, people can communicate with one another anywhere, anytime. On the production side, we are witnessing that new media are much further developed than in previous years. Datafication refers to the fact, users even if they are not so aware of their mediatized lifeworld (and with it the communicative construction of reality), they are increasingly influenced by the media software and technical infrastructure.

The "Communicative Figurations" research network hypothesizes that these trends will lead to certain consequences, such as segmentation, optionality, spatial extension of communication and blurring of social borders. This will have consequences for the communicative construction of social domains as well (for the trends and consequences, see Hepp and "Communicative Figurations", research network 2017, 12–14).

The crucial question now remains how can we analyze these changing communicative constructions of reality and relate the trends as well as the consequences to one another. To analyze the communicative constructions of religion or rituals, we need an analytical heuristic to comprehend this mediatized lifeworld. As the name indicates, the "Communicative Figurations" research network offers an approach as an enhancement of the different mediatization approaches. It should "not be confused with a specific method. Rather it is a heuristic concept that offers a systematization of the field" (Radde-Antweiler 2017b, 211).

Communicative Figuration – an Analytical Concept of Researching Religion in Times of Deep Mediatization

So, how do communicative practices change in times when actors live in a qualitatively and quantitatively expanded media environment and to what extent does this – and especially these trends – affect their understanding of religion? The proposed research heuristic is based on Elias's concept of figuration as "networks of individuals" (Elias 1978, 15) and allows for the analysis of "patterns of processes of communicative interweaving that exist across various media and have a thematic framing that orients communicative action" (Hasebrink and Hepp 2013, 10). It distinguishes between different structural layers of analysis:

1 A specific actor's constellation,
2 A thematic framing,
3 The related communicative practices.

This is of specific importance, because "the figurational approach allows for a holistic picture of the interrelationship between what we have traditionally thought of in different domains of study within communication and media studies: texts, audiences, uses, practices, and actors and production" (Lohmeier and Böhling 2018, 348).

Applying this model to the religious field, we can specify the three different layers as follows:

1   The actors' constellations refer to individuals, groups, organizations or institutions that define themselves as religious or which, depending on the concrete research question, are part of or connected to the religious field.
2   The frame of relevance identifies the communicative figuration "and therefore character of a communicative figuration as a social domain" (Hepp and "Communicative Figurations", research network 2017, 18). Even if the dominant frame is religion, it is possible to define more specific frames, i.e., frames such as ritual, depending on the respective research question.
3   We define the respective modes of communication and the involved media as communicative practices. They include not only the different types of communication such as direct communication, mutual, produced or virtualized media communication (cf. Krotz 2007), but also refer to the media used. However, from my perspective, a distinction must be made here: While we can find media – especially social media – that allows the actors to communicate with each other, we also have media where religion is (re)presented, such as journalistic media. We have to make a further distinction, in relation to media, between media environments and media repertoires. Whereas a media environment is defined as any media available in society (Livingstone 2001, 30), the media repertoire refers to the medium/media actually used by the actor.

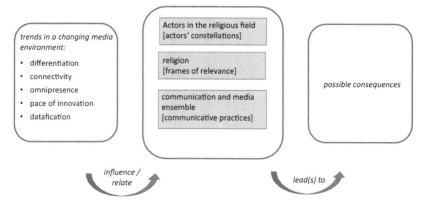

Figure 12.1 Religion as a Communicative Figuration (based on Hepp and "Communicative Figurations", research network 2017, 18, Figure 1).

Applying this model to the Philippines case study, we are able to identify the different structural layers:

1 Actors' constellations: The respective actors' constellations can refer to the engaged ritual participants, ranging from people such as Ruben Enaje, who crucifies himself, to the local audience during this ritual, to the people helping conduct the ritual (e.g., by offering water on the way to the cross, by crucifying him), and even the people who watch the videos played on television or on YouTube. Furthermore, actors who do not take part in the ritual, but are linked to it, can be part of the actors' constellation. A prominent example in the case study is the Philippines Roman Catholic Church that comments most critically on the ritual in online and off-line media and therefore positions it as a practice not accepted by the official church (cf. also Bautista 2018). In this sense, the different settings (in relation to media as well as to the specific countries) have to be taken into consideration.

2 Frame of relevance: Depending on the research question, we could define the frame of relevance in our case study as a ritual in a narrow sense.

3 Communicative practices: We found many communicative practices in the Philippines example. These range from representations in travel books, television broadcasts or press articles to smartphones which are used by audiences during the ritual to take pictures as well as to search for the best nearby hotels or to call themselves an Uber. However, interesting observations can be found regarding the involved ritual actors. Whereas actors not explicitly active within the religious field (tourists, journalists, etc.) used media to represent this ritual, the majority of the ritual actors (such as Ruben Enaje) did not use digital media such as Facebook or Twitter as a platform for presenting their performance or their person. Only reports about the actors in the whole, but not by themselves, are visible. Furthermore, the videos or pictures presented are primarily discussed by people not engaged in the ritual. People from different religions or Christian dominations in particular had intense discussions about the meaning of the ritual. For example, a video by a Baptist reverend entitled "Catholic 'Holy Week' in the Philippines" criticized the ritual while documenting it and labeling it complete blasphemy. In addition, the comments on this video also stressed a critical relationship to the Roman Catholic Church:

> A picture is worth a thousand words. Rome has many versions of the "truth" from "her history books," and she uses the appropriate "version" at the appropriate time. Keep believing what she tells you, and you'll wind up in hell with the rest of Bible rejecting humanity. Your blinded countrymen are not the only

Catholic people who practice this form of penance. Flagellation as mortification has been taught for centuries (see I Cor. 9:27; Col 2:23 in a Roman Catholic Bible). Repent or Perish.

(Flang 2009)

Within the Catholic field, one can also find discussions on this topic. An example is the article "Philippines bishops disapprove of Holy Week self-crucifixion and flagellation" (Catholic News Agency n.d.) by the Catholic News Agency, a Catholic news provider. It is quite clear in this article that the official church, namely the Philippines bishops, disapproves of these rituals as a non-proper-Catholic performance. Letters to the editor stress this dichotomy of right and wrong Catholicism.

An important question regarding the communicative practices is whether we can find the same media usage for all actors or groups involved. Are there different communicative practices entangled with media ensembles? In cases of religious organizations, it is possible to observe differences "between the media ensemble that is offered by the organization and the media repertoire that is actually used by its local representatives is also obvious in the local representatives' communicative practices." (Radde-Antweiler, Grünenthal and Gogolok 2018, 277). A further research question is thus whether we can find different degrees of mediatization regarding the different actors. If so, do these different degrees of mediatization produce different tempi of transformations?

Conclusion

Regarding research on media and religion, it becomes obvious that we have to involve various layers in researching multilevel transformations: the religious actors' constellations; their communicative practices; as well as the respective media used in these communicative practices; and furthermore the respective thematic frame.

If we want to evaluate the relationship between changing media and religion in its different forms (such as religious authority and identity), an analytical concept like communication figuration is quite helpful. This is because it focuses on the different structural layers. Instead of presupposing a monolithic block or religion as such, it focuses on the communicative construction of religion and asks how such a communicative construction changes (has changed) in relation to media. Based on a figurational approach that focuses on the interrelations between the related actors; the concrete thematic frame; as well as the communicative practices; and the media related to them, we can gain a more differentiated picture of changing religion in times of deep mediatization.

Researching specific case studies has to focus, of course, on a specific level and cannot include all different layers. It must rather take on a layer as a starting point. As we can see in the chapters presented in this edited volume, the focus is always different. On the one hand, the chapters by Birgit Staemmler on Japanese online forums; Tan Meng Yoe on Malaysian communities across the Internet and social media platforms; Narges Valibeigi on Shia Iranians on Instagram; and Ruth Tsuria and Heidi A. Campbell on the digital construction of religion in relation to gender and sexuality, diasporic identity and social media in Israel focus on communicative practices (specifically on media for communication). On the other hand, the chapters by Wai-yip Ho on Chinese Muslims' websites and by Sam Han on South Korean televised talk shows used communicate practices in forms of media representations as a starting point. Hew Wai Weng writes on both the online and off-line strategies of two Chinese Muslim preachers in Indonesia; Pauline Hope Cheong comments on spiritual institutions and lay followers in Singapore and Dhanya Fee Kirchhof on Ravidassias, a socioreligious community of North Indian origin; and Gregory Grieve, Christopher Helland and Rohit Singh discuss the digitalization of the Tibetan Buddhist ceremony of the 33rd Kalachakra. All started with a focus on specific actors' constellations.

An additional benefit of the communicative figuration research heuristic is its focus on structural elements that can be found worldwide. Even if this concept, as well as its mediatization approaches, were developed primarily for analyzing European and North American regional contexts, it can (from my perspective) easily transfer to the relationships between religion and media in Asia. Instead of presupposing certain outcomes of mediatization as Hjarvard suggested, the model of communicative figurations allows a differentiation of specific structural elements and then asks what role media plays in the specific context.

Based on these results, we can further ask (with regard to the respective culture) how an evolving media environment leads to changes in religion as a social domain. What trends can be found, which cannot? For example, does the "connectivity" trend really offer all actors worldwide connectivity? Is the "datafication" trend the same in each country? In which countries can we observe reluctance to adopt this? What does that mean for communication processes; especially regarding religion? Based on this, we can draw a differentiated picture of the respective degrees of mediatization. With such a figuration model, a non-eurocentric perspective on changing religion in relation to a changing media environment will be possible. Furthermore, we can compare the different findings in the various Asian as well as Non-Asian countries and cultures and evaluate possible structural similarities as well as differences.

References

Altheide, D. L. and Snow, R. P., 1979. *Media Logic*. Beverly Hills: Sage.
Bautista, J., 2011. The Bearable Lightness of Pain: Crucifying Oneself in Pampanga. In: Dańczak, A. and Lazenby, N., eds. *Pain: Management, Expression and Interpretation*. Oxford: Interdisciplinary Press, 151–159.

Bautista, J., 2018. On the Anthropology and Theology of Roman Catholic Rituals in the Philippines. *International Journal of Asian Christianity*, 1(1), 2542–4246.

Bräunlein, P., 2010a. *Passion/Pasyon. Rituale des Schmerzes im europäischen und philippinischen Christentum*. Paderborn: Wilhelm Fink Verlag.

Bräunlein, P. J., 2010b. Flagellation. Religions of the World. In: Baumann, M. and Melton, J. G., eds. *A Comprehensive Encyclopedia of Beliefs and Practices*. Santa Barbara: ABC-CLIO, 1120–1122.

Catholic News Agency, n.d. Philippines Bishops Disapprove of Holy Week Self-crucifixion and Flagellation. *Catholic News Agency, News, Asia-Pacific*. Available at www.catholicnewsagency.com/news/philippines_bishops_disapprove_of_holy_week_self-crucifixion_and_flagellation, accessed 13 July 2018.

Cornelio, J. S., 2016. *Being Catholic in the Contemporary Philippines*. New York: Routledge.

Couldry, N. and Hepp, A., 2013. Conceptualizing Mediatization: Contexts, Traditions, Arguments. *Communication Theory*, 23, 191–202. doi:10.1111/comt.12019.

Elias, N., 1978. *What Is Sociology?* London: Hutchinson.

Flang, D., 2009. Catholic *"Holy" Week in the Philippines*, [YouTube video] 16 March 2009. Available at www.youtube.com/watch?v=1BsnE88gfk4, accessed 13 July 2018.

Gladigow, B., 1988. Gegenstände und wissenschaftlicher Kontext von Religionswissenschaft. In: Cancik, H., Gladigow, B. and Laubscher, M., eds. *Handbuch religionswissenschaftlicher Grundbegriffe* 1. Stuttgart: Kohlhammer, 26–40.

Hasebrink, U. and Hepp, A., 2013. Human Interaction and Communicative Figurations: The Transformation of Mediatized Cultures and Societies. *Communicative Figurations Working Papers*, 2. Available at www.kommunikativefigurationen.de/fileadmin/redak_kofi/Arbeitspapiere/CoFi_EWP_No-2_Hepp_Hasebrink.pdf, accessed 22 May 2017.

Helland, C., 2000. Online-Religion/Religion-Online and Virtual Communitas. In: Hadden, J. K. and Cowan, D. E., eds. *Religion on the Internet. Research Prospects and Promises*. London: JAI Press, 205–223.

Hepp, A. and "Communicative Figurations" Research Network, 2017. Transforming Communications. Media-Related Changes in Times of Deep Mediatization. *Communicative Figurations Working Paper*, 16. Available at www.kofi.uni-bremen.de/fileadmin/user_upload/Arbeitspapiere/CoFi_EWP_Hepp-Research-Network.pdf, accessed 1 June 2017.

Hjarvard, S., 2008. The Mediatization of Religion. A Theory of the Media as Agents of Religious Change. *Northern Lights*, 6, 9–26.

Hjarvard, S., 2013. *The Mediatization of Culture and Society*. London: Routledge.

Kelller, R., Knoblauch, H. and Reichertz, J., 2012. *Kommunikativer Konstruktivismus*. Springer: Wiesbaden.

Knoblauch, H., 2014. Benedict in Berlin. The Mediatization of Religion. In: Hepp, A. and Krotz, F., eds. *Mediatized Worlds. Culture and Society in a Media Age*. Basingstoke: Palgrave Macmillan Limited, 143–158.

Knoblauch, H., 2017. *Die kommunikative Konstruktion von Wirklichkeit*. Wiesbaden: VS-Verlag.

Krotz, F., 2001. *Die Mediatisierung kommunikativen Handelns. Der Wandel von Alltag und sozialen Beziehungen, Kultur und Gesellschaft durch die Medien.* Opladen: Westdeutscher Verlag.

Krotz, F., 2007. *Mediatisierung: Fallstudien zum Wandel von Kommunikation.* Wiesbaden: VS Verlag für Sozialwissenschaften.

Krotz, F., 2008. Media Connectivity: Concepts, Conditions and Consequences. In: Hepp, A., Krotz, F., Moores, S. and Winter, C., eds. *Connectivity, Network and Flows. Conceptualizing Contemporary Communications.* Cresskill: Hampton Press, 13–32.

Livingstone, S. M., 2001. Children and Their Changing Media Environment. In: Livingstone, S. M. and Bovill, M., eds. *Children and Their Changing Media Environment. A European Comparative Study.* London: Lawrence Erlbaum, 307–333.

Lohmeier, C. and Böhling, R., 2018. Researching Communicative Figurations: Necessities and Challenges for Empirical Research. In: Hepp, A., Breiter, A. and Hasebrink, U., eds. *Communicative Figurations. Transforming Communications—Studies in Cross-Media Research.* Cham: Palgrave Macmillan, 343–362. doi:10.1007/978-3-319-65584-0_11.

Lonely Planet, n.d. *Top Things to See in the Philippines.* Available at www.lonelyplanet.com/philippines/top-things-to-do/a/poi/357304, accessed 13 July 2018.

Lövheim, M., 2011. Mediatization of Religion: A Critical Appraisal. *Culture and Religion,* 12(2), 153–166.

Luckmann, T., 2006. Die kommunikative Konstruktion der Wirklichkeit. In: Tänzler, D., Knoblauch, H. and Soeffner, H. G., eds. *Neue Perspektiven der Wissenssoziologie.* Konstanz: UVK, 15–26.

Lundby, K., ed., 2009. *Mediatization: Concept, Changes, Consequences.* New York: Peter Lang.

Radde-Antweiler, K., 2012. Authenticity. In: Campbell, H., ed. *Digital Religion. Understanding Religious Practice in New Media Worlds.* London: Routledge, 88–103.

Radde-Antweiler, K., 2017a. Digital Religion? Media Studies from a Religious Studies Perspective. In: Nord, I. and Zipernovszky, H., eds. *Religious Education in Mediatized Worlds.* Stuttgart: Kohlhammer, 138–150.

Radde-Antweiler, K., 2017b. How to Study Religion and Video Gaming. A Critical Discussion. In: Šisler, V., Radde-Antweiler, K. and Zeiler, X., eds. *Methods for Studying Video Games and Religion.* London and New York: Routledge, 2017–2216.

Radde-Antweiler, K. and Grünenthal, H., forthcoming. Investigating Media Appropriation: Photo Elicitation as a Tool for Narrative Storytelling. In: Krüger, O. and Rota, A., eds. *The Dynamics of Religion, Media and Community.* Special Issue of *Online – Heidelberg Journal of Religions on the Internet.*

Radde-Antweiler, K., Grünenthal, H. and Gogolok, S., 2018. 'Blogging Sometimes Leads to Dementia, Doesn't It?' The Roman Catholic Church in Times of Deep Mediatization. In: Hepp, A., Breiter, A. and Hasebrink, U., eds. *Communicative Figurations. Transforming Communications—Studies in Cross-Media Research.* Cham: Palgrave Macmillan, 267–286. doi:10.1007/978-3-319–65584-0_11.

Waardenburg, J., 1986. *Religionen und Religion. Systematische Einführung in die Religionswissenschaft.* Leipzig: Göschen.

Index

Note: Boldface page numbers refer to tables; italic page numbers refer to figures and page numbers followed by "n" denote endnotes.

Printed and bound by CPI Group (UK) Ltd, Croydon, CR0 4YY

30/10/2024

01781308-0001